insight

Upper-Intermediate Workbook

Rachael Roberts   Mike Sayer

Great Clarendon Street, Oxford, OX2 6DP, United Kingdom

Oxford University Press is a department of the University of Oxford. It furthers the University's objective of excellence in research, scholarship, and education by publishing worldwide. Oxford is a registered trade mark of Oxford University Press in the UK and in certain other countries

© Oxford University Press 2014

The moral rights of the author have been asserted

First published in 2014

2021

18

No unauthorized photocopying

All rights reserved. No part of this publication may be reproduced, stored in a retrieval system, or transmitted, in any form or by any means, without the prior permission in writing of Oxford University Press, or as expressly permitted by law, by licence or under terms agreed with the appropriate reprographics rights organization. Enquiries concerning reproduction outside the scope of the above should be sent to the ELT Rights Department, Oxford University Press, at the address above

You must not circulate this work in any other form and you must impose this same condition on any acquirer

Links to third party websites are provided by Oxford in good faith and for information only. Oxford disclaims any responsibility for the materials contained in any third party website referenced in this work

ISBN: 978 0 19 401114 3

Printed in China

This book is printed on paper from certified and well-managed sources

ACKNOWLEDGEMENTS

The authors and the publisher would like to thank Jane Cammack and Richard MacAndrew *for the material they contributed to this book.*

The author and the publisher would also like to thank the many teachers who contributed to the development of the course by commenting on the manuscript, taking part in lesson observations, focus groups and online questionnaires.

The authors and publisher are grateful to those who have given permission to reproduce the following extracts and adaptations of copyright material: p.85 Extract from Oxford Bookworm Library Stage 6: *Jane Eyre* by Charlotte Brontë, retold by Clare West. © Oxford University Press 2008. Reproduced by permission. p.87 Extract from Oxford Bookworm Library Stage 5: *The Great Gatsby* by F. Scott Fitzgerald, retold by Clare West. © Oxford University Press 2008. Reproduced by permission. p.91 Extract from Oxford Bookworm Library Stage 6: *Oliver Twist* by Charles Dickens, retold by Richard Rogers. © Oxford University Press 2008. Reproduced by permission. p.93 Extract from Oxford Bookworm Library Stage 5: *Great Expectations* by Charles Dickens, retold by Clare West. © Oxford University Press 2008. Reproduced by permission.

The publisher would like to thank the following for their permission to reproduce photographs: Alamy Images pp.5 (hoodies/Ace Stock Limited), 6 (refugee boys/Friedrich Stark), 7 (Marie Curie/Pictorial Press Ltd), 8 (knife crime/imagebroker), 12 (Canna school/pictureditor), 15 (Sungai Tembeling, Taman Negara National Park/Robert Harding World Imagery), 17 (classroom/Remember), 20 (game cartridges/Radhard Images), 22 (box/Neil Overy), 22 (plaque/DWImages Scotland), 26 (antique telephone/Adrian Sherratt), 29 (ambulance/Kevin Britland), 30 (mouse/Deco Images II), 32 (hand illustration/Ikon Images), 34 (dog cartoon/Igor Zakowski), 36 (notes/Marek Uliasz), 37 (blackboard/CNCCRAY), 37 (student/OJO Images Ltd), 46 (snow sculptures/Swapnali), 48 (film SLR/Sergey Parantaev), 52 (*Gulliver's Travels* by Jonathan Swift/Lebrecht Music and Arts Photo Library), 63 (BBQ/Mouse in the House), 63 (stir fry/foodfolio), 65 (cattle/Mark Downey), 69 (blurry beings/Stocksnapper), 76 (autumn landscape/AA World Travel Library); Corbis pp.5 (Craig and Marc Kielburger/Biserka Livaja), 9 (restaurant/Helen King), 13 (Royal Flying Doctor Service/Kit Kittle), 15 (Batu Caves/Jochen Schlenker/Robert Harding World Imagery), 21 (Upcycled fashion/Rob Sheppard/Demotix), 22 (pink kimono/Sean Gallagher/National Geographic Society), 23 (Mortuary Temple of Queen Hatshepsut/Dave Bartruff), 32 (running android/Oliver Burston/Ikon Images), 40 (e-book/Jim Craigmyle), 40 (brain graphic/Oliver Burston/Ikon Images), 44 (Bob Woodward & Carl Bernstein/Bettmann), 47 (early projector/Bettmann), 49 (Apollo 11 mission/NASA/Reuters), 53 (Paul Newman/Twentieth Century Fox Film Corporation/Sunset Boulevard), 60 (Irish famine print), 62 (picnic/Drew Myers), 64 (logging/Marcelo Sayao/epa), 68 (Project Glass/Google), 79 (Ronald Reagan/Wally McNamee), 80 (Prince William and Catherine, Duchess of Cambridge/John Stillwell/POOL/Reuters), 81 (King Harald V/Jim Gehrz/ZUMA Press); Getty Images pp.26 (diamond ring/Robert Kirk), 28 (Helen Keller/Hulton Archive), 31 (H G Wells/Fox Photos), 36 (baby with tablet/Yuji Kotani/Digital Vision), 45 (Andy Carvin/Ricky Carioti/The Washington Post), 45 (celebrity/Tom Merton/OJO Images), 46 (snowman/richierocket on www.flickr.com), 46 (sand sculptures/Matt Cardy), 46 (Russian sand castle/Andrey Smirnov/AFP), 46 (Brighton Sand Sculpture Festival 2013/Erhan Elaldi/Anadolu Agency), 49 (Don McCullin 1986/Alex Bowie), 49 (soldiers raising the American flag, Iwo Jima/SuperStock, Inc.), 54 (teen boy/Vincent Besnault), 62 (sushi bar/Andrea Chu/Photodisc), 62 (friends eating/Three Images), 71 (Alexander Graham Bell/Dorling Kindersley), 72 (playing guitar/John Lund/Marc Romanelli), 77 ('Shoeless Joe' Jackson/Sporting News), 78 (meeting/Steve Debenport), 81 (The Royal Family/Samir Hussein/WireImage), 89 (The Grand Canal in Venice/Hulton Archive); Kobal Collection pp.42 (*The Great Gatsby* 2013/Bazmark Films), 85 (*Jane Eyre* 1944/Twentieth Century Fox), 87 (*The Great Gatsby* 1974/Paramount), 91 (*Oliver Twist* 2005/R.p. Productions/Runteam Ltd./Guy Ferrandis), 93 (*Great Expectations* 2012/BBC Films); Oxford University Press pp.4 (female DJ/Corbis), 18 (teen boy/Digital Vision), 18 (boy outside/Chris King), 63 (frying pan/Dorling Kindersley RF), 84 (*Jane Eyre* book cover), 86 (*The Great Gatsby* book cover), 88 (*And All For Love...* book cover), 90 (*Oliver Twist* book cover), 92 (*Great Expectations* book cover), 99 (Leaving home/Design Pics), 102 (Stack of dictionaries/Oleksiy Mark), 108 (Boy asleep/Gareth Boden), 108 (Teens playing with games console/Image Source), 108 (Laptop/Ocean); Rex Features pp.6 (RSPCA centre/Geoff Robinson), 7 (Tegla Loroupe/Tom Oldham), 14 (1970's Manhattan/Everett Collection), 16 (Ruhagurika Catch-Up Class/Eye Ubiquitous), 24 (Forrest Fenn/Most Wanted), 31 (*The Time Machine* poster/Everett Collection), 55 (Mark Wahlberg/Canadian Press), 57 (rolling dice/Darren Greenwood/Design Pics Inc.); Shutterstock pp.14 (New York City/Songquan Deng/Shutterstock.com), 18 (teen with laptop/racorn), 21 (beggar/Halfpoint), 22 (copper bowl/Dimitar Sotirov), 26 (leather jacket/alltoz696), 26 (trophy/jayfish), 29 (homeopathy/Alexander Raths), 45 (photographers/cinemafestival/Shutterstock.com), 56 (fortune cookie/viviamo), 61 (chopsticks/SFC), 62 (eating chocolate/aastock), 63 (pot/Coprid), 63 (gas cooker/OZaiachin), 63 (toaster/John Kasawa), 73 (vintage room/Vita Khorzhevska), 74 (girls with phones/nenetus), 105 (Businessman choosing worker/Dooder), 105 (Business management diagram/graphixmania); South West News Service p.57 (rainbow lightning/Rob Bass/Newsteam).

Cover: Nikali Larin/Image Zoo/Alamy.

Unit	Vocabulary	Grammar	Listening, speaking and vocabulary	Vocabulary and grammar	Reading	Writing
1 Inspiration p4	Challenges	The 'we' generation	Do the right thing	Belief and commitment	New York mugging takes a surprising turn	An article
Progress check p11						
2 The world around us p12	Real education	Life on the edge	Urban stories	Songlines	Educating the world's children	Describing a place
Progress check p19						
3 Things that matter p20	Hoarders	What's left behind	One man's trash …	Lost treasures	The thrill of the chase	A story
Progress check p27						
4 Mind and body p28	Perfect people	Fact or fiction	Face value	Frankenstein	Is the genetically-modified athlete on the way?	A letter to a newspaper
Progress check p35						
5 Words p36	A word is born	Fast track to fluency	A good read	Shakespeare	More speed, less analysis?	A book review
Progress check p43						
6 The media and the message p44	Who controls the news?	The big picture	Making the headlines	Truth or lies?	The life of a war photographer	An article
Progress check p51						
7 That's life p52	Before I die …	Lucky break or lucky escape?	The golden years	The Road Not Taken	Serendipity – how we make our own luck	An opinion essay
Progress check p59						
8 Food and ethics p60	A right to eat	Wet wealth	Feeding the world	The origins of food	Designer shoes and the Amazon rainforest	A for and against essay
Progress check p67						
9 Technology p68	What's new?	Young minds	Digital footprints	First?	Living without technology	A report
Progress check p75						
10 Power p76	Utopia?	Dirty sport	Have your voice heard	The power of words	Making the case for the monarchy	A for and against essay
Progress check p83						

Literature insight p84

Exam insight p94

Grammar reference and practice p109

Wordlist p129

1 Inspiration

Vocabulary Challenges

Describing qualities

1 Match the words below to statements 1–6.

- perfectionism ■ commitment ■ perseverance
- compassion ■ optimism ■ ingenuity

1 I have lots of great ideas. ....
2 I don't give up easily. ....
3 I often feel that what I do isn't quite good enough. ....
4 If I promise to do something, you can be sure that I will do it. ....
5 I can't bear to see other people suffer. ....
6 I usually expect things to work out well. ....

insight Synonyms

2 Complete the text with the words below. Sometimes more than one answer is possible. Use each word only once.

- get over ■ problem ■ ground-breaking ■ overcome
- innovative ■ hindrance

Norfolk's newest internet radio station, South Norfolk Youth Action Radio (SNYA), was officially launched on Saturday.

The brainchild of fourteen-year-old Josh Worley, SNYA is ¹............... in being the first radio station run by and for young people in south Norfolk. Josh first started broadcasting from his bedroom, but was determined to make it bigger and better. Having no money was a bit of a ²..............., so he approached South Norfolk District Council who helped him to find organizations that could fund the project. Little by little, Josh managed to raise the money for his dream studio and all the equipment. 'I was very impressed that someone so young was so determined to ³............... any ⁴............... to set up a project like this,' says Lucy Norris, from one of the organizations that helped Josh.

The station is now up and running, with presenters aged between thirteen and twenty-one.

Josh was recently recognized for his ⁵............... idea and hard work with a Cultural Achiever award at the Bernard Matthews Youth Awards. 'Even if young people don't want to work in radio or even the media at all, SNYA Radio gives them an amazing experience, develops their key life skills and helps them to ⁶............... any lack of self-confidence.'

Ways of looking

3 Choose the correct words to complete the sentences.

- gawping ■ glaring ■ glancing

1 a 'Don't say that!' he said, ... at me furiously.
  b 'What are you .... at? It's rude to stare!'

- gaping ■ gazing ■ squinting

2 a 'I can't quite see what it says,' she said, ... at the postcard.
  b 'I think I'm in love with you,' he said, ... into her eyes.

- glared ■ peeked ■ glimpsed

3 a 'Were you at the concert last night? I thought I .... you in the distance.'
  b 'I think this letter is from Kieron,' she said, 'I .... at the handwriting.'

4 Complete the text with the words below. There are two words that you do not need.

- gawp ■ benefit ■ overcome ■ obstacles ■ ingenuity
- perseverance ■ glimpse ■ ground-breaking

Having fallen out with his mum and her new partner, Billy ended up living on the streets at the age of seventeen. His life looked hopeless, but he was lucky enough to find the ¹............... programme AIR Football, which helps homeless people to ²............... their difficulties through sport. Set up by Colm Witty in 2006, it's a charity that uses football to help young people get off the streets and change their lives.

When he was younger, Billy had hoped to become a professional footballer, but there were just too many ³............... in his way. Now, however, Billy is going to represent England at the next Homeless World Cup, in Poznan, Poland.

It's clear that AIR Football has been of huge ⁴............... to many young homeless people. More than 70% of players from previous years have gone on to make significant changes in their lives after taking part in the competition, such as finding a home or a job.

'It's an opportunity for them to ⁵............... the future, to see how things might be different,' said one of the coaches. 'Billy will still need some ⁶............... to succeed, but we have every faith in him.'

5 CHALLENGE! Write about an obstacle in your life that you have successfully overcome. What was it? How did you manage to overcome it? What qualities did you need to do this?

Grammar The 'we' generation

Tense revision

1 Complete the text with the correct form of the verbs in brackets. Use the present simple, past simple, present perfect or past perfect.

Marc and Craig Kielburger are best known for their involvement in Free the Children, a charity that they ¹................. (found) in 1995. But Marc ²................. (begin) doing good deeds some years before then. When he was thirteen, he ³................. (develop) environmentally-friendly cleaning products as part of a school science project and ⁴................. (start) collecting names on various petitions to protect the environment. The boys' passion for saving the environment and encouraging social change through making responsible lifestyle choices ⁵................. (be) key to all their activities since then. In 2008, they ⁶................. (set up) a new organization, called 'Me to We', which ⁷................. (produce) ethically-made goods and ⁸................. (raise) social awareness by offering leadership training and volunteer trips. Craig also regularly ⁹................. (appear) on Canadian TV, giving responsible lifestyle tips in segments called 'Living Me to We'. The brothers say, 'Me to We was created to help transform consumers into socially conscious world changers, one transaction at a time.'

2 Choose the correct answers.
1. Marc and Craig **have done / have been doing** volunteer work for over two decades now.
2. They came up with the idea to start Me to We while they **built / were building** a school in Ecuador.
3. In 2012, the Me to We organization **helped / was helping** to plant 195,000 trees.
4. So far, between them, they **have published / have been publishing** eleven books about their charitable work.
5. They both regularly **contribute / are contributing** to numerous newspapers and magazines.
6. In their newspaper column *Ask the Kielburgers*, they **offer / are offering** tips on ways to give back to the world.
7. Currently, the brothers **prepare / are preparing** their next annual We Day event.
8. Since 1995, 278,000 people **have attended / have been attending** a We Day event.

3 Complete the second sentence so that it has a similar meaning to the first. Use the words in brackets.
1. Megan started working for the charity when she was fourteen.
   Megan .... (been)
2. I've never taken part in a We Day event before.
   It's .... (first)
3. There is no decision yet about the funding for the project.
   They .... (still)
4. They didn't begin their speech until everyone had entered the room.
   They waited until .... (before)
5. You're over an hour late!
   I .... (waiting)
6. It was the first time they had travelled abroad to do volunteer work.
   They .... (never)
7. The charity has been helping women in Africa for over six years now.
   The charity .... (started)
8. There has been an increase in the number of people joining our organization.
   More and more .... (are)

4 Complete the text with the correct form of the words in brackets. Sometimes more than one answer is possible.

As a young boy, Dennis Gyamfi ¹................. (live) in Ghana with his grandparents. His life wasn't easy. He ²................. (have to) work hard to help his family. During that time, his parents ³................. (live) in London and when Dennis was ten, they ⁴................. (decide) to bring him to England. That's when his life ⁵................. (take) a turn for the worse.
Dennis's parents ⁶................. (work) long hours, day and night, and there was nobody to look after him. As a result, Dennis ⁷................. (start) spending time hanging about on the streets and ⁸................. (get) involved in gangs and street crime.
Luckily for him, Dennis ⁹................. (meet) a man called Solomon who worked for an organization called X-it, set up by people who ¹⁰................. (escape) gang life. The programme ¹¹................. (connect) youths at risk with mentors who ¹²................. (experience) similar issues when they were young.
Dennis eventually ¹³................. (become) a mentor himself and he now ¹⁴................. (work) as a youth counsellor for X-it. Not only that, but he ¹⁵................. (recently / win) a public service award for his efforts.

5 CHALLENGE! Do some research on organizations for young people or set up by young people in your country. Then select one and write about its organizers, history and activities.

Listening, speaking and vocabulary Do the right thing

V | insight Words with *self-*

1 Match the words below to definitions 1–7.

■ self-interest ■ self-defence ■ self-control ■ selflessness
■ self-assurance ■ self-preservation ■ self-sacrifice

1 protecting yourself in a dangerous situation: ....
2 being able to remain calm, even if you are angry, excited, etc.: ....
3 thinking more about the needs of other people than your own: ....
4 doing or saying something to protect yourself: ....
5 not letting yourself have or do something in order to help other people instead: ....
6 believing in your own strengths and abilities: ....
7 the act of thinking only about yourself and not caring about other people: ....

Choosing a charity

2 🔊 **3.01** Listen to a school committee deciding which charity to raise money for. Which of the following charities do they NOT mention?

1 Animal Rescue
2 Heart Health Foundation
3 Disaster Relief
4 Help for the Homeless
5 International Aid
6 Youth Sports Foundation

3 🔊 **3.01** Listen again and match speakers Jill (J), Steve (S), or nobody (N) to opinions 1–6.

1 Larger charities spend too much money on advertising. ....
2 Smaller charities are usually run by volunteers. ....
3 They should choose a charity which helps young people. ....
4 It's a good idea to raise money for a charity that has helped you or your family. ....
5 Animal charities are very well supported. ....
6 People care more about animals than people, so they should choose an animal charity. ....

4 🔊 **3.01** Complete the sentences with one word in each gap. Then listen again and check.

1 Well, my .... is that we should choose a smaller charity.
2 Could you .... what you mean?
3 Jill, I do understand that .... of view, but I think … .
4 Ah, that makes .... to me now.
5 But, ... me, I still think a smaller charity might be better.
6 I see where you're .... from, but do we have to limit it to young people?
7 I think we need to .... what will be a popular charity to raise money for.
8 Are you .... that people care more about animals than people … ? That's silly.

5 Match sentences 1–8 in exercise 4 to categories A–C below.

A Giving an opinion: ..1.., ..., ...
B Acknowledging an opinion: ...., ..., ...
C Asking for clarification: ...., ...

6 Complete the dialogue with the phrases below.

■ for me ■ Are you saying that ■ The point is that
■ What do you mean exactly ■ That makes sense to me
■ we need to consider ■ I understand that point of view

Tom   Well, in deciding on a charity to raise money for, **1**.......... two things: which charity do we feel is the most worthwhile, and which charity will be easiest to raise money for?
Olivia   I don't understand what point you're trying to make. **2**..........?
Tom   Well, if we choose a charity which we personally think is great, but which no one else wants to support, we won't raise very much money, will we?
Olivia   Oh, OK. **3**.......... now.
Tom   So, I'd like to suggest that we don't choose an animal charity.
Olivia   **4**.......... people don't like animals, or that it isn't worthwhile?
Tom   Well, **5**.........., people are more important than animals.
Olivia   Well, I suppose **6**.........., but I don't personally agree with it. **7**.......... there's no reason why we shouldn't raise money for animals. What about protecting endangered species, for example?

7 Which of the charities in exercise 2 would you choose to raise money for? Which one would you not choose? Justify your answers.

Vocabulary and grammar Belief and commitment

V insight Word analysis

1 Complete the text with the words below. There is one word that you do not need.

■ gradual ■ interim ■ haggard ■ a great deal
■ attentive ■ conundrum ■ penalized

Tegla Loroupe is a highly-successful Kenyan long-distance track and road runner. Her passion for running started when she was seven and she had to run ten kilometres to school every morning. She soon found that she loved it, and that she was very good at it.

However, her father (who had four wives and twenty-three other children) was not a very ¹......... parent, and at one point he stopped Tegla from running altogether, saying it was not ladylike. Tegla faced a ²......... . She wanted to be a good daughter, but she didn't want to be ³......... for being a girl. Supported by her mother and her older sister, she kept running and made ⁴......... but steady progress.

In 1994, Loroupe was the first African woman to win the New York Marathon, and became an important sporting role model. During the 2000 Summer Olympics in Sydney, Loroupe was expected to do very well. However, on the night before the race, she went down with severe food poisoning. Although she felt exhausted and looked tired and ⁵......... the next day, she still managed to complete the marathon in thirteenth place and the 10,000 metres in fifth place.

She retired from running in 2003 and now devotes ⁶......... of her time to humanitarian and peace activities.

V Qualities of a hero

2 Match the words below to comments 1–7.

■ compassionate ■ courageous ■ dedicated
■ determined ■ inspirational ■ resourceful ■ willing

1 His life story gave me many new ideas and motivated me to change a few things in my own life. ....
2 They never object to doing anything I ask them to do. ....
3 She devoted all of her time to researching the next medical breakthrough. ....
4 She cares for and understands people who are suffering. ....
5 They weren't afraid of jumping into the water to save the children. ....
6 He always finds new ways of doing things. ....
7 She wasn't willing to change her mind about moving abroad to continue her studies. ....

Past perfect and past perfect continuous

3 Choose the correct answers.

1 When Tegla got to school on her first day, she was exhausted. She .... ten kilometres to get there.
   a had run   b had been running
2 Tegla .... in many school races before she realized she was good at running.
   a had taken part   b had been taking part
3 The Kenyan athletics federation .... in her until she won a barefoot race in 1988.
   a hadn't believed   b hadn't been believing
4 By 1994, Tegla .... long distances for fourteen years.
   a had run   b had been running
5 Tegla was delighted. She .... the New York Marathon.
   a had won   b had been winning

4 Complete the text using the past simple, past perfect simple or past perfect continuous. Sometimes more than one answer is possible.

Dr Marie Skłodowska-Curie was born in 1867 in Warsaw, Poland, into a poor, but well-educated family. Her father ¹........................... (be) a maths and physics teacher and her mother ²........................... (be) a teacher before she sadly ³........................... (die) when Marie was still quite young.

Although Marie ⁴........................... (do) very well in her studies before she ⁵........................... (graduate), she was unable to go to the University of Warsaw because at the time it ⁶........................... (only accept) male students.

Marie ⁷........................... (want) to study abroad, but couldn't afford to do so. So she agreed with her sister Bronisława that Marie would work to support Bronisława while she ⁸........................... (study), and then Bronisława would support her in return.

In 1891, Marie ⁹........................... (manage) to enrol at the Sorbonne University in Paris and completed her master's degree in 1893. Around this time, she was introduced to French physicist Pierre Curie, who ¹⁰........................... (work) with one of her colleagues. Together, they ¹¹........................... (continue) her research into uranium and ¹²........................... (discover) polonium and radium, which ultimately ¹³........................... (lead) to the invention of X-ray machines.

5 CHALLENGE! Think about an inspirational person from your country. Make a list of some of the key events in their life. Then use your list to write about their life.

Reading New York mugging takes a surprising turn

1 Look at the opinions. Which ones do you agree with? Which ones do you disagree with?
  1 An armed mugging should be punished by time in prison.
  2 An armed mugging is only carried out because the mugger is desperate and doesn't have other options. That person should be helped.
  3 If you are kind to people, they will always be kind to you in return.
  4 If you show someone kindness and interest, it makes them feel better about themselves.
  5 It's fake to be kind to people who have treated you badly.
  6 People are usually only nice when they want something.

2 Read the article. Which statements in exercise 1 would the author agree with?

3 Read the article again and choose the correct answers.
  1 What do the police suggest you should do if you are mugged?
    a Avoid getting into an argument.
    b Show the mugger you are not afraid of them.
    c Try to defend yourself if possible.
    d Try talking reasonably with your mugger.
  2 How did the mugger respond when Julio offered him his coat?
    a He was furious and reacted with violence.
    b He was astounded and didn't know how to respond.
    c He took Julio's coat as well.
    d He didn't bother turning round.
  3 Which of the benefits of following the Golden Rule is NOT mentioned in the article?
    a It generally results in being treated well yourself.
    b It encourages people to look after each other.
    c It makes people feel better about themselves.
    d It helps different cultures to understand each other.
  4 What argument does the writer give for trying to get the mugger arrested?
    a It would have taught the boy not to do it again.
    b It would have been the safest thing to do.
    c It could have prevented Julio being hurt.
    d It would have been what most people would have done.
  5 Which sentence best sums up the writer's attitude to what Julio Diaz did?
    a It was too risky and overall it was a stupid thing to do.
    b It was unlikely to have any real effect on the boy.
    c It was likely to have a positive impact on the boy.
    d It was a way for Julio to feel good about himself.

New York mugging takes a surprising turn

What would you do if someone pulled a knife on you, demanding your wallet? Police advice is that, rather than attempting any form of self-defence, you should accede to any demands and avoid being antagonistic. The situation can very quickly turn ugly, particularly if a weapon is involved. Research shows that one in three victims of mugging experiences some sort of physical injury.

So, if you were mugged, once you'd complied with a demand for your wallet, would you offer anything else? Your ring? Your watch? Or perhaps your nice warm coat?

Julio Diaz, a thirty-one-year-old social worker, did just that. Preoccupied with thoughts of what he would order for dinner at his favourite diner that evening, Julio stepped off the New York subway to be confronted by an aggressive teenage boy, holding a knife and demanding his wallet. Julio silently handed over his wallet, but then called after the boy, who was rapidly making away with it. 'Hey, wait a minute. You forgot something. If you're gonna be robbing people for the rest of the night, you might as well take my coat to keep you warm.' The boy simply gaped at him. He looked even more bewildered when Julio offered to treat him to dinner.

It was a risky response. The teenager might have thought he was being ridiculed, lost his temper and stabbed him. And even if he didn't, why on earth would Julio want to have dinner with someone who had just robbed him at knifepoint?

Julio's offer was in response to a gut feeling that the boy needed some kind of help. And the boy seemed willing to take it, following Julio to his usual booth in the diner. Over their meal, the boy was uncommunicative and guarded, but he closely observed how the manager, the waiters and even the dishwashers all stopped by to chat to Julio. Bemused, he wondered if Julio owned the restaurant. Why was he so nice to everyone?

Julio's behaviour embodied the principles of the 'Golden Rule', which says we should behave towards others as we would like them to behave towards us – a principle which has its roots in
45 almost every culture and religion and plays a vital role in building a cohesive society. However, following the Golden Rule is not purely altruistic, as ultimately we, like Julio, are likely to reap the rewards of people being friendly and happy to see
50 us. We also gain improved psychological welfare simply through the satisfaction of knowing that we behaved well.

When the time came to pay the bill, Julio asked for his wallet back so he could pay, and the
55 boy handed it to him without a murmur. Julio then gave him a twenty dollar bill, and asked for the knife in exchange. The boy handed it over. His cooperation gave Julio hope for the boy's future. Perhaps it signified that Julio's interest and
60 kindness to him made him feel valued, increased his sense of self-worth and allowed him to feel that he could have a different type of life?

Of course, it could all have ended very differently. The mugger might have just taken Julio's coat and
65 raced off. Or Julio might have found himself the victim of a vicious assault. Even if Julio hadn't been hurt, one might argue that by letting the boy off the hook, Julio was not actually doing the boy, or society, any favours. Perhaps Julio should have gone
70 straight to the police, let the boy learn his lesson and helped protect others from being assaulted.

However, perhaps it's possible that by treating him with kindness and compassion, Julio may have enabled the teenager to see that life can be lived
75 in a very different way, and perhaps even changed the course of his future.

As Julio said, 'If you treat people right, you can only hope that they treat you right. It's as simple as it gets in this complicated world.'

4 Match the highlighted adjectives in the article to definitions 1–6.
1 confused and puzzled: ...., ...
2 behaving in a hostile, angry or forceful way: ...., ...
3 extremely violent: ....
4 caring about other people more than you care about yourself: ....
5 not giving much information: ....
6 thinking so much about something that you don't notice other things: ....

5 Choose the correct answers.
1 Being a social worker is hard work and badly paid. You need to be quite ....
   a bemused   b altruistic   c antagonistic
2 When I refused to give him my wallet, he became .... and started shouting and waving his fist.
   a guarded   b preoccupied   c aggressive
3 Her tone of voice was .... ; she was looking for a fight.
   a bewildered b antagonistic c bemused
4 He was attacked by a(n) .... criminal and badly beaten.
   a vicious   b altruistic   c preoccupied
5 I couldn't understand what was happening to me. I just felt completely ....
   a antagonistic b vicious   c bewildered
6 His answer was .... ; he was cautious about what he said.
   a aggressive b guarded   c bewildered
7 I was completely .... by the way he behaved. It just didn't seem at all logical.
   a preoccupied b guarded   c bemused
8 She's obviously .... with something – I can't get her to concentrate at all.
   a bewildered b preoccupied   c guarded

6 CHALLENGE! Write or talk about the questions below. Give reasons and examples.
1 If someone is antagonistic or aggressive towards you, how do you usually react? Why?
2 When you meet someone for the first time, are you usually quite open with them, or a bit guarded until you get to know them better? Why?
3 Do you think that anyone is ever truly altruistic, or is there always a benefit in behaving well towards others?
4 Were you bemused by Julio's actions, or do you think he did the right thing? Why?

Inspiration 9

Writing An article

1 Read the beginning of a newspaper article. Do you agree with what the writer says? Make a list of five points or examples to support your view.

Young people just want an easy life

The number of sixteen- to twenty-four-year-olds not working has risen to more than one million, and almost half have never worked at all. Clearly the economic situation isn't helping, but it is also evident that most young people simply don't want to work very hard. They are quite happy just to be given money, sit back and do nothing. There are plenty of opportunities out there, but they simply aren't capable of rising to the challenge …

2 Look at the task below and write a plan of your article.

Write an article in response to the newspaper article in exercise 1 for your school's online magazine. Give examples of teenagers who have successfully taken on challenges.

3 Read the article. Does the writer make any of the same points that you thought of?

I recently read a newspaper article which made me very angry. It claimed that young people nowadays just want an easy life and aren't capable of taking on real challenges. The author also seemed to believe that high youth unemployment was a result of young people not wanting to work hard. This was ¹**such / so** a ridiculous argument that I felt I had to write an article in response to this.

In my experience, young people work extremely hard. Nowadays, we have to take more exams and get higher grades than ever before ²**so that / so as to** stand a chance of getting a good job. ³**As a result / So as to**, we are studying much harder than our parents did. Many students also work part-time ⁴**in order to / as a consequence** help their parents, and there are more and more young entrepreneurs setting up their own businesses.

For example, a few days ago, I read about a young man who had become homeless at the age of sixteen. Rather than give up, however, he was ⁵**such / so** determined that he first managed to get a job delivering papers and then, eventually, set up his own delivery business. That's definitely a real challenge.

To conclude, I think it's very easy for older generations to blame young people for today's problems. I have also heard young people complaining that their problems have been caused by decisions made by previous generations. Ultimately, I would like to see everyone working together ⁶**so that / in order to** we can face today's challenges and overcome them.

V Purpose and result

4 Read the article again and choose the correct answers in 1–6.

5 Complete the sentences with a suitable purpose or result clause.
1 The idea that young people don't want to work hard is .... insulting that I can't believe the article was ever published.
2 In fact, I have never heard .... a ridiculous argument.
3 Nowadays, even jobs that aren't well-paid demand qualifications. .... young people are having to pass more exams than ever before.
4 University is more expensive than it used to be. ...., many young people have to work as well as study.
5 They need extra money .... afford books and computers.
6 However, they still need enough time to study .... they can get good grades.

6 Which of the following elements of the writing process have you already completed?
■ incorporating changes ■ writing the final draft
■ self-correction ■ publishing a blog post
■ peer-correction ■ brainstorming ■ planning
■ emailing it to the teacher ■ writing the first draft

WRITING GUIDE

■ **Task** Write your own response to the task in exercise 2.

■ **Ideas** You should already have decided whether you agree or disagree with the statement and thought of some ways to support your argument. Think of any additional points you want to make and at least one example of a person whose story supports your points.

■ **Plan** Follow the plan:
Paragraph 1: Outline the argument given in the task and introduce your point of view.
Paragraph 2: Introduce supporting evidence.
Paragraph 3: Give an example (or examples) of a person who has shown they can work hard and rise to a challenge (or the opposite).
Paragraph 4: Sum up your arguments.

■ **Write** Write your article. Use the paragraph plan to help you.

■ **Check** Check the following points.
■ Have you responded to the opinion in the task?
■ Have you included arguments that support your opinion?
■ Have you checked grammar, vocabulary, spelling and punctuation?

Progress check Unit 1

Read 1–10 and evaluate your learning in Unit 1. Give yourself a mark from 1 to 3. How could you improve?
1 I can't do this.   2 I have some problems with this.   3 I can do this well.

A Challenges	Mark (1–3)	How can I improve?
1 Give two examples of questions to 'ask' the author while reading critically.		
I can think critically while reading a text.		
2 Complete the following definitions with a suitable quality. a If you have ...., you have sympathy when others are suffering. b If you show ...., you are able to accept others being different.		
I can describe different qualities.		
3 Write suitable synonyms for the words below. a obstacle / .... b get over something / .... something c innovative /		
I can use synonyms.		

B The 'we' generation	Mark (1–3)	How can I improve?
4 Explain the difference between these two sentences. a When I arrived, he left. b When I arrived, he had already left.		
I understand when to use the past perfect and the past simple.		
5 Explain the difference in meaning between the underlined verb forms. A What <u>are you doing</u> now? B <u>I'm studying</u>. A What about tonight? Do you fancy going out? B Sorry, I can't. <u>I'm studying</u>. A You<u>'re always studying</u>!		
I can use present, past and perfect tenses.		

C Do the right thing	Mark (1–3)	How can I improve?
6 Give a word with *self-* which means: a being able to stop yourself from doing something. b being confident about your own abilities.		
I can use a variety of words with *self-*.		
7 Give one way of giving an opinion, one way of acknowledging an opinion and one way of asking for clarification.		
I can give and acknowledge opinions.		

D Belief and commitment	Mark (1–3)	How can I improve?
8 What impact did Nelson Mandela's choices have on his mother's life?		
I can understand an autobiographical text.		
9 Explain the difference between these sentences. a They had been driving for hours and were feeling exhausted. b He had driven for hours to reach the house.		
I can understand different uses of the past perfect simple and past perfect continuous.		

E An article	Mark (1–3)	How can I improve?
10 Replace the underlined result and purpose clauses with other suitable phrases. a He studied hard. <u>As a result</u>, his grades were very good. b He went to university <u>so that</u> he could become a teacher.		
I can use different result and purpose clauses.		

2 The world around us

Vocabulary Real education

insight Word analysis

1 Choose the sentence that best describes the meaning of the word in bold.

1 We face **profound** challenges.
   a We face difficult challenges that will be hard to overcome.
   b We face straightforward challenges that are easy to deal with.
2 It was a **harsh** environment.
   a The environment was cold, empty and difficult to live in.
   b The environment was warm, green and easy to grow food in.
3 The benefits of learning English seem **remote**.
   a The benefits of learning English are clear.
   b It is difficult to see the benefits of learning English.
4 We'll **inevitably** lose.
   a Our team is hopeless. We'll lose. There's no chance of winning.
   b Although our team isn't very good, we might not lose if we try hard.
5 On the art course, the atmosphere was **stifling**.
   a On the art course, the atmosphere was very positive – we were encouraged to be creative.
   b When I was on the art course, the atmosphere didn't allow me to really express myself.
6 **Subsistence** farming was going on in the village.
   a In the village, the people involved in farming only grew enough food for themselves.
   b Farming in the village produced enough food for the people to sell fruit and vegetables at the market.

insight Nouns + prepositions

2 Read the extracts from a blog about life in an island community and choose the correct answers.

1 There isn't much **respect / responsibility** for people who don't work hard in the community. Everyone expects other people to do their best.
2 The islanders have a good **benefits / grasp** of local history. They understand when and how their way of life began.
3 A lot of students at the local school don't see the **demand / relevance** of studying foreign languages if they don't intend to live abroad.
4 The school on the island only has fifty students, so that's why there are only a **handful / grasp** of teachers here.
5 These days, there is an increased **demand / sense** for mobile phones and computers on the island. Young people there want to be in touch with the rest of the world.
6 Young people on the island feel they have a **responsibility / knowledge** for looking after older residents. Life is hard, so it's important to help other people.

The natural world and outer space

3 Choose the correct answers.

1 Which of the following is always flat?
   a a plain   b a peninsula   c a glacier
2 Which word describes a small, narrow river?
   a a pond   b a stream   c a swamp
3 What do you call the place where a large river widens and flows into the sea?
   a a glacier   b a bay   c an estuary
4 Which of the following is usually wet?
   a a plain   b a tundra   c a swamp
5 What is Venus?
   a a solar system   b a constellation   c a planet
6 What do you call something that moves around another planet?
   a a galaxy   b a moon   c a universe

4 Choose the correct answers.

The empty schools of Rum and Canna

The islands of Rum and Canna are a long way from the coast of the Scottish mainland. In fact, they are so ¹**remote / stifling / harsh / profound** that it takes hours to travel to either island by boat or plane. The islands are very beautiful, though. On Rum, there is a mountain ²**plain / group / range / reach** in the centre with small, natural ³**floes / swamps / estuaries / streams** that run down to the coast. In the north, there is a large ⁴**tundra / swamp / range / bay** with a fine beach and the remains of a village. That's where ships come in to dock, away from the strong winds.

One of the ⁵**grasps / benefits / responsibilities / demands** of living on a small island is the ⁶**grasp / sense / handful / responsibility** of community people feel. When there are only a handful ⁷**of / from / for / on** families in one place, everybody gets to know everybody else very well and they find time to help and support each other. The problem on Rum and Canna, however, is that one of the most important parts of their community is missing. There are so few children on the islands that the schools are empty. Islanders have no ⁸**relevance / knowledge / responsibility / respect** of a time when both schools were empty before and the concern is that without a school they will never be able to attract young families to live on Rum and Canna again. That's why they are keeping the schools open, hoping and waiting for the day when pupils might once more return to the islands and their schools.

5 CHALLENGE! Imagine you and your family have just moved to the island of Canna and that you are one of a handful of students at the school. What are the advantages and disadvantages of going to a small school in a remote island community?

12 The world around us

Grammar Life on the edge

Future tenses

1 Complete the dialogues with the correct future form of the verbs in brackets.

1
Matt Do you have any plans for next Saturday, Sarah?
Sarah Yeah, I .... (meet) Tim and Louise at the shopping centre at two o'clock. Do you want to come?

2
Emily Are you ready for the start of the race?
Tom Yes, I am. I'm excited. I don't know why, but I think Jo .... (win) today.

3
Eddie When's the next tour?
guide It .... (start) at half past four.

4
Tom Wow! A baby! Congratulations! When?
Louise Three months from now. I .... (have) twins! I'm so excited!

5
Sophie I have to get this parcel to the post office today and I don't have time.
Robin Don't worry. I .... (take) it there for you. It's on my way.

6
Sam Have you told Todd about the party?
Ruth I .... (tell) him tonight. It's on my list of things to do.

7
waiter What would you like?
Frank Oh, I think I .... (have) the fish, please.

8
Ben One day, I .... (be) the richest man in the world.
Dad Oh, stop dreaming and do your homework!

Future continuous, future perfect and future perfect continuous

2 Lizzie and Harry have just got married. Use the prompts to write about their hopes, dreams and expectations. Use the future continuous, future perfect and future perfect continuous.

1 At this time next week, / they / sit / on a beach on their honeymoon

2 By the end of March, / they / move into their new house

3 In mid-May, / Lizzie / study French at evening college

4 By July, / Harry / start his new job

5 By September, / Lizzie / buy a new car

6 By December, / they / live / in their new house for nine months

3 Complete the text with the correct future form of the verbs in brackets.

Royal Flying Doctor Service of Australia

Since the 1920s, the Royal Flying Doctor Service has helped thousands of sick or injured people in remote regions of central and northern Australia. Kerry Lee Cochrane is a 'flying doctor' and she **1** .... (work) all day tomorrow. According to her schedule, her day's work **2** .... (start) at 6 a.m. and **3** .... (end) at 6 p.m. 'We work long hours,' says Kerry Lee, 'but it's an exciting job. At seven tomorrow morning I **4** .... (probably / fly) over the Australian outback on my way to help somebody.' Right now, however, Kerry Lee is at the small hospital in Tennant Creek, packing her medical kit for tomorrow. 'I take as many things as I can,' she says. 'Anything **5** .... (happen). You just never know.' She's also packing plenty of anti-mosquito spray. 'Have you seen the weather forecast?' she asks. 'I have! It **6** .... (rain) tomorrow and that brings out the mosquitoes.' By 6 p.m. tomorrow, Kerry Lee **7** .... (fly) hundreds of kilometres across Australia, and, hopefully, she **8** .... (help) a lot of people. 'It's a very rewarding job,' she says, with a smile, 'and I've decided that I love it so much that I **9** .... (continue) to do it for as long as I can.'

4 CHALLENGE! Think about the next twelve months and write answers to the questions below.
- What arrangements for the weekend do you have?
- What do you think the weather will be like and will it affect your arrangements?
- What will you have achieved by the end of this month?
- What are your plans for the next school holidays?
- What dreams, hopes and expectations do you have for the coming year?

The world around us 13

Listening, speaking and vocabulary Urban stories

insight Antonyms: urban regeneration

1 Choose the correct answers.

A New York in the 1970s

In the 1970s, New York was a violent and dangerous city. In areas such as Harlem and the Bowery, many of the buildings looked ugly and ¹**worthwhile / unappealing**. The people who lived in them often didn't have electricity or running water. Some buildings had been ²**efficient / neglected** for decades and had begun to fall down. Other areas of the city were full of empty buildings which had been ³**thriving / abandoned** because a lot of people had left the city to live in the suburbs. And the city was very badly organized, which resulted in a ⁴**wasteful / pointless** use of resources, and rising levels of crime. In 1977, the electricity went off for twenty-five hours and nearly 4,000 people were arrested for committing robbery and vandalism in the dark city streets.

B New York today

Today, New York is a completely different city. In fact, it's really ⁵**thriving / declining** – it's getting richer and its population is growing. There are over 8 million people in the city now – so many people that almost every house or apartment is ⁶**destroyed / inhabited**. Areas which were once poor and ugly are now wealthy. People there spend time and money doing repairs, so the properties are ⁷**efficient / cared for** and the exteriors of the buildings are now quite ⁸**attractive / worthwhile** – they look beautiful again. It is now one of the most exciting cities to visit in the world.

V Urban landscape

2 Complete the compound words.
1 We live on the top floor of a high-............... building in the city centre. There are great views from the living room window.
2 Most of the shops in the mall are boarded-............... . They have closed down because very few people go shopping in that area of the city.
3 There are many factories and businesses on the new industrial .... on the edge of the city.
4 I go to work on my bike on cycle .... because they're safer than using the main road.
5 Always use a pedestrian .... to go from one side of a busy city centre street to another.
6 The local council has put speed .... in place on roads near our house to stop drivers from going too fast in residential areas.

Deciding on a new redevelopment scheme

3 The local government has given Walton High School €50,000 to redevelop an old building in the school grounds into a new and useful space. Look at the development schemes below and choose three that you would choose to spend money on if Walton High was your school. Think of two reasons for choosing each of the three schemes.

- a new computer room   ■ an after-school study centre
- a new library   ■ a common room for students
- a snack shop   ■ a gym   ■ an extra classroom
- a music room   ■ a dance studio

4 🔊 3.02 Listen to three people from the school, Kelly, Simon and Mr Lewis. Which schemes in exercise 3 do they each suggest?

5 🔊 3.02 Listen again. Match the speakers, Kelly (K), Simon (S) or Mr Lewis (L) to opinions 1–6.
1 Not many students would use a music room. ......
2 Selling poor quality food in a school isn't a good idea. ......
3 Providing computers for all the students in the school who need them is important. ......
4 The space should be used for a facility that is available when the rest of the school is closed. ......
5 All students should have the opportunity to learn the piano, guitar or some other instrument. ......
6 The new facility should only be made available to some of the school's students. ......

6 🔊 3.02 Look at the phrases from the dialogue. Write who uses each phrase (Kelly (K), Simon (S) or Mr Lewis (L)). Sometimes more than one person uses a phrase. Then listen again and check.
1 My main concern is … . ..K.. , ...
2 That should be a priority. ......
3 It might be an idea to have … . ...
4 I'm not convinced. ......
5 It's important to draw attention to … . ...
6 What we really need is … . ... , ...
7 It's important to highlight … . ...
8 It's probably not that useful or practical. ......
9 It could be useful for … . ...
10 For me, it's a must. ......

7 Match phrases 1–10 in exercise 6 to categories A–D according to their use in the dialogue.
A Introducing requirements: ...1.. , ... , ...
B Essential requirements: ...... , ... , ...
C Desirable requirements: ......
D Evaluating requirements: ...... , ... , ...

8 Imagine that your school has received some money to redevelop a room or building into a new and useful space. Think of three possible uses for the room or building. Then decide which new use you prefer and why.

14 The world around us

Vocabulary and grammar Songlines

V insight Adjective suffixes: -able and -ible

1 Complete the sentences with the correct form of the words below. Add the correct adjective suffix, -able or -ible.

▪ collect ▪ treat ▪ fashion ▪ sense ▪ terror

1 David spends all his money on .... designer clothes. His clothes are always new and modern.
2 The essay was ....! The grammar and spelling were so awful that it was impossible to understand.
3 Some of these diseases are .... The problem is that we can't afford the medicines in this poor country.
4 It is .... to buy a good pair of hiking boots for walking in the mountains.
5 Old stamps are .... items. Some people have hundreds of them and will pay a lot of money to buy one.

2 Write the correct letter to complete the adjective suffixes. Then complete the text with the adjectives.

▪ advis........ble ▪ incred........ble ▪ navig........ble
▪ consider........ble ▪ access........ble ▪ valu........ble
▪ aud........ble ▪ ed........ble ▪ flex........ble ▪ vis........ble

The Batu Caves
The Batu Caves lie not far to the north of Malaysia's capital city, Kuala Lumpur, and they are easily ¹................................ by train or by car. At weekends, hundreds of local people visit, so it's ²................................ to go during the week if you can. When you arrive, the first thing you'll see is an enormous staircase that climbs up the side of the mountain to the mouth of the caves and a golden statue of the Hindu war god Lord Murugan. You can't miss the statue! It's so tall that it's ³................................ from miles away. There are 272 steps up to the caves, so it takes a ⁴................................ amount of time and energy to walk up. It's a sensible idea to wear good, ⁵................................ walking shoes – if they bend easily they will be good for going up so many steps. On the way up, you'll see lots of monkeys which will steal any ⁶................................ items, as well as things they can't eat! For example, they've been known to take ⁷................................ items like cameras and mobile phones, so be careful! In the caves, there is a Hindu temple with lots of statues and there are hundreds of bats flying around. The pitch black caves are ⁸................................ for bats because they use sonar to find their way around, producing sounds which are so high that they aren't ⁹................................ to humans. Once a year, in January or February, the Batu Caves are the scene of a really ¹⁰................................ Hindu festival. Thousands of people walk for seven hours to the temple in the caves, many of them carrying heavy containers of milk.

Future time clauses

3 Choose the correct answers.

1 If you walk up the steps to the Batu Caves, your feet will hurt **unless / as long as** you wear good walking shoes.
2 We will visit the Batu Caves **after / when** we are in Malaysia.
3 It won't be very crowded at the caves **in case / as long as** you go on a weekday.
4 **Supposing / Unless** the caves are closed, what other places can we visit near Kuala Lumpur?
5 Take an umbrella **in case / suppose** it rains on the way to the caves.
6 **As soon as / Until** they see tourists with food, the monkeys will try to steal it.
7 You'll be very tired **by the time / as long as** you reach the top of the staircase.

4 Complete the sentences with the phrases below. Use each phrase only once.

▪ suppose ▪ in case ▪ as long as ▪ unless ▪ after ▪ before

1 .... you go to the Batu Caves in January or February, you won't see the festival.
2 We will go inside the temple and caves .... we walk up the 272 steps.
3 Keep your camera in your bag .... the monkeys try to steal it.
4 .... it rains heavily, will we still be able to walk up the steps and visit the caves?
5 You will see the statue of Lord Murugan .... you arrive at the mouth of the Batu Caves.
6 .... you are reasonably fit, it won't be difficult to climb up the 272 steps.

5 CHALLENGE! Some of your friends are going on a walking holiday in the Taman Negara rainforest in Malaysia. Read the advertisement and offer them some advice about what to take, wear, see and do.

The oldest rainforest reserve in south-east Asia.
See wild animals including elephants, bears and monkeys.
Camp overnight in the middle of the rainforest.
Go white water rafting on the river.
But watch out for insect bites, sunburn and heavy rainfall!

The world around us 15

Reading Educating the world's children

1 Look at the headlines. In your opinion, which ones are surprising and which ones are not surprising?

1. **MORE CHILDREN THAN EVER ARE ATTENDING SCHOOL**

2. **LITERACY RATES ARE ON THE RISE**

3. **10% OF THE WORLD'S CHILDREN DON'T GO TO SCHOOL**

4. **GIRLS ARE MORE LIKELY THAN BOYS TO BE DENIED ACCESS TO EDUCATION**

5. **CHILDREN IN AFRICA ARE LEAST LIKELY TO GO TO SCHOOL**

2 Read the article. Match questions 1–5 to paragraphs A–E that answer the questions.
1. Why are some children not able to attend school?
2. Is access to education generally improving?
3. What should we do to help improve access to education?
4. Why is education important?
5. How many children don't go to school?

3 Match sentences a–g to gaps 1–5 in the article. There are two sentences that you do not need.
a. More people in the world can read and write than ever before.
b. The improvement in school attendance is a sure sign that these measures are working.
c. Many developing countries have to repay large amounts of money in debt to wealthier countries.
d. Consequently, for poor families, it makes more sense to send their boys to school.
e. However, a lot of mothers can neither read nor take care of their children.
f. However, this is not true.
g. In such circumstances, children often get caught up in their nation's conflict.

Educating the world's children

A ....
Everyone knows how important it is to educate the world's children. But is the world really doing enough to educate its youth, or are we letting young people down by failing to provide opportunities to learn? On the plus side, it seems that access to education is better than it was. In 2008, UNESCO, the United Nations organization that focuses on education, carried out research which was largely encouraging. They published figures to show that, overall, since the 1970s, there has been a considerable rise in school attendance in both primary and secondary schools across the world and the amount of time young people spend being schooled has lengthened, too. [1] .... This is very good news, as rising literacy rates suggest that both access to and quality of education are getting better around the world.

B ....
Unfortunately, these generally positive statistics can't hide the fact that a worrying number of young people are still not getting the educational opportunities they should. Recent UNESCO figures show that almost 60 million children of primary school age don't attend school at all, which is about ten per cent of the world's population. In parts of sub-Saharan Africa and south and west Asia, the young children who are privileged enough to receive any schooling at all are in a minority.

C ....
There are a lot of factors that stop children from getting an education. For example, if a country is at war or going through a period of political problems, school attendance will inevitably drop. [2] .... Currently, about 300,000 children in the world are child soldiers. Economic factors are also a key reason why children don't go to school. According to UNESCO figures, 215 million children are already working and their incomes are often essential for their families. In the developing world, it's much more likely that girls are denied a good education. Sometimes, cultural and religious factors may prohibit girls from getting a good education, but, more often than not, the reasons are economic. Adult males have more opportunities to earn if they have an education. [3] .... Thirty-nine thousand girls under the age of eighteen get married every day, so one reason why many teenage girls don't go to school is that they already have children of their own.

D ....

It is reasonable to ask what relevance education has for children and their families in poverty-stricken countries. For people living in remote communities, bringing up children in harsh conditions and often relying on subsistence farming to survive, education may not seem important. ⁴.......... Education is vital to people who live in countries in the developing world, where incomes and opportunities are low. In the next few decades, jobs in technology and communications, which require literacy and numeracy skills, will replace manual jobs more and more. Experts estimate that every additional year of education will increase the income of a person in a poor country by ten per cent. And educated people don't just make money for themselves – they are the entrepreneurs and the inventors who, in the future, are going to create jobs and wealth for other people.

E ....

In the developed world, children are fortunate to have access to a good education. This should be available for everyone. It is important that governments around the world take action and there are a lot of things they can do. For example, rich countries can relieve poor countries from debt. ⁵.......... By cancelling or reducing these debts, wealthy countries allow poorer countries to spend more money on education. Policy makers in developing countries can also make a difference by investing resources in education, in the knowledge that having a well-educated population is a way of improving a country's economy. Well-educated people set up businesses, create jobs and are able to take on the responsibilities of professional careers, such as medicine, teaching and the law, which improve the lives of everybody in their country.

4 Study the article and the sentences in exercise 3 and complete the phrasal verbs in the sentences below with the correct prepositions. Then match the phrasal verbs to the correct synonyms, a or b.

1 If you don't work hard at school, you'll **let** .... your parents and yourself.
 a disappoint b please
2 We **got caught** .... in the demonstrations against the education cuts.
 a participated by chance b looked at
3 Sociologists have **carried** .... research into how to improve access to education in developing countries.
 a performed b attempted
4 In Britain, a growing number of young people are being **brought** .... by only one parent.
 a educated b raised
5 Many people have **set** .... companies to advise school leavers on their career prospects.
 a started b closed
6 You shouldn't **take** .... more work unless you know that you can do it.
 a refuse b accept

5 Complete the text with the correct form of the phrasal verbs in exercise 4.

American high school drop-outs

According to a statistical analysis which experts ¹.......... in 2013, over 3 million teenagers drop out of school every year. By doing so, they ².......... themselves .... badly, since statistics show that a high school graduate who works throughout his or her adult life will earn about $260,000 more than a drop-out. Often, high school drop-outs have been ³.......... without good role models and they sometimes find themselves ⁴.......... in a life of poverty and crime. Remarkably, 75% of US crimes are committed by high school drop-outs! Currently, education experts are trying to think of new ways to persuade young people to attend school every day. People who are successful at school are more likely to ⁵.......... their own businesses or ⁶.......... demanding, but well-paid professional jobs.

6 CHALLENGE! How important is education to you? Answer the questions.

1 What would you be doing if you weren't at school?
2 Why do you want to study?
3 How do you think you benefit from being at school?
4 Is getting good grades important to you? Why / why not?

Writing Describing a place

Modifying adverbs with gradable and non-gradable adjectives

1 Choose the correct answers.

1 Our tour guide was **extremely** ………..
   a knowledgeable b spellbinding c amazing
2 Buenos Aires, the capital of Argentina, was a **totally** ……….. city to visit.
   a diverse b overwhelming c vibrant
3 The day we spent in the museum was **a bit** ……….
   a tedious b awesome c incredible
4 Parts of the countryside are **utterly** ………..
   a diverse b incredible c recognizable
5 The view from the top of the mountain was **absolutely** ……….
   a interesting b exciting c magnificent
6 The view of the opera house was **very** ……….
   a disappointing b enormous c diverse

2 Read extracts A–D. Then match them to four of the text types below.

- an encyclopaedia entry ■ emails ■ a newspaper article
- a history book ■ a tour promotion leaflet ■ a travel guide
- messages on a social networking site ■ a novel

A
Riga Riga is Latvia's capital city. It lies on the Gulf of Riga and it is a major seaport and financial centre in the Baltic Sea Region, with a population of over 650,000. The city was founded in 1201 and its historical centre features old wooden buildings and Art Nouveau architecture from the nineteenth and early twentieth centuries.

B
A city with a fascinating history and amazing architecture, museums, cafés and restaurants. Explore its narrow streets and magnificent buildings at your leisure. Enjoy delicious food at Riga's excellent restaurants. And don't forget to try Riga's famous chocolate! You'll love Riga. It's the ideal place to spend a long weekend.

C
Riga Walking Tour
Experienced local guide, Ilse, will introduce you to unseen Riga. We start at the Freedom Monument, near the well-known Laima Clock. First, we will walk to the top of Bastion Hill for views of the city. Next is the fascinating War Museum. Then, we visit the trendy shops and cafés near the old city walls before visiting Riga Cathedral and the Occupation Museum. Book now. Places are limited.

D
view previous comments

- **Greg** On my way back from Riga! Awesome place!
- **Omar** Cool! ;)
- **Lucy** What was it like?!
- **Greg** Did walking tour. Knowledgeable guide but v. boring! Views from hill magnificent! Art Nouveau buildings extraordinary!
- **Omar** What else was cool?
- **Greg** Busy, crowded squares, great food esp. chocolate! War Museum tedious but Occupation Museum fascinating.
- **Lucy** Well, glad you had a good time!!
- **Greg** Sure did! Check out my photos!

Write a comment…   Report

3 Match the style descriptions below to the extracts in exercise 2 that they best describe.

1 It uses simple, repetitive sentences and the personal pronoun *We*. ……….
2 It uses long, complex sentences, passive forms and full forms. ……….
3 It uses abbreviations, idiomatic and colloquial language, and exclamation marks for emphasis. ……….
4 It uses imperatives, personal pronouns and descriptive adjectives. ……….

WRITING GUIDE

■ **Task** Imagine that you are Greg. Write a travel blog post about your trip to Riga, what you did and what you saw.

■ **Ideas** Use the information in the texts to brainstorm ideas for your description of Riga. Make notes about:
- when you decided to go and why.
- what impressions you had of the city.
- what you saw and did on the walking tour.
- what you think about the place.

■ **Plan** Follow the plan:

Paragraph 1: Opening paragraph. Describe when and why you decided to go and your first impressions of the place.
Paragraph 2: Describe what you did, what you saw and what you liked or didn't like.
Paragraph 3: Sum up the main features of the place and what makes it an interesting destination.

■ **Write** Write your description. Use the paragraph plan to help you.

■ **Check** Check the following points.
- Is your style consistent?
- Does your description use gradable and non-gradable adjectives?
- Have you checked grammar, vocabulary, spelling and punctuation?

Progress check Unit 2

Read 1–11 and evaluate your learning in Unit 2. Give yourself a mark from 1 to 3. How can you improve?
1 I can't do this. 2 I have some problems with this. 3 I can do this well.

A Real education	Mark (1–3)	How can I improve?
1 Name two things that Wagner Iworrigan can do that most people can't.		
I can understand a text about the meaning of school.		

2 Complete the sentences with the correct prepositions.
  a What are the benefits .... getting a good education?
  b There is not much demand .... manual workers nowadays.		

I can use nouns with dependent prepositions.		

B Life on the edge	Mark (1–3)	How can I improve?

3 Choose the best future form in each of these sentences.
  a I've just checked the timetable. The next bus **leaves / will leave** at three.
  b I've written the appointment in my diary. I **'m seeing / will see** the doctor tomorrow.
  c By Friday, we **will finish / will have finished** the essay.		

I can understand and use future forms.		

C Urban stories	Mark (1–3)	How can I improve?
4 What are the antonyms of the adjectives below? a inhabited b renovated c efficient		
I can use antonyms to describe urban regeneration.		
5 What is the SIER hierarchy?		
I can apply strategies for active listening.		
6 Give one way of introducing a requirement and one way of evaluating a requirement.		
I can introduce, express and evaluate requirements.		

D Songlines	Mark (1–3)	How can I improve?
7 What are songlines?		
I can understand a text about songlines.		
8 Complete the adjectives with -*able* or -*ible*. a flex......... b advis......... c ed.........		
I can use adjectives with -*able* or -*ible*.		

9 Join the clauses with one word.
  a Bring a jumper with you in .... it's cold at the barbecue.
  b We'll spend the day outside as .... as the weather stays fine.		

I can use future time clauses.		

E Describing a place	Mark (1–3)	How can I improve?

10 Which of the adjectives below can go with the modifier *extremely* and which can go with *utterly*?
  a overwhelming   b vibrant
  c spellbinding d diverse		

I can use gradable and non-gradable adjectives and modifying adverbs.		
11 Name a style of writing that uses contractions and exclamation marks or capital letters for emphasis.		
I can recognize different styles of writing.		

3 Things that matter

Vocabulary Hoarders

V insight Synonyms

1 Replace the words in italics with the correct form of the synonyms below.

- accumulate ■ get rid of ■ stacks ■ products ■ junk
- belongings

1 My room looks quite tidy, but there's a lot of *rubbish* .... under the bed!
2 I don't think he's ever *thrown* .... anything *out*!
3 When I moved house I couldn't believe how much stuff I had *amassed* ....
4 My dad still has *piles* .... of old records, but no record player!
5 I keep all my precious *possessions* .... in a tin box, where I know they're safe.
6 The bathroom is full of *stuff* .... that I have only used a couple of times.

V insight Phrasal verbs with *out*

2 Choose the correct answers.

Next time your parents are ¹**clearing out / dropping out of** the loft or garage, make sure they don't ²**wear out / throw out** their old video games. Games from the 1980s are becoming collectible items.

Joel Cassidy was ³**helping out / opting out** at his local charity shop when the manager pointed to a whole heap of 1980s video games which were ⁴**running out / spilling out** of a cupboard. The manager asked Joel to ⁵**sort them out / pick them out**, and, knowing Joel had an old games console, the manager told him he could ⁶**pick out / clear out** any he wanted to take home. Joel ⁷**spread them out / took them out** on the counter and saw that one of them was *Pepsi Invaders*, a rare game worth over £1,000.

V British vs American English

3 Replace the British English words in italics with the appropriate American English words.

1 Put the saucepan on top of the *cooker* .... for now; I'll put it away later.
2 He lived in a very small *flat* .... with just one bedroom.
3 She liked sitting in the *garden* .... when it was sunny.
4 Just put the bread in the *dustbin* ....; it's going mouldy.
5 I need to go through what's hanging in my *wardrobe* .... and sort out the clothes that don't fit me any more.
6 How do you manage to live in a building with no *lift* ....?
7 Pull the *curtains* ....; it's getting dark.
8 Oh no, it's really dark out here. Where's the *torch* ....?

4 Complete the text about feng shui for teenagers with the words below. There are two words that you do not need.

- piles of ■ drop out of ■ chest of drawers ■ possessions
- throw out ■ curtains ■ clutter ■ help out ■ reach out

Feng shui for teenagers

Feng shui is the ancient Chinese art of designing your room and placing objects to create a positive environment, influencing your emotions and behaviour, and perhaps even how other people treat you. The first step is to ¹.......................... all the stuff you don't really need. According to feng shui, holding onto ².......................... will hold you back in life.

Then, think about where to place the bigger items of furniture. For example, the ³.......................... should be in a different position, depending on what it is made of. For example, if it's made of wood, place it in the east corner. The bed should never be underneath a window, even if you have ⁴.......................... . Try not to place your desk with ⁵.......................... books behind it. Feng shui says this will make people gossip about you.

There are also some other things you can do to improve your life. Put a lamp in the north-east of your room for educational success, or, if you want to ⁶.......................... to someone and create a better relationship, place a picture of that person in the south-west corner. Want to achieve something in particular? Feng shui could ⁷.......................... if you place anything related to your goal on the south wall of your room.

5 CHALLENGE! Prepare a description of your room. In what ways could you improve it to follow the rules of feng shui?

Grammar What's left behind

Articles

1 Complete the text with *a / an*, *the* or – (no article).

Homeless man returns valuable ring

Sarah Darling, **1**......... American businesswoman, was walking past **2**......... homeless man sitting on a street corner in Kansas City. Feeling sorry for him, she reached into her purse and gave him **3**......... handful of coins. Only later did she realize that amongst **4**......... coins was her very valuable engagement ring, which she had taken off earlier that day because it was uncomfortable. **5**......... ring was made from platinum and diamonds and was worth thousands of dollars. Two days later, Sarah returned to find **6**......... homeless man, Billy Ray Harris, and asked him about the ring. To her amazement, he immediately handed it back to her. He explained that **7**......... honesty was very important to him. His grandfather had brought him up properly.
It shows that **8**......... people shouldn't jump to **9**......... worst conclusion and assume that **10**......... homeless are more likely to be dishonest than any other group of people. In fact, Billy Ray Harris had taken the ring to **11**......... jeweller, who had offered him $4,000 for it. However, although he only usually received a few dollars **12**......... day, Harris decided to keep the ring in case the owner came back for it.

2 Read the rest of the text. In each sentence there is an unnecessary word, a word missing or an incorrect word. Circle the mistakes and write the corrections.

Sarah gave Billy all money she had in her wallet as a reward, but it still didn't feel like enough. So later, she and her husband, Bill, set up the fund for Harris. They wanted to raise a $4,000 he had been offered for the ring. As story spread, however, they ended up raising more than $186,000. Billy was also offered the part-time job. Best of all, he has also been given second chance with his family. His sister, who is living miles away in the Texas, recognized him on TV. A family has now been reunited.

Determiners

3 Complete the text with the determiners below. Do not use a determiner more than once. Sometimes more than one answer is possible. There are two determiners that you do not need.

■ far too much ■ many ■ several ■ little ■ a little ■ a few
■ almost none ■ some ■ much ■ a lot of ■ hardly any

TRASH TO TREND

We're all familiar with the idea of recycling waste, but what about *upcycling* it? Trash to Trend (TTT) is a new organization that decided that **1**......... material was being wasted in the fashion industry. When clothes are made, **2**......... scraps of material are thrown away. In fact, according to one designer, many companies bin as **3**......... as 20% of the material they buy and **4**......... of it is even recycled. TTT came up with the idea of encouraging clothes manufacturers to provide information about how much scrap material they have, the kinds of materials and so on. With this information, TTT can contact independent designers and offer them the material for free, or for very **5**......... money.

Trash to Trend started in Estonia and spread to other countries in the area. **6**......... of the designers, such as Reet Aus, are becoming quite well known. Now TTT are looking to find partners in as **7**......... countries as possible. **8**......... of the fashion made by their designers can be bought on the Trash to Trend website and they're about to open **9**......... stores in Tallin and other cities as well. There's even a new Master's degree in fashion upcycling at the Estonian Art Academy.

4 CHALLENGE! Think about a time when you lost something valuable or important to you. Prepare answers to the questions and write or tell the story of what happened.

1 When did this happen? How old were you?
2 Where were you? What were you doing?
3 Was there a particular reason why you lost the item?
4 Did you ever find the item? Did someone find it for you?
5 How did you feel about losing it / finding it?

Things that matter

Listening, speaking and vocabulary One man's trash …

V Adjectives describing objects

1 Choose three different adjectives from the list below to describe each photo. Then complete the sentences about each object using your chosen adjectives in the correct order.

- antique ■ beaten ■ copper ■ delicate ■ flowery ■ silk
- tiny ■ square ■ wooden

1 He put the ring in a .... box.
2 She was delighted with the gift of a .... kimono.
3 In the museum, I saw a .... bowl.

2 In each of the following sentences, one adjective is in the wrong place. Rewrite the adjectives in the order they should appear.

1 We gazed at the blue, slow-moving, narrow river far below us.
2 The sculpture was made from plastic, crushed, transparent cups.
3 The divers found a rectangular, metal, rusty box.
4 When we finally opened the old desk, there was a pile of tangled, silk, decaying ribbons.
5 The man was flying a colourful, huge, paper kite.
6 How much did you pay for that leather, dated, ripped jacket?

Selecting things for a time capsule

3 A time capsule is a collection of objects buried for future generations to find, so that they can discover things about our lives now. Think of six objects people might put in a time capsule.

4 3.03 Listen to Jim and Sue discussing what to put in a time capsule. Which of the following items do they agree to include?

- a popular toy ■ a newspaper ■ a DVD ■ a receipt
- a memory stick ■ an item of clothing ■ food
- photographs ■ a letter

5 3.03 Listen again and match the speakers, Jim (J) or Sue (S), to opinions and suggestions 1–7.

1 Newspapers are old-fashioned. ....
2 Food is an impractical idea. ....
3 Fifty years isn't long enough to keep the time capsule buried. ....
4 Only quite cheap items should be included. ....
5 A memory stick will be useless in the future. ....
6 It isn't vital that people will be able to read information on the memory stick. ....
7 A picture of clothes could be better than the real thing. ....

6 3.03 Complete the phrases from the dialogue. Listen again and check.

1 Right. Our main .... is to give people in the future some idea about what life was like for us, isn't it?
2 Well, we .... have something like today's newspaper, couldn't we?
3 How about .... some typical food?
4 Mmm. I don't think that's the best .... Won't it just go bad?
5 I'm not .... Even tinned food doesn't last more than a few years.
6 Actually, I think that's an .... point. How long are we planning to leave the time capsule buried?
7 Yes, that .... like a really good idea. We don't want people to forget it's there.
8 I think we should definitely have some modern technology. It will help to .... that our society was quite technologically advanced.
9 Now, we shouldn't forget that one of our main .... involves choosing objects that represent the whole community.
10 But thinking about it, wouldn't clothes take up a lot of space? .... we should think again.
11 OK, ... look at another way of showing what people wore. How about some photographs?

7 Match sentences 1–11 in exercise 6 to categories A–D.

A Stating aims: ...1..., ...
B Making suggestions: ...., ..., ...
C Approving suggestions: ...., ..., ...
D Rejecting suggestions: ...., ..., ...

8 Imagine you are planning to bury a time capsule. Decide which of the items in exercise 4 you would include to help people from the future understand how young people lived today. Add any other items you think are important. Then use your ideas to write a dialogue in which you discuss what to include and why. Include some of the language in exercise 6.

22 Things that matter

Vocabulary and grammar Lost treasures

insight Compounds with participles

1 Complete the text with the words below. There are two words that you do not need.

- mind-blowing ■ heartfelt ■ never-ending ■ handmade
- broad-minded ■ breathtaking ■ well-earned
- highly-respected ■ much-anticipated

Although several ¹............ experts had announced that there was nothing of any significance still to be found in the Valley of the Kings, in 1917 Howard Carter resumed his seemingly ²............ search for the tomb of Tutankhamun. A set of beautiful ³............ items bearing Tutankhamun's name had already been found, and this proved, he believed, that the tomb must be there somewhere, too.

In November 1922, after five years of searching, even Lord Carnarvon, Carter's sponsor, was ready to give up. Carter made one last ⁴............ plea for more time and Carnarvon reluctantly agreed.

Only a few days later, Carter finally found the ⁵............ tomb, and, on opening the door, he was greeted by a sight of the ⁶............ treasure within. His ⁷............ place in the history books was assured.

Objects in a museum

2 Complete the sentences with the words below. There are two words that you do not need.

- coins ■ helmets ■ jewels ■ masks ■ mummy ■ pottery
- sculpture ■ statues ■ tablets ■ tools ■ vase ■ weapons

1 Once people had discovered how to make iron, they were able to make .... to help with farming.
2 Stoke-on-Trent was an area of England famous for making ...., such as plates, bowls and cups.
3 Soldiers have always worn .... to protect their heads.
4 The museum had a fine collection of old ...., such as swords, bows and arrows.
5 The Crown ...., which belong to the Queen of England, are only worn on special occasions.
6 It's incredible to think that the .... used to be a living person.
7 It was impossible to recognize anyone because they were wearing ....
8 Many famous people have had .... made of them.
9 She carefully arranged the flowers in a tall ....
10 Before paper was invented, people would write on stone ....

Verb patterns

3 Complete the second sentence so that it has a similar meaning to the first. Use the correct form of the words in brackets.

1 It's vital that you bring in your homework today.
   You must .... (remember)
2 I think it would be a good idea for you to tell me what's happening.
   I .... (suggest)
3 She wasn't allowed to stay out late – her parents were very strict.
   Her parents .... (let)
4 I'm sure I made the right decision to leave.
   I have never .... (regret)
5 You should take an umbrella – it's raining.
   It's raining, so you'll .... (need)
6 I advise you to get a lawyer.
   I .... (recommend)
7 Don't force him to do it if he doesn't want to!
   Don't ....! (make)
8 I should ring Jane later. Can you remind me?
   Can you make sure I don't ....? (forget)

4 Complete the text about visiting the Valley of the Kings with the correct form of the verbs in brackets.

Valley of the Kings

Have you ever imagined ¹............ (visit) the great Valley of the Kings in Egypt and seeing for yourself the tomb of Tutankhamun? If you can afford ²............ (do) it, it is certainly a mind-blowing experience.

I would recommend ³............ (hire) an experienced local guide. Someone who knows a lot about the site will really help you ⁴............ (visualize) how it must have looked in ancient times. Don't forget ⁵............ (make) a visit to the Egyptian Museum in Cairo as well. You'll want ⁶............ (go) there in order to see the fantastic treasures that were found in the tomb.

If you are considering ⁷............ (stay) longer in Egypt, you could also go on ⁸............ (see) the famous temples at Luxor. The modern town of Luxor is, in fact, the ancient city of Thebes, once the capital of Egypt. Even today, the huge Temples of Karnak, which together are over a kilometre wide, show the vast power and might of the Egyptian Empire, but you should also try ⁹............ (make) time to visit the smaller Luxor Temple in the town itself. Over 5,000 years old, it's an amazing sight, especially floodlit at night. I'd also suggest ¹⁰............ (visit) the Luxor Museum, where many of the relics from the temples are to be found. After all this sightseeing, why not take a well-earned rest, relaxing as a *felucca* (a traditional boat) takes you gently down the Nile?

◀ PREV   NEXT ▶

5 CHALLENGE! Think of a historical site you have visited and write a similar text to the one in exercise 4. Try to include some compound adjectives and remember to use correct verb patterns.

Reading The thrill of the chase

1 Read *The thrill of the chase* and answer the questions.
   1 What kind of text is this?
      a an autobiography
      b a narrative
      c an article
      d a news report
   2 What is the writer's main aim in writing the article?
      a To create a sense of excitement about the treasure hunt.
      b To warn people to take care when treasure hunting.
      c To explain Forrest Fenn's reasons for hiding the treasure.
      d To give his or her opinions about the treasure hunt.

2 Read the article again. Choose the correct answers.
   1 Fenn has placed his autobiography in the treasure chest so
      a anyone who finds the treasure will know it was his.
      b he will become famous when the treasure is found.
      c he can sell more copies of his book.
      d as to encourage people to look for the treasure.
   2 The author's view of Fenn's autobiography is that it is
      a somewhat unbelievable.
      b rather long and boring.
      c compelling reading.
      d very well written.
   3 The authorities are worried about people
      a digging up national parkland.
      b fighting each other for the treasure.
      c being attacked by wild animals.
      d getting lost or hurting themselves.
   4 According to Fenn, his family are
      a very upset about losing the wealth.
      b mostly uninterested in the treasure.
      c very worried about his mental health.
      d definitely planning to look for it themselves.
   5 The writer implies that Fenn's old friends are
      a only contacting him because they want the treasure.
      b pleased to have the opportunity to get back in touch.
      c following him every time he leaves home.
      d sending him thousands of emails every day.
   6 The author believes Fenn's treasure hunt isn't just about selling books, because he
      a has done this kind of thing before.
      b has shown the treasure to other people.
      c doesn't need to make any more money.
      d is a very serious man.

The thrill of the chase

Imagine finding a treasure chest straight from ancient times, with piles of rare gold coins, antique jewellery, gold nuggets and a sprinkling of gold dust. Just a dream? Not at all! One day
5 someone will find this treasure chest, hidden by eighty-two-year-old eccentric millionaire Forrest Fenn, in a secret location somewhere in the wild American countryside.

Estimated to be worth at least one million dollars,
10 Fenn's treasure was amassed over a lifetime of collecting. Included in the chest are some of his most prized possessions, such as an ancient Indian necklace covered in jewels. And, at the bottom of the chest, in a small glass jar, is his autobiography, so
15 that even if the chest is opened thousands of years from now, the finder will know who the hoard belonged to.

All you have to do to find these unimaginable riches is to decipher nine clues contained in
20 a mysterious poem, which can be found in Fenn's autobiography, *The thrill of the chase*. The autobiography is well worth a read for its own sake: a fascinating story of a boy from a poor family who grew up to be a fabulously wealthy art dealer. Fenn
25 didn't even go to college; instead, he spent nearly twenty years in the Air Force, accumulating quite a collection of medals for bravery. Later, he returned

24   Things that matter

to Texas and started a business as an art dealer, making his fortune from trading art and antiquities.
30 His customers included many famous Hollywood actors and political leaders.

Many of the treasure hunters believe that, as well as the poem, there may be more clues in Fenn's life story; that the treasure is probably buried
35 somewhere that he knows well. Fenn has said that the treasure is more than 1,500 m above sea level, causing many people to start digging in the mountains near his Santa Fe home. Others have concentrated their efforts on Yellowstone
40 National Park, where Fenn spent most of his childhood holidays learning to find his way round the winding trails.

The number of inexperienced city dwellers descending on these wild areas has raised some
45 safety concerns. Only a few weeks ago, a woman from Texas got lost in the huge mountainous area near Los Alamos and had to spend the night outside before being rescued the next day. Officials have warned people to make sure they
50 are properly prepared for the great outdoors.

According to Fenn, he is the only person who knows the location of the treasure chest. Even his wife and daughters have no idea. Asked if his children mind his hiding quite a significant
55 part of their inheritance for a stranger to find, Fenn replied, 'They've been saying for years that I'm crazy.' He doesn't think his daughters would have any interest in it, though perhaps his grandchildren might.

60 Fenn is also finding himself at the centre of a lot of unwanted attention. He has already received over 9,000 emails and even has people ringing his doorbell, or trying to follow him whenever he leaves the house. He has also found a lot of old
65 friends contacting him out of the blue. The reason for their sudden interest isn't exactly a mystery!

Of course, no one can be absolutely sure that Fenn has actually hidden the treasure at all. While the treasure certainly exists and many people
70 have seen it, the whole idea of the treasure hunt might just be an elaborate joke. Some people have even suggested that it was simply a way to sell thousands of copies of his autobiography.

Given, however, that Fenn does indeed have a
75 considerable personal fortune, it seems unlikely that it is just about selling books. His friends also claim that he is absolutely serious. It seems that, after a lifetime of treasure hunting, Fenn simply wants to give others the opportunity to
80 experience the thrill of the chase for themselves. So the treasure is out there somewhere, and, one day, someone will find it. Could it be you?

3 Match the adjectives in A to the nouns in B to make adjective–noun collocations. Then check your answers in the article.

A

■ ancient ■ prized ■ unwanted ■ elaborate ■ personal ■ unimaginable ■ winding ■ antique

B

■ trails ■ attention ■ riches ■ jewellery ■ possessions ■ times ■ fortune ■ joke

1 ....
2 ....
3 ....
4 ....
5 ....
6 ....
7 ....
8 ....

4 Complete the sentences with the collocations in exercise 3.

1 The history of the Native Americans can be traced back to ....
2 Can you really not hear that noise, or is this all just some kind of ....?
3 It is rumoured that the former President used his time in office to amass a vast ....
4 There have always been stories of .... to be found in sunken ships.
5 She gazed at the rings, brooches, necklaces and other items of ....
6 The best way to deal with .... is to ignore the person.
7 She felt the wind in her hair as she climbed up the ....
8 My car is one of my most .... I don't know what I'd do without it.

5 CHALLENGE! Think about one of your most prized possessions. Prepare answers to the questions and write or tell the story of how you got it.

1 What is the possession? Describe it.
2 Was it given to you, or did you buy it? How long have you had it?
3 Why do you value it so much? Would other people feel the same about it, or is it just special to you?

Writing A story

1 Look at the objects. Write a short description of each one. What era do you think each one comes from? Who would have owned them and what would they have done with them? What stories might they tell if they could speak?

2 Read the story. Which object is it about?

Suddenly, the noise of a bell rang out. Looking up from her book, Cecily wondered what on earth it could be. It wasn't the doorbell, which was far less shrill and insistent. The sound continued. Feeling a little anxious, she put her book down and walked out into the hall. She was just in time to see Alfred, her husband of twenty-five years, march towards the hall table. Of course! The telephone!

'Hello, Redhill 2453,' he announced into the receiver.

How could she have forgotten the arrival of the telephone? Having been one of the first people to get one, Alfred was terribly pleased with his decision. The only problem was that they didn't really know anyone else who had a telephone, so there was no one to call them. In fact, this was the first time she had ever heard the telephone ring at all. As she thought this, she heard Alfred draw in a sharp intake of breath. 'Yes,' he said urgently. 'Yes, I quite understand.'

Cecily's heart started to beat faster. What had happened? As she hurried down the hall, she reached for Alfred's arm.

'What is it?' she asked. But Alfred was too busy writing something down on a little note-pad he had put by the telephone. Looking at the pad, she saw the name of a hospital.

'What is it?' she asked, more anxious than ever. After carefully putting down the receiver, Alfred turned to look at her.

'Our first grandchild,' he said, a tear in his eye. 'She's just been born at the hospital. Everything's fine. Let's go and see them now.'

3 Put the following events from the story in the order in which they actually happened (not necessarily the same order that they are told in the story).

1 Cecily heard the telephone for the first time. ……….
2 Alfred decided to get a new telephone. ……….
3 Cecily and Alfred went to the hospital. ……….
4 Cecily and Alfred's daughter had a baby girl. ……….
5 Alfred answered the telephone. ……….

4 Rewrite the sentences from the story, replacing the words in italics with a different structure for ordering events in a story. Make any other changes necessary.

1 *Looking* up from her book, Cecily wondered what on earth it could be.

2 *As she thought* this, she heard Alfred draw in a sharp intake of breath.

3 *As she hurried* down the hall, she reached for Alfred's arm.

4 *Looking* at the pad, she saw the name of a hospital.

5 *After carefully putting down* the receiver, Alfred turned to look at her.

WRITING GUIDE

■ **Task** Choose one of the other objects in exercise 1 (or another object of your choice) and write a story about something that happened to the object, or while the object was being used.

■ **Plan** Follow the plan:

Paragraph 1: Begin your story. Introduce the object and the main characters. Decide if the story is going to be in the first or third person. Are you going to tell the story chronologically, or have a flashback?

Paragraph 2: Develop the story. What happens to the object? What impact does it have on the main characters? Try to show what the characters are seeing, hearing, feeling and thinking.

Paragraph 3: End your story. What happens to the object and the main characters? Try to add a twist or something unexpected.

■ **Write** Write your story. Use the paragraph plan to help you.

■ **Check** Check the following points.
- Does your story start in an interesting way?
- Does it make you want to learn more about the characters?
- Does it have a beginning, middle and end (though the events don't need to happen chronologically)?
- Have you checked grammar, vocabulary, spelling and punctuation?

Progress check Unit 3

Read 1–14 and evaluate your learning in Unit 3. Give yourself a mark from 1 to 3. How can you improve?
1 I can't do this.   2 I have some problems with this.   3 I can do this well.

A Hoarders	Mark (1–3)	How can I improve?
1 Give three reasons why people might find it difficult to throw things away.		
I can understand a text about hoarding.		
2 How can you decide what the purpose of an article is?		
I can detect the writer's purpose in writing a text.		
3 Write three synonyms for *belongings*.		
I can use a variety of synonyms.		
4 Give two phrasal verbs using *out* that both mean *to discard something*.		
I can use a variety of phrasal verbs with *out*.		

B What's left behind	Mark (1–3)	How can I improve?
5 Give three reasons for using the definite article (*the*).		
I can state reasons for using different articles.		
6 Explain the difference between *few*, *a few*, *little* and *a little*.		
I can use determiners accurately.		

C One man's trash …	Mark (1–3)	How can I improve?
7 Put the following types of adjectives in the order they go before a noun. a opinion b age c colour d size		
I can put adjectives in the correct order before a noun.		
8 What was Schult's main goal in making *Trash People*?		
I can understand a radio interview about an artist's work.		
9 Give two different ways of making a suggestion and two ways of responding (one approving and one rejecting).		
I can make and respond to suggestions.		

D Lost treasures	Mark (1–3)	How can I improve?
10 Give two reasons why a museum might not want to return an item to its country of origin.		
I can understand a text about museums.		
11 Give examples of two compound adjectives made with an adverb + past participle and two made with a noun + present participle.		
I can understand and use compound adjectives.		

12 State the difference in meaning between these pairs of verbs.
  a stop to do something / stop doing something
  b forget to do something / forget doing something		

I can use the *-ing* or infinitive form of a verb correctly.		

E A story	Mark (1–3)	How can I improve?
13 Explain when you would use the structure *having* + past participle.		
I can use different structures to order events in a story.		
14 Give two ways of starting a story in an interesting way.		
I can write an engaging story.		

4 Mind and body

Vocabulary Perfect people

insight Verbs and nouns with the same form

1 Read the news story and the blog entry. Complete the blog entry with the words in bold in the news story.

> An American company that employs **engineers** to design lifting machinery that can **shift** heavy boxes from one part of a warehouse to another is in the news. It wants to **screen** its employees to find out whether they are genetically likely to develop certain diseases. The company's factories produce chemicals which, in rare cases, **cause** cancer. Some employees don't **mind** undergoing the process. However, opponents say that it is unfair to tell employees that they are likely to suffer from a rare disease, as this is a great **burden** to carry through life.

MickeyJ   Home   Profile   Account

> What sort of cruel ¹................. could think of a plan that is likely to ²................. workers with information they really don't want to hear? Every day, on TV, the company spokesperson ³................. public opinion by arguing that the process is good for employees. I disagree. This is a ⁴................. I strongly believe in and I hope to create a ⁵................. in attitude on this matter. I'm organizing a petition. It's on my computer ⁶................. right now. I'm hoping to get enough signatures to ban the company's poisonous chemicals.

insight Noun suffixes: -ness, -ity, -ion

2 Read about the famous people. Change the adjectives below to nouns and match them to the descriptions.

- addicted
- bald
- deaf
- disabled
- short-sighted

1 Alexander Graham Bell is famous for inventing the telephone, but did you know that his wife, Mabel Gardiner Hubbard, wasn't able to hear it ring?

2 Film star Johnny Depp is often seen in glasses. He finds it difficult to see objects that are far away.

3 Franklin Delano Roosevelt was President of the United States from 1933 to 1945. He was paralyzed by polio in 1921, but only used his wheelchair in private.

4 Julius Caesar was one of the most powerful leaders in history. He also had no hair on his head!

5 French writer Honoré de Balzac drank hundreds of cups of coffee a day. He just couldn't stop!

Phrases with *mind*

3 Complete the sentences with the correct form of the words below.

- make
- cross
- slip
- change
- take
- give

1 Write important things down so that they don't .... your mind, especially if you're forgetful.

2 I didn't think you'd want to come, so it never .... my mind to tell you about the party.

3 I was so upset about breaking up with Charlie that I went on holiday with friends just to .... my mind off him.

4 I haven't .... up my mind which team to play for. I'll decide tomorrow.

5 I was so angry with Peter that I .... him a piece of my mind. I really told him what I thought!

6 I .... my mind about what colour to paint my room. It's going to be orange now, not green.

4 Complete the text about Helen Keller. Use the correct form of the words in brackets, or, if the word *mind* is in brackets, complete the phrase with *mind*.

Helen Keller

Helen Keller was a world-famous writer and public speaker who overcame blindness and ¹................. (deaf) to become influential in the world of American politics. Helen lost her sight and hearing following a childhood illness. However, she didn't sink into ²................. (depress) or go ³................. (mind). With the help of her teacher, Anne Sullivan, she learned to communicate with the outside world. Anne spelled words into Helen's hand with her finger. At first, Helen didn't understand and became ⁴................. (aggression), but, eventually, she understood what Anne was doing. Helen's parents were ⁵................. (mind) about whether to send their daughter to school or not, but eventually she attended college and became the first deaf and blind woman to get a degree. Helen's life and achievements show that what may seem like an ⁶................. (imperfect) need not hold anyone back in life.

5 CHALLENGE! In what ways have the people below overcome disabilities? Research one of the people and describe their achievements. Then describe the achievements of a person with a disability who is famous in your country.

- David Weir
- Stevie Wonder
- Evelyn Glennie

Grammar Fact or fiction

Talking about habitual behaviour

1 Choose the correct answers.
1. I **used to be / would be** a big fan of medical dramas when I was younger.
2. My aunt **often watches / is often watching** daytime TV. She really enjoys it and so do I!
3. George Clooney **would be / used to be** in the TV medical drama *ER* before he became a major movie star.
4. My sister is so annoying! She **always complains / is always complaining** about how much TV I watch!
5. Every Saturday evening, my family and I **will sit / are sitting** in front of the TV, waiting for our favourite programme.
6. I have two cousins who **used to work / would work** in a hospital.

2 Complete the sentences with the past form of the verbs in brackets. Use *used to* or *would* whenever possible. If it is not possible, use the past simple. If you can use either *used to* or *would*, use *would*.

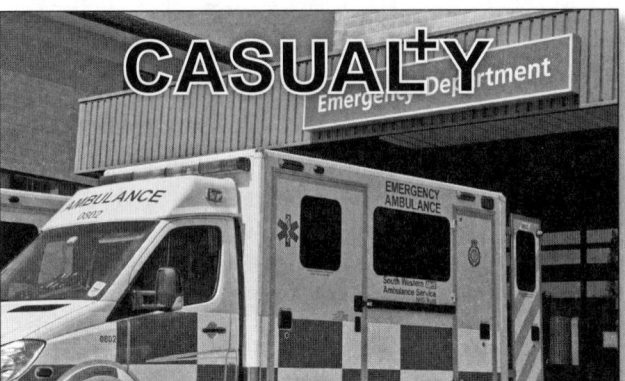

Casualty is the longest-running medical drama series in the world. It ¹_____ (begin) in 1986 and is set in a fictional casualty unit in a British hospital. The series ²_____ (be filmed) in Bristol, but nowadays, they film each episode in Cardiff. In the 1980s and 1990s, they ³_____ (broadcast) the show on Friday nights. However, these days, it's usually shown on Saturday evenings at around eight o'clock.

In the early years, each episode ⁴_____ (start) with an accident. Then the storyline ⁵_____ (tell) the story of the person in the accident, but there ⁶_____ (be) a lot of scenes about the doctors and nurses at the hospital, too. Nowadays, the stories are similar, but they vary the way the programme starts, and, of course, most of the cast is different. There is one exception: one character, a nurse called Charlie, has been in the series since 1986!

Some famous actors, including Kate Winslet and Orlando Bloom, ⁷_____ (play) a role in one or two episodes of the series before they ⁸_____ (become) famous. In fact, in the 1980s and 1990s, a lot of promising young actors ⁹_____ (apply) for parts in the series because it was a great chance to be on TV for the first time.

3 Rewrite the sentences using *used to*, *be used to* or *get used to*.
1. When she was young, Polly **enjoyed** watching medical dramas on TV every weekend.
2. I'm **becoming more familiar with** my new job. It's hard work, but I'm starting to learn what to do.
3. Tom felt tired because he **wasn't accustomed to** getting up so early in the morning.
4. **Were you** a nurse?
5. At her old school, Sylvia **was accustomed to** being top of the class.
6. Wendy is **becoming familiar with** having a lot of free time now that she's finished her studies.

4 Read the text and choose the answers which cannot be used to complete the text.

Alternative medicine – is it nonsense?

Until recently, I ¹**believed / would believe / used to believe** in the benefits of many different alternative medicines. I ²**will take / would take / used to take** homeopathic medicines and dietary supplements on a regular basis. However, now, my views have changed. I ³**don't use / used to use / won't ever use** medicines which haven't been properly tested.

Why? Well, I recently read a book called *Do you believe in magic?* by medical expert Dr Paul A Offit, which separates fact from fiction on the subject of alternative medicine. It describes how many of us ⁴**have got so used to taking / so used to take / are so used to taking** alternative medicines that we have come to believe in them even though there is no medical proof that they work. He criticizes celebrities who ⁵**are always promoting / will be ever promoting / constantly promote** alternative practices. And he points out that, although some alternative medicines seem to work because of the 'placebo' effect (we take them and imagine we're getting better), others are actually bad for our health. In the past, older generations ⁶**never used to trust / were never trusting / would never trust** alternative medicines, and he argues that, for the most part, we should not trust them today.

5 CHALLENGE! Read the statements below and decide whether you think they are fact or fiction. Justify your opinions.
- Alternative medicines don't work and can't be trusted.
- Celebrities are constantly trying to make us buy products that they don't really believe in.
- Medical dramas and other TV programmes used to be better in the past.

Mind and body 29

Listening, speaking and vocabulary Face value

V Phrases with body parts

1 **Complete the sentences using idioms with the words in brackets.**
   1 People think Penny is quiet and shy, but actually she's ambitious and strong-minded. (eye)
     There's ....
   2 Julia felt relieved after she had completed the course. (shoulders)
     It ....
   3 Sally refused to admit that she was wrong. (heels)
     She ....
   4 Amy found it difficult to accept so much criticism after she had worked so hard on her performance. (swallow)
     It ....
   5 At first, Claire was rude to all her friends because she was so angry with them. (senses)
     Later, she ....
   6 Debbie was really upset when she didn't get a place at drama school. (heart)
     It ....

Discussing a controversial topic

2 **Look at the photo of the 'ear mouse'. Read the text and answer the questions.**

The ear mouse

The idea of growing an ear on the back of a mouse used to belong in science fiction stories, but not any more. Researchers are fine-tuning a technology that will allow us to regrow ears and noses. A mould is placed on the animal's back and covered in cartilage cells. Then, over time, the cells develop and replace the mould to form a real ear. Researchers believe that it will be possible to then remove the new ear and connect it to a person's head. The animal, meanwhile, should be able to survive the operation and lead a normal life.

   1 Which of the following statements are true according to the text?
     a Scientists are able to grow human ears on the back of a mouse.
     b Scientists have already successfully transplanted ears from animals to humans.
     c Scientists expect the mouse to die after the ear is removed.
   2 What is the purpose of the text?

3 🔊 **3.04** Listen to Martin and Fiona discussing the idea of using mice to produce new human ears or noses. Who is in favour of the idea?

4 🔊 **3.04** Complete the phrases from the discussion. Then listen and check.
   1 There's no .... in my mind that … .
   2 I'm not .... that's true.
   3 Oh, ... on!
   4 I see where you're .... from, but … .
   5 I'm not .... by that argument.
   6 I .... believe it's … .
   7 I know what you're .... at, but … .
   8 That's .... not true.

5 **Match phrases 1–8 in exercise 4 to categories A–D.**
   A Expressing doubts: ...., ...
   B Expressing your point of view forcefully: ...1..., ...
   C Being diplomatic: ...., ...
   D Being undiplomatic: ...., ...

6 **Read the text about recent Japanese research into using animals to provide new body parts. Underline two arguments in favour of the research and three arguments against.**

Animals to provide new body parts

Japanese scientists are planning to place human stem cells inside the embryo of a pig. This embryo will then grow a perfect human organ (a heart, a kidney, a liver, etc.) which can be removed from the pig and transplanted into a person. The team hope to be able to grow a number of different human organs inside each pig, which will make it a practical and cost-effective method of providing transplant organs.

Animal rights campaigners are concerned that using an animal to carry human organs may be cruel. Others believe that it is ethically wrong to genetically alter animals and that there may be health risks in using organs that are produced in this way. Social scientists also point out that rich people could rear pigs carrying their organs, but poorer people couldn't, creating a very unfair situation. There is a shortage of transplant organs, so this may be a solution that will save thousands of human lives, but the ethical considerations are considerable.

◀ PREV   NEXT ▶

7 **Decide whether you are in favour of the Japanese research or against it. Then discuss the pros and cons. Express doubts about the arguments you do not support, and express your own point of view forcefully.**

Vocabulary and grammar Frankenstein

V insight Word analysis

1 Choose the correct answers.

1 an adjective that describes something as negative, grey and boring
   a dreary   b failing   c shrivelled
2 an adjective that describes eyes that look sad as if they have been crying
   a pearly   b watery   c terrible
3 an adjective that describes skin which has dried up in an unattractive way
   a dull   b flowing   c shrivelled
4 an adjective that means lifeless and not moving
   a inanimate   b failing   c flowing
5 a noun for a creature that people feel pity for because it is so miserable
   a monster   b wretch   c thing
6 an adjective that describes things that are very white
   a failing   b pearly   c dismal

V Body parts

2 Put the body parts below into the correct category 1–3. Which body part can go in two of the categories?

■ arteries ■ skull ■ lungs ■ spine ■ stomach ■ heart
■ ribs ■ veins ■ liver

1 Body parts that are made of bone: ...., ..., ...
2 Body parts that pump or carry blood: ...., ..., ...
3 Internal organs that perform specific functions: ...., ..., ..., ...

Future in the past

3 Choose the correct answers.

1 You're back early. I thought you .... play tennis with Jack this evening! That was your plan, wasn't it?
   a were about to   b were going to
2 Wendy came round to my house just as I .... go out. I had already put my coat on.
   a would   b was about to
3 According to the programme, the play .... start at seven, but they decided to delay it because of the traffic.
   a was to   b would
4 I used to believe that life in the neighbourhood .... improve one day. I no longer believe that.
   a was to   b would
5 The drummer left the band just as they .... go on tour.
   a were about to   b would
6 Simon was shy at school. I had no idea that one day he .... become a famous film star.
   a was about to   b was going to

4 Read what H.G. Wells says about his future (in 1890). Then read the encyclopaedia entry about his life and complete it with the correct form of the future in the past. When more than one answer is possible, explain the difference in meaning.

'My name is H.G. Wells and it is 1890. I am to write novels that are to influence how others see the future and make predictions about how the world is about to change, and how mega-cities will grow and the atomic bomb will be invented. My family don't know that I'll be famous one day. They think I'm going to be a sportsman or a teacher, but I have other plans. I will become a visionary writer.'

H.G. Wells – the father of science fiction

In his lifetime, Herbert George (H.G.) Wells (1866–1946) ¹.............. write a number of science fiction novels in English which ².............. influence our vision of the future. They included *The Time Machine* (1895), *The Invisible Man* (1897) and *The War of the Worlds* (1898). In his novels, and in his non-fiction book *Anticipations*, Wells described how he believed the world he lived in ³.............. change. He expected these changes to happen soon. In his works, he predicted that cities ⁴.............. grow into huge mega-cities and that people ⁵.............. invent an atomic bomb.

When he was young, Wells's parents had no idea that he ⁶.............. become a famous novelist. He enjoyed cricket, so they thought he ⁷.............. play professional cricket like his father. He also trained as a teacher, so they thought he ⁸.............. teach. In the end, he ⁹.............. become one of the most visionary writers in the English language.

5 CHALLENGE! H.G. Wells's parents had no idea what he would make of his life. Prepare some plans and predictions about your life. Then imagine it is one hundred years from now. Describe your life in the past tense, including information about your plans and predictions and what happened to them.

'One day I'll become a scientist and I'll travel the globe .... I'm going to make an important discovery that is going to change the world ....'
In her lifetime, Jo Bloggs would become one of the world's most important scientists .... .

Mind and body 31

Reading Is the genetically-modified athlete on the way?

1 What do you think about genetics and sport? Discuss the questions.

1. Should we look at what genes children have in order to discover their athletic potential?
2. Do scientists already know how to modify genes to improve athletic performance?
3. Should we discourage young people from taking up sport these days?
4. Are some athletes already modifying their genes to cheat?
5. Would enjoyment of sport be affected if it became normal to modify athletes' genes?
6. Might knowledge of the connection between genes and performance change sportspeople's approach to achieving sporting success?
7. Do scientists already know which genes affect aspects of athletic performance?

2 Read the article. Match five of the questions in exercise 1 to paragraphs A–E that discuss them. There are two questions that you do not need.

3 Read the article again. Are the statements true (T), false (F) or not given (NG)?

1. Olympic athletes have always analysed their genetic make-up to find out how successful they will be.
2. If you want to be a top athlete, training hard will always be more important than having the right genes.
3. Scientists know which of our genes affect athletic performance.
4. Screening young people's genes to find out what sports they are good at may happen in the future.
5. The writer sees no advantages to screening kids to find out about their genes.
6. It is already possible to modify a person's genes to improve athletic performance.
7. In the writer's opinion, genetic modification will become very common in the future.
8. We know for sure that some top athletes already have modified genes.

Is the genetically-modified athlete on the way?

A

To become an Olympic champion, athletes have always needed dedication and perseverance, as well as natural ability. In the past, athletes would spend hours training in the gym and would make sure they ate all the right foods. However, neither they, nor anybody else, felt the need to analyse their genes to test whether they were likely to succeed in their chosen sport. This may well be about to change. Our understanding of the connection between our genes and sporting performance is growing and this understanding may soon radically transform the way we select and train the athletes of the future.

B

Research has shown that, in many sports, genes are as important as hard work. The 'right' genes can, for example, affect our cardiovascular capacity – the heart's ability to deliver oxygen to the muscles – and they can also affect the muscles' ability to turn oxygen into the fuel needed for muscles to contract quickly and powerfully. Any athlete with these genes has an advantage over people who don't have them because they allow them to train longer and harder, to recover from exercise more quickly and to produce power more efficiently. Scientists have identified a variant of a gene called ACTN3 which is associated with the presence of a muscle protein found only in particular muscle fibres. It is effectively a 'power gene' which enables sprinters to react explosively and to start running very quickly. Any 100-metre sprinter with this gene clearly has a distinct advantage over an athlete who doesn't have it. In fact, many would now argue that it is essential to have this gene to win gold in a sprint event.

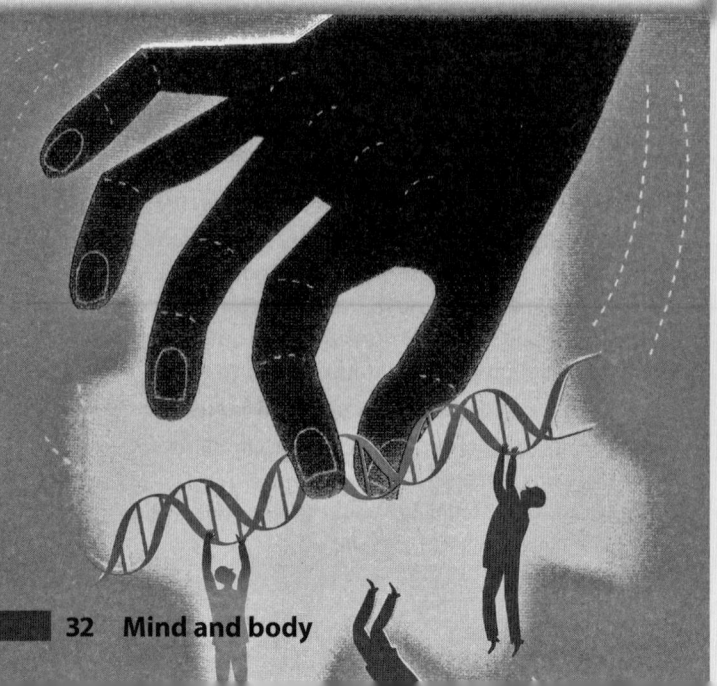
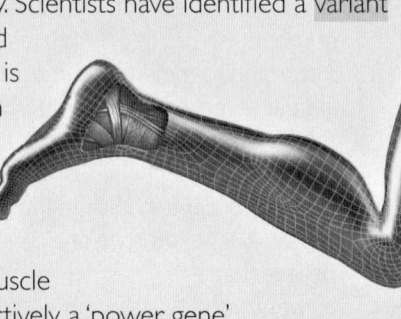

C

The importance of the genetic component in sporting ability has many implications for the future. Currently, we're used to the idea of encouraging every young person to have a go at different sports. Kids find out what they're good at and what they enjoy. But what if sports clubs screened kids to see whether they were genetically disposed to particular sports? As a society, we would uncover talent quickly and put young athletes with genetic potential on the right path to athletic achievement, but, individually, finding out, at a young age, that we were never going to be good at a chosen sport would be very demoralizing. It also undermines much that is positive about sport, such as the fact that it is about enjoyment and challenge and testing personal limits. Sport should not be about trying to achieve genetic potential.

D

Even more disturbing is the possibility that some countries might consider using our rapidly growing knowledge of how genes work to engineer the make-up of a young athlete's genes in order to turn them into a 'superman' or 'superwoman'. Scientists might, for example, inject a gene into an athlete's cells that increases muscle growth, making him or her faster and stronger. As yet, there is no evidence that this has happened. However, the technology is in place to modify genes and research has been carried out on mice that shows how effective genetic modification can be. A major concern is that nobody knows what the long-term consequences of altering genes might be for humans. It could result in all sorts of appalling health problems.

E

So, what of the future? Will top athletes be selected at a young age because of their genes, and will it become commonplace to modify an athlete's genes? Both are worrying scenarios. If selection were to happen, especially at a young age, sports would stop being about personal achievement and mental endurance and would become games for super-humans. If modifying genes were to become an accepted part of elite sport, the pressure on athletes and sports bodies to alter people's genes would be overwhelming. It is a disturbing thought. The age of the genetically-modified super-athlete may soon be upon us.

4 Study the highlighted words in the article. Then match each word to the correct meaning a–c.

1 perseverance
 a determination
 b uncertainty
 c stubbornness
2 radically
 a slightly
 b completely
 c interestingly
3 variant
 a slightly different form
 b identical form
 c only form
4 distinct
 a slightly different
 b recognizably different
 c unfair
5 uncover
 a lose
 b remove
 c discover
6 demoralizing
 a discouraging
 b unprincipled
 c critical
7 modify
 a destroy
 b replace
 c change
8 commonplace
 a rarely seen
 b often seen
 c never seen

5 Complete the sentences with the words in exercise 4.

1 This new disease is a .... of diseases we already know. Its biology is like that of many well-known illnesses.
2 Sports centres are .... in my country. You can find them almost everywhere.
3 The new design .... differed from the old one. It didn't look like the old one at all.
4 Zoologists hope to .... the secrets of how the tiger hunts at night.
5 Billy didn't give up and eventually finished the marathon. He showed a lot of ....
6 The culture of the northern part of the country is .... from that of the south. It has its own identity.
7 Amy trained hard, but was told she wasn't good enough to play for the team. It was a very .... experience.
8 Architects want to .... part of the stadium so that it can hold more spectators.

6 CHALLENGE! Which sports do you enjoy doing and which sports are you good at? In what ways do you think you have been influenced to take up different sports by the following factors?

- your genetics (your height, size, body build, etc.)
- your environment (your school or the interests of your family and friends, for example)
- your culture (popular sports, sports that are on TV)

Mind and body 33

Writing A letter to a newspaper

V Addition and contrast

1 Read the letter and choose the correct answers.

> To the Editor
>
> **A** Firstly, it is worth stating that, **¹no matter what / despite** other people may think, losing a family pet can be a very upsetting experience and pet cloning may one day genuinely offer a way of helping families get over that sense of loss. **²Moreover, / Although,** many families get used to the personality of a pet dog or cat. What better way of replacing the perfect pet than with another animal that is identical in every way?
>
> **B** I was fascinated by your article on cloning animals. My family and I have recently lost our much-loved pet, a dog called Henry, and the idea of being able to clone him and have him back with us is very appealing. **³Also / While** I accept that there are ethical issues involved, I feel strongly that the option of cloning a favourite pet is one that should be available to people in the future.
>
> **C** In conclusion, the benefits to pet owners of being able to have their perfect pet back with them, in cloned form, outweigh any drawbacks. Pet cloning is a way of reuniting families with their loved animals. **⁴In addition, / Whereas,** it is not harmful to animals and the current imperfections in the science of cloning will soon be sorted out. I strongly believe that cloning pets will become commonplace and will be a good thing.
>
> **D** Secondly, to my mind, I don't see that the techniques involved in cloning are in any way harmful to animals. **⁵What's more / Even though** the science is at an early stage of development and not every cloned animal survives, it is clear that no animal is being hurt. In time, once the initial problems have been solved, this will become a simple and safe procedure.
>
> Yours faithfully

2 What is your reaction to the issue described below? Should we be able to clone our pets or not? Write down two arguments to support your point of view.

> ## Pet cloning – is it here to stay?
> How long will it be before pet-lovers will be able to clone their favourite pet? Some people think it will be the best thing that could happen for owners who have lost loved pets. Others are worried that we shouldn't be interfering with nature. One thing is certain: we have the technology, so it will probably happen soon. Tell us what you think.

3 Read the letter in exercise 1 again and put the four paragraphs in the correct order. Does the letter support or oppose pet cloning?

4 Read the letter again. Choose the sentence that best describes the writer's point of view.
a The writer supports pet cloning.
b The writer opposes pet cloning.
c The writer doesn't express a view.

5 What arguments does the letter make in support of its point of view? Are any of the arguments similar to your ideas in exercise 2?

WRITING GUIDE

■ **Task** Read the newspaper extract. Decide on your reaction to the issue of genetically modifying fish. Write a letter to the editor. Include arguments to support your point of view.

> ### Genetically-modified pets kids will love
> The zebrafish is a small, attractive freshwater fish from India. Recently, an American company genetically modified the fish by injecting its eggs with jellyfish DNA. As a result, it glows in the dark and you can buy the fish (for only $5!) in a variety of bright colours.

■ **Ideas** Make notes about:
- your view: do you agree or disagree with the point of view in the extract?
- your main ideas: what ideas illustrate your point of view?
- arguments and examples you will use to support your ideas.

■ **Plan** Follow the plan:

Paragraph 1: Introduce your reason for writing. Mention your personal situation if relevant.
Paragraph 2: Present your first idea, with supporting arguments and examples.
Paragraph 3: Present your second idea, with supporting arguments and examples.
Paragraph 4: Conclusion: sum up your point of view.

■ **Write** Write your letter. Use the paragraph plan to help you.

■ **Check** Check the following points.
- Are your point of view and the main ideas clearly stated?
- Has each idea got supporting arguments and examples?
- Have you checked grammar, vocabulary, spelling and punctuation?

Progress check Unit 4

Read 1–13 and evaluate your learning in Unit 4. Give yourself a mark from 1 to 3. How can you improve?
1 I can't do this.   2 I have some problems with this.   3 I can do this well.

A Perfect people	Mark (1–3)	How can I improve?
1 Give two 'imperfections' that Anton doesn't have because the geneticist has removed his problem-causing genes.		
I can understand an article about the issue of genetic engineering.		
2 Explain the noun and verb meanings of the words below. a screen b shift c burden		
I can use nouns and verbs with the same form.		
3 Add noun suffixes to the words below. a imperfect b bald c obese		
I can use noun suffixes.		

B Fact or fiction	Mark (1–3)	How can I improve?
4 Explain the difference between *used to* and *would*.		
I can use *used to* and *would* to talk about habitual behaviour.		
5 Which tense do you use to express irritation?		
I can talk about habitual behaviour in the present.		
6 Who is completely happy with his new routine – Bob or Bill? Bob is getting used to the early mornings. Bill is used to the early mornings.		
I can talk about becoming accustomed to new situations.		

C Face value	Mark (1–3)	How can I improve?
7 Why did Vanilla and Justin decide to have cosmetic surgery?		
I can understand a radio programme about cosmetic surgery.		
8 What idioms do you know with the words below? What do they mean? a shoulders b eye c heart		
I can use phrases with body parts.		
9 Give one way of expressing a doubt, one way of expressing your point of view forcefully and one way of being diplomatic.		
I can express a doubt, express my point of view forcefully and be diplomatic.		

D Frankenstein	Mark (1–3)	How can I improve?
10 Who wrote *Frankenstein* and how old was she when she wrote it?		
I can understand a text about *Frankenstein*.		
11 When do you use future in the past?		
I can use future in the past.		
12 What three names did Frankenstein give to his creation?		
I can analyse words.		

E A letter to a newspaper	Mark (1–3)	How can I improve?

13 Complete the sentences with a linker of addition or contrast.
  a .... I don't agree with cloning, I believe that it will happen one day.
  b Genetic engineering will change the face of farming. ...., it will help feed the world.		

I can express addition and contrast.		

5 Words

Vocabulary A word is born

insight Phrasal verbs with *on*

1 Rewrite the sentences by replacing the words in italics with the correct form of the phrasal verbs below.

■ add on ■ carry on ■ cheer on ■ cling on ■ move on
■ slip on ■ switch on

1 If you *continue* speaking to me like that, I'm leaving!
   ....

2 I loved my smartphone when I bought it two years ago, but technology has *developed* since then.
   ....

3 I have a season ticket and go to every football game. I think it's important to be there to *encourage* my team.
   ....

4 The little boy was *firmly holding* his mother's legs.
   ....

5 As he *started* the engine, the car jumped forward.
   ....

6 In America, prices in menus don't include tax. When you pay, the restaurant *includes* the tax.
   ....

7 It's only sensible to *wear* some strong walking shoes when you go hiking.
   ....

insight Verb prefixes: *en-* and *em-*

2 Complete the text with the correct form of the words below. The verb prefix has already been added.

■ power ■ able ■ courage ■ danger ■ sure ■ title ■ trust

At present, there are nearly 7,000 languages being used around the world. However, more than 40% of those are ¹en............ and are likely to become extinct within the next 100 years. Why does this matter? It's because different languages ²en............ us to see the world through different eyes. When a language is lost, so is a culture.
The Endangered Languages Project has been set up to ³en............ people to take an interest in saving these languages. The website asks people to submit samples of languages at risk in both written and audio forms. In this way, it hopes to ⁴en............ that, at the very least, these languages are not lost forever.
However, the project also wants to ⁵em............ people to take responsibility for keeping their language alive. For example, it supports communities who are fighting for their children to be ⁶en............ to learn the language at school. Previous generations have ⁷en............ us with this rich cultural heritage. We mustn't throw it away lightly.

Acronyms

3 Replace the phrases in italics with an acronym below. There are two acronyms that you do not need.

■ FYI ■ BTW ■ FWIW ■ TIA ■ IMHO ■ IDK ■ TMI ■ ASAP
■ YOLO ■ LOL ■ AFAIK ■ BFN

1 That joke you sent me was great. *Really funny!* ....
2 *I'm not sure, but I think* it's true. ....
3 I need to speak to you *immediately*. ....
4 *You might like to know that* John's leaving next week. ....
5 Can you find out what the homework is for me? *Cheers for that*. ....
6 *I think* videos of cats are really silly. ....
7 That picture of your toenail was disgusting. *I didn't need to see that!* ....
8 You should definitely go to the concert. *Life's too short to worry about the cost!* ....
9 Is Jake going to the party? *I have no idea*. ....
10 I need to go now. *See you later*. ....

4 Complete the text with the correct form of the words below. There are two words that you do not need.

■ entitle ■ keep on ■ slip on ■ endanger ■ turn on
■ ensure ■ enable ■ encourage ■ switch on

¹............ your tablet and switch off your vocabulary?

Experts say that too much time is being spent on tablets and computers, ²............ children's ability to learn new words. Rather than talking to each other, we are too quick to ³............ the computer, meaning that young people are not being ⁴............ to listen to a wide range of words. Research shows that it is important to ⁵............ that children actually *hear* new words, as this develops the language learning area of the brain.
According to the findings, if children ⁶............ learning visually, rather than through hearing words in conversation, it is likely that future generations will have smaller vocabularies. Talking and reading to children will best ⁷............ them to take in new vocabulary.

5 CHALLENGE! Is it important to protect endangered languages, or would it be better if we encouraged everyone to speak just one language? Write or speak about your opinion.

Grammar Fast track to fluency

Advice, obligation and prohibition

1 Choose the correct answers.

Learning from your mistakes

Einstein once said, 'Anyone who has never made a mistake has never tried anything new.' This doesn't mean that you **¹**........ try and make as many mistakes as possible, but it does mean that you **²**........ accept that making mistakes is a natural part of the learning process. This is particularly true when you are learning a language. When you make a mistake and the teacher corrects it, there is a great opportunity for you to learn and improve your language skills.

Although correction can be very helpful, we **³**........ be careful not to overdo it. One famous study found that when parents corrected their young children's language, believing that their children **⁴**........ say things like, 'Daddy gone work', their children's language actually got worse rather than better!

Of course, we **⁵**........ assume that learning a second language is exactly like learning our first language. It's very different; we're older and more intellectually developed, for a start. Nonetheless, teachers usually **⁶**........ correct every single mistake we make; furthermore, if they do, we may find we lose all confidence, especially at lower levels.

1 a ought to	b needn't	c had better not
2 a mustn't	b needn't	c need to
3 a must	b mustn't	c ought not to
4 a need to	b had better not	c don't need to
5 a mustn't	b don't need to	c must
6 a must	b should	c don't need to

2 Complete the second sentence so that it has a similar meaning to the first. Use the words in brackets.

1 Don't forget your homework again, or you'll be in trouble! (better)
   You ....
2 Joe should try to work a bit harder. (ought)
   Joe ....
3 It's not necessary to bring your book. (needn't)
   You ....
4 It is forbidden for students to chew gum on school premises. (must)
   Students ....
5 It is important to work hard if you want to do well at school. (need)
   If you want to do well at school, ...
6 It is a good idea to revise new vocabulary regularly. (should)
   You ....

Past modals

3 Complete the dialogue with the words and phrases below. Sometimes more than one answer is possible.

- needn't have ■ had to ■ didn't need to ■ ought to have
- shouldn't have ■ didn't have to

Beth   You really **¹**............ said that to the waiter! It was so rude.
Sarah But I felt I **²**............ complain. There was a dead insect in my salad, after all.
Beth   I still think you **³**............ speak so loudly. Everyone in the restaurant must have heard you.
Sarah Well, they **⁴**............ washed the salad more carefully!
Beth   But it wasn't the waiter's fault. You **⁵**............ shout at him.
Sarah I didn't shout at him. I was just being assertive.
Beth   I still think you **⁶**............ made such a fuss.
Sarah Just because I prefer to stand up for myself ... .

4 Choose the correct answers.

A new way to learn a language

A few months ago, I decided that I **¹needed to improve / needn't have improved** my spoken German. I was already having lessons, so I felt I **²didn't need to / ought not to** find a teacher; what I needed was someone to practise speaking with. So I decided to join an online language-exchange website which puts you in touch with someone who wants to learn a language you speak. You help them to learn and get credit which you can then use to pay someone else to help you with the language you want to learn.

I **³should have paid / had to pay** a small fee to create a profile on the site, listing the languages I already speak and the languages I want to learn. I realized later that I **⁴shouldn't have listed / didn't have to list** all the languages I speak, because some of them I speak very badly and I was asked to teach them to other people! In fact, I **⁵ought to have / needn't have** just listed English as the language I spoke, and German as the language I wanted to improve – this would have created far less confusion!

I was worried it would take a long time to find someone to teach me German, but I **⁶didn't need to / needn't have** worried. I **⁷didn't have to / ought not to** wait very long before I met Steffi. My German has really improved and we've become very good friends, too!

5 CHALLENGE! Imagine that you are going to teach someone to speak your language. What is particularly easy or difficult about it? What advice would you give them? Complete the sentences below and add your own ideas.

- You should remember that ... .
- You needn't worry too much about ... .
- You don't have to ... .
- You'd better not ... or you might offend someone.
- It can be difficult to ... , so you ought to ... .

Words 37

Listening, speaking and vocabulary A good read

V Phrases with *point*

1 Complete the sentences with the phrases below.

- at some point ■ there's no point in ■ take your point
- on the point of ■ up to a point ■ from my point of view
- the point is ■ point out

1 I ...., but I still think it would be better to go with the first option.
2 It's not important why you didn't listen to me. .... that you didn't.
3 Please try to look at this .... I know it's a great opportunity, but Sydney is so far away!
4 I agree with you ...., but not completely.
5 .... getting upset; it's too late to change it now.
6 I was just .... leaving when the phone rang.
7 I'd just like to .... that I did warn you not to do that.
8 I don't know where my purse is. I must have dropped it .... during the evening.

Choosing together

2 🔊 3.05 Jack and Marie are members of a school council. They represent other students and work together with the teachers to make some of the decisions about the school. Listen to part of a school council meeting. What does the teacher think about their ideas and what does she propose?

3 🔊 3.05 Listen again and complete the notes. Use no more than two words in each gap.

> Minutes of school council meeting
> 1 Congratulations on raising £650.00
> 2 Discussion about how best to spend the money. Two possible proposals from students:
> New photo editing software
> Positive points:
> * It is really needed for ¹...................... and photography.
> * The ²...................... department could use it as well.
> Negative points:
> * Likely to be very ³...................... .
> Books for school library
> Positive points:
> * Would encourage more people to use ⁴...................... .
> * Something that ⁵...................... would be able to use.
> Negative points:
> * People might not use the library as they prefer to do their reading ⁶...................... .
> Next steps:
> Marie: To find out the exact ⁷...................... of the software package.
> Jack: To make ⁸...................... of useful books.

4 🔊 3.05 Rewrite the sentences from the dialogue, replacing the phrases in italics with the phrases below. Then listen again and check.

- Surely you have to agree ■ Doesn't it make more sense
- I was wondering if any of you ■ let's sleep on it
- I was hoping we could ■ shall we go for
- Could you tell us a bit more about
- Wouldn't it be better to

1 *Perhaps somebody* would like to make a suggestion.
 ....
2 Well, *I'd really like us to* get some more software for the computers.
 ....
3 *Please explain* what kind of software you have in mind.
 ....
4 *Shouldn't we* spend the money on something that would make more impact on the school?
 ....
5 *It's obvious* that we should buy something that everyone will be able to use.
 ....
6 *Isn't it a more sensible idea* to get something more up-to-date?
 ....
7 Both are good ideas, but which one *should we choose*?
 ....
8 OK, *let's decide tomorrow*, then.
 ....

5 Put this dialogue between three speakers in the correct order. Then write two more lines of dialogue using the phrases in exercise 4.

..... Well, we've got some quite interesting stuff. There's a great article on our town in the year 1900.
..1.. OK, so we have to decide which article to use as the front page in the student magazine this month. Leah, I was wondering if you could tell us all about what we have to choose from?
..... Mmm … I'm not sure people will be interested in that. Wouldn't it be better to have something about life today?
..... But not everyone is interested in sport. Doesn't it make more sense to have something of general interest? I still think the historical article is the best.
..... OK, well, if you want something more up-to-date, Josh has written something about a recent ski trip he went on.
..... Skiing sounds a bit more interesting, I think.

38 Words

Vocabulary and grammar Shakespeare

V insight Word analysis

1 Complete the text with the words below. There are two words that you do not need.

- abuse ▪ chilling ▪ preface ▪ pinnacle ▪ protagonists
- quirky ▪ ruthless ▪ transcend

> If you are an aspiring writer, you need to read a lot of books. Whether you enjoy Magnus Mills' **1** .... comic novels about bus drivers or the **2** .... horror stories of Stephen King, reading will help you create great literature. Observe other people and their behaviour to get ideas for the **3** .... of your story. A powerful account of the human experience can **4** .... time and place. You'd better get practising if you want to reach the **5** .... of your writing powers, so start with a blog if you haven't got an idea for a great story yet. Edit all your work and be **6** .... in your criticism. Keep on editing until it's not just great, but perfect.

V Book structure

2 Complete the sentences with the words below. There are two words that you do not need.

- back cover ▪ bibliography ▪ contents page
- dust jacket ▪ front cover ▪ hardback ▪ imprint page
- index ▪ spine ▪ title page

1 Most people usually take the .... off their hardback books when reading them.
2 I hate it when people open a book so wide that they break the ....
3 The list of books the author has read or referred to is called the ....
4 The .... has information about the publisher.
5 If you want to find a specific topic in the book, the easiest thing is to look at the ....
6 The .... repeats the information on the cover.
7 If I'm buying a book for studying, I usually look at the .... to see what's in it.
8 There's usually a 'blurb' on the .... saying what the book is about.

Talking about ability

3 Complete the text about David Harewood. Use the correct form of *can* where possible. Where that isn't possible, use the correct form of *manage to*, *be able to* or *succeed in*.

> The actor David Harewood was born in Birmingham in 1965. His father was a long-distance truck driver and his mother a caterer, and it seemed unlikely that David would become an actor, especially a Shakespearian actor.
>
> By his own admission, he didn't do well at school, saying that the only way he felt he **1** .... get attention was to act the clown. He assumed he would leave school at sixteen and, if he **2** .... get a job at all, it would probably be in one of the nearby factories. However, his English teacher **3** .... see that he had talent and encouraged him to apply to drama schools. To his parents' surprise, he first **4** .... earning a place on a short course at the National Youth Theatre and then a place on a three-year training course at the Royal Academy of Dramatic Art.
>
> David decided that he **5** .... not succeed as a classical actor with his distinctive Birmingham accent, so he **6** .... train himself to speak with a more neutral accent. He has also **7** .... produce such an authentic-sounding American accent for the TV series *Homeland* that many Americans are shocked to learn that he's actually British.
>
> As well as a career in films and television, David has **8** .... realizing his ambition to become a great Shakespearian actor, playing the roles of Antony in *Antony and Cleopatra*, Othello and Romeo to great critical acclaim.

4 Complete the sentences with the correct form of the verbs below. Some verbs can be used more than once.

- could ▪ be able to ▪ manage to ▪ succeed in ▪ can

1 .... use different accents is an important skill for an actor.
2 David's family .... believe it when he was accepted for drama school.
3 Not many people .... becoming well-known actors.
4 David .... speak in a very convincing American accent.
5 David hopes he'll .... play James Bond one day.
6 Although it was difficult, the kids .... put on the performance in just five days.

5 CHALLENGE! What talents do you have? Write or speak about the things below.

1 something you can do very well
2 something you could not do when you were a child, but you can do now
3 something you are proud of having succeeded in doing

Words 39

Reading More speed, less analysis?

More speed, less analysis?

In many ways, the internet has been a boon for the written word. [1]......... How much of our days are now taken up with reading and writing emails, tweets, status updates and blog posts?

However, though we may be reading and writing a great deal more than we used to, we are doing it in very different ways. Take letters and emails, for example. In the past we would sit down with a piece of paper and a pen and think carefully about what we wanted to say, knowing that any changes would result in ugly crossings out, or in having to start again from scratch. Now we can fire off an email in seconds.

The way we read has also changed. We talk about reading a book from cover to cover, because traditionally we start at the beginning and read through to the end. However, this is not how we read online. Instead, we start on a particular page, but may not even finish that page, as a link takes us off to a passage on another page, and so on. [2]......... This is known as 'associative' thinking and it uses the brain in a very different way from 'linear' reading.

There are certainly advantages to developing associative thinking skills. Using the brain in this way means that we are getting better than ever at multi-tasking. It ensures that we can work at speed and develops our ability to think outside the box. Being able to switch backwards

---

1 Read the article and decide whether the author would agree or disagree with the following statements.

  a People don't read and write as much these days.
  b The way we read online is different from the way we read books.
  c Multi-tasking is a useful skill.
  d If we don't read deeply, we may stop being able to do so.

2 Read the article again and match sentences A–F to gaps 1–5. There is one sentence that you do not need.

  A People have always been reluctant to accept change.
  B These neural pathways only develop as we need to use them, and if we don't use them, they won't develop at all.
  C Rather than going through a piece of text in order, we are skipping about, and this means we have to hold onto lots of different threads or ideas simultaneously.
  D People are reading and writing more than ever.
  E Although the brain continues to develop throughout life, new circuits are not created overnight.
  F Some prominent researchers would agree.

3 Study the highlighted phrases in the article. Then match them to the definitions below.

  1 completely involved in: ....
  2 redo from the beginning, not using all the work you have already done: ....
  3 forget what you are thinking or talking about: ....
  4 quickly send: ....
  5 the whole thing: ....
  6 have original and creative ideas; see things from a new perspective: ....

and forwards between emails and other tasks is useful in a working environment, but constant distractions make it very difficult to read at a deeper level. We are therefore much less likely to be critically analysing what we read, making inferences, thinking in an abstract way or gaining any real insight.

In his article *Is Google making us stupid?*, Nicholas Carr suggests that we are not only less likely to be reading deeply, but that we may be becoming less capable of doing so. Reflecting on his own experience and that of his contemporaries, he concludes that many people, including 'literary types', are no longer able or willing to become immersed in a book or a longer article. They become fidgety or lose their train of thought. And, Carr argues, this may be not just because it's more convenient to read associatively, but because the way people think is actually changing, too. **3** .... The work of Gary Small, a professor of psychiatry at the University of California, concludes that being constantly exposed to new media strengthens new neural pathways – connections between different parts of the brain – that are related to associative thinking, but also simultaneously weakens the pathways which enable us to follow a narrative or fully digest and understand information.

4 .... We might, therefore, face the prospect of a whole new generation that lacks the ability to think critically and deeply about what they are reading.

But haven't we been here before? **5** .... The Ancient Greek philosopher Socrates was very suspicious of the written word, concerned that people would lose the ability to memorize long texts. He was, of course, quite right, but future generations, who increasingly became used to having books, no longer saw a need for this skill, and now, in our modern world, it is not valued at all.

Ultimately, the world is changing and our brains are probably changing in line with the new demands they face, just as they have always done throughout history. However, while we may not be bothered about having lost our once prodigious ability to memorize, are we as willing to lose our ability to read deeply? If not, we need to consider just how we can maintain our critical, deeper reading skills, while also engaging in our daily digital diet.

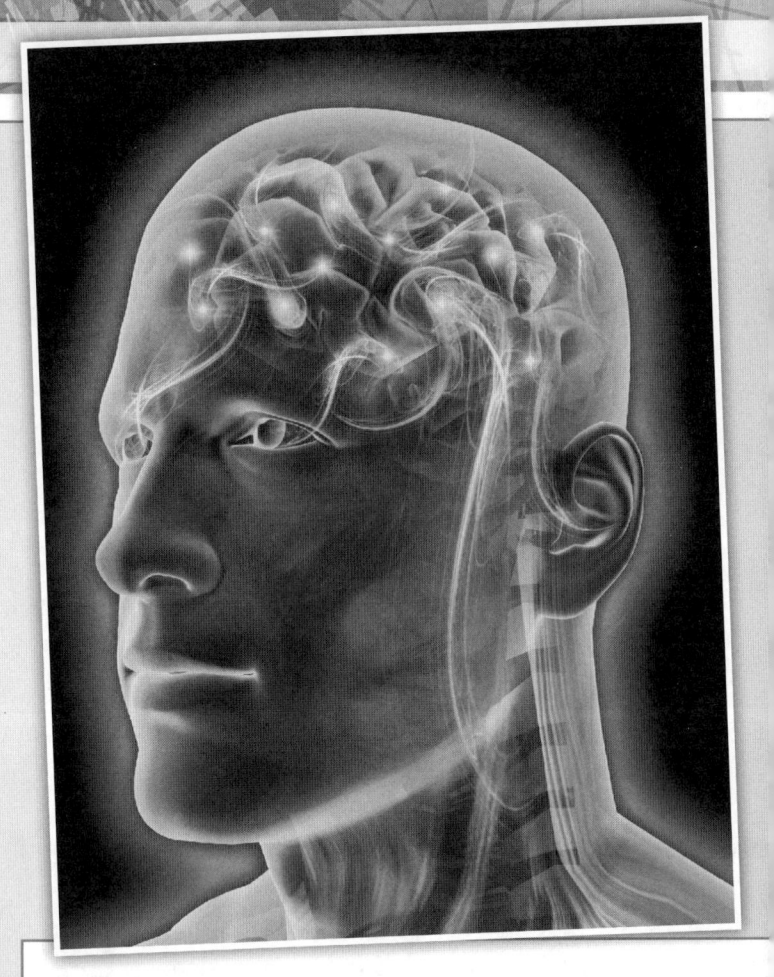

4 Complete the sentences with the correct form of the phrases in exercise 3.
1. Goodness – you read quickly! Have you read that novel from .... in just one afternoon?
2. I was so .... my book that I didn't even hear the doorbell ring.
3. It was hard to concentrate with all the noise. I kept ....
4. I was so angry that I sat down straight away and .... a letter of complaint.
5. This advertising agency needs people who can ....
6. This essay just doesn't make sense. I'm afraid you're going to have to ....

5 CHALLENGE! Answer the questions about yourself.
1. How do you feel about having to start things again from scratch – for example, if you have to redo an essay? Does it annoy you, or do you feel it's important to get things right?
2. Do you think you're the kind of person who can think outside the box? Give an example of when you've done this.
3. How often do you sit down and read a book from cover to cover? Has this changed in recent years?
4. Do you like to work with music on, or does it make you lose your train of thought? What other things help or prevent you from concentrating?
5. What possible problems could be caused by firing off an email without thinking about it first?
6. Are you more likely to get immersed in a book or in a film? Why?

Writing A book review

V insight Synonyms: adjectives describing stories

1 Complete each sentence with two of the words below.

- complex ■ expressive ■ gripping ■ insightful ■ intricate
- meaningful ■ moving ■ perceptive ■ riveting
- touching

1 The film's unusually ……………… / ……………… plot and dense dialogue made it difficult to follow.
2 The plot was surprisingly ……………… / ……………… . I even forgot to eat my popcorn!
3 The final reunion was so ……………… / ……………… , I found myself in tears.
4 As well as being very funny, the movie was also surprisingly ……………… / ……………… about the issues raised. I learned a lot.
5 The look on the actor's face was very ……………… / ……………… . It was easy to see how she felt.

2 Read the review of the film version of *The Great Gatsby*. Which did the reviewer prefer: the book, or the film based on the book?

3 Read the review again and complete the gaps with the phrases below. There is one phrase that you do not need.

a I couldn't really identify with
b I was disappointed with
c There's a dramatic twist at the end
d I was captivated by
e the film fails to
f The film opens with
g the biggest problem was
h the film would appeal to anyone who

4 Study the underlined words in the text. Write what each word refers to.

1 These: ……………………
2 did so: ……………………
3 his: ……………………
4 This: ……………………
5 one: ……………………
6 It: ……………………

The Great Gatsby is a subtle and insightful novel which raises some big questions about the nature of love and the effects of money and materialism. Having loved the book, ¹……… Baz Luhrmann's new film version, which has plenty of materialism, but absolutely no subtlety whatsoever.

²……… Nick Carraway, the narrator of the story, looking back at his memories of the Roaring Twenties. <u>These</u> centre around Nick's fabulously wealthy neighbour, Jay Gatsby, and the extravagant parties he throws. Nick is flattered when Gatsby befriends him, but he soon discovers that he only <u>did so</u> in order to get close to <u>his</u> cousin, Daisy, with whom Gatsby was in love before the First World War. Daisy married someone else, but her husband, while rich, is unfaithful and a bully. <u>This</u> gives Gatsby hope that he can win her back.

³……… the spectacle of the film. Luhrmann certainly knows how to put on a show and the film is full of glitz and glamour. However, ⁴……… be at all moving and it feels quite unrealistic. Frankly, ⁵……… any of the characters. Seen through the eyes of the narrator, Nick, the book encourages us to feel fascinated by Gatsby and a little in love with Daisy. In the film, however, it is obvious from the start that Daisy is shallow and even Gatsby shows no signs of hidden depths. This is not the first film of *The Great Gatsby* and nor is it the first <u>one</u> to fail at portraying the complex characters. <u>It</u> is a challenging task, but I had hoped for more.

Superficially, ⁶……… enjoyed Luhrmann's previous films. The plot is quite gripping. For me, however, ⁷……… that it just didn't touch me at all.

WRITING GUIDE

■ **Task** Choose a film you have seen that is based on a book. Plan and write a review.

■ **Ideas** Make notes about:
- the name of the film, the book it is based on and the film director.
- the setting, main themes and characters.
- the plot.
- what you liked and didn't like about the film.
- how and why the film is better than / not as good as the book.
- whether you would recommend it, who you would recommend it to and why.

■ **Plan** Follow the plan:

Paragraph 1: Introduction. Tell the reader what the film is called, what book it is based on and who the director is.
Paragraph 2: Concise summary of the plot. Is the story different from the book?
Paragraph 3: Your opinion. What did you like or dislike about the film? How does it compare with the book?
Paragraph 4: Conclusion. Summarize your opinion and write whether you would recommend the film.

■ **Write** Write your review. Use the paragraph plan to help you.

■ **Check** Check the following points.
- Have you used a clear paragraph structure?
- Have you managed to avoid repetition?
- Have you made clear comparisons between the film and the book?
- Have you checked grammar, vocabulary, spelling and punctuation?

Progress check Unit 5

Read 1–14 and evaluate your learning in Unit 5. Give yourself a mark from 1 to 3. How can you improve?
1 I can't do this.   2 I have some problems with this.   3 I can do this well.

A A word is born	Mark (1–3)	How can I improve?
1 Give three ways in which new words come into a language.		
I can understand a text about new words.		
2 Give two possible strategies you can use when you come across an unknown word when you are reading.		
I can deal with unknown words in reading texts.		
3 Give two phrasal verbs with *on* which have the meaning *continue*.		
I can use phrasal verbs with *on*.		
4 Give three words beginning with the prefix *em-* or *en-*.		
I can correctly form verbs with the prefixes *em-* and *en-*.		

B Fast track to fluency	Mark (1–3)	How can I improve?

5 Explain the difference in meaning between
   a *had better* and *should*.   b *have to* and *must*.
   c *shouldn't* and *mustn't*.		

I can use modals to express advice, obligation and prohibition.		
6 Explain the difference between the following two sentences. a I didn't need to go. b I needn't have gone.		
I can use past modals correctly.		

C A good read	Mark (1–3)	How can I improve?
7 Give a phrase using *point* which means a *In my opinion* … . b *I accept what you're saying*.		
I can use a variety of expressions with *point*.		
8 Give four things people can do in public libraries apart from read a book.		
I can understand a radio interview about public libraries.		
9 Give two different ways of politely asking for more information and two ways of persuading someone.		
I can make and respond to suggestions.		

D Shakespeare	Mark (1–3)	How can I improve?
10 Give four reasons that Shakespeare is still popular today.		
I can understand a text about Shakespeare.		
11 What are *tales that transcend time*?		
I can understand and use a range of words related to literature.		
12 Choose the best answer to complete the sentence. Explain your choice. The window was stuck, but I **could / managed to** open it in the end.		
I can use modal verbs of ability correctly.		

E A book review	Mark (1–3)	How can I improve?
13 Write a synonym for each of the following adjectives. a touching b intricate c perceptive d riveting		
I can use a variety of adjectives to describe a book or film.		
14 Give three ways of avoiding repetition.		
I can avoid repetition in my writing.		

6 The media and the message

Vocabulary Who controls the news?

insight Collocations: journalism

1 Complete the sentences with the words below. There are two words that you do not need.

■ expose ■ set ■ spread ■ trace ■ fall for ■ make ■ lack ■ go

1 It is difficult to .... sources of information on the internet because people prefer to remain anonymous.
2 Many commentators on political websites want to .... corruption by politicians. They want to tell the world what they're doing.
3 The opinions of many people online .... credibility because they don't support their views with hard facts.
4 It's easy to .... rumours on the web. People will read a piece of gossip and then pass it on to all their friends online.
5 The remarkable events in the Middle East are going to .... headlines all over the world.
6 Recently, bloggers have begun to .... the agenda for news sites everywhere. They decide what news is important.

insight Word analysis

2 Match the words in bold to the correct definitions, a or b.

1 The workers in the factory are **vulnerable** to exploitation by the management.
   a powerful and in a strong position
   b having little power and in a weak position
2 The election was **rigged** and the ruling political party remained in power.
   a corrupt and dishonest
   b well-organized and fair
3 Bloggers have no **accountability** so they can write anything they want.
   a no responsibility to be fair or honest
   b no clear understanding of what is happening
4 Many people believe that the police should always be **armed**.
   a carrying guns
   b having special powers of arrest
5 The photojournalist **scrambled** to the top of the staircase in order to take some good photos.
   a climbed up slowly and very carefully
   b climbed up quickly and with difficulty
6 When Susie heard that she had lost her job, she felt **devastated** and couldn't stop crying.
   a very upset
   b a little upset

Headlines

3 Replace the words in italics in the headlines with the correct form of the words below. There are three words that you do not need.

■ plea ■ back ■ quit ■ curb ■ riddle ■ vow ■ ban ■ bid ■ axe

1 TOP COMPANY *CUTS* .... JOBS
2 COACH *SUPPORTS* .... PLAYER
3 MINISTER *RESIGNS* .... POST
4 COUNCIL *PROHIBITS* .... MARCH
5 ACTOR'S *REQUEST* .... FOR PRIVACY
6 BILLIONAIRE *PROMISES* .... TO SAVE RAINFOREST

4 Choose the correct answers.

The Watergate Scandal

In June 1972, five men were arrested as they broke into the Watergate office building in Washington, D.C. Two journalists, Bob Woodward and Carl Bernstein, decided to delve ¹........ the crime. They believed that the 'burglars' were members of the CIA, the American security service, who were breaking into the building to place bugs. They also believed that President Richard Nixon knew about the break-in and was guilty of a ²........ . These days, speculation about the crime would ³........ viral, but back in 1972, it was left to the two *Washington Post* journalists to set the ⁴........ and to put pressure on the President by ⁵........ his behaviour in the media. In 1974, a recording of President Nixon talking about blocking an investigation into what had happened was discovered. Nixon was forced to resign. The headlines across the US read: PRESIDENT ⁶........! It sent shock waves around the world.

1 a into   b in
   c on   d onto
2 a break-down   b cover-up
   c turn-over   d set-down
3 a do   b take
   c go   d make
4 a agenda   b scam
   c source   d footage
5 a tracing   b exposing
   c spreading   d covering-up
6 a ends   b stops
   c quits   d axes

5 CHALLENGE! Choose one of the headlines below. Then prepare and tell the news story that goes with the headline. Use at least five of the words below.

■ spread ■ eyewitness ■ expose ■ footage ■ trace
■ defamatory ■ fall for ■ vulnerable

ROCK STAR RUMOURS GO VIRAL

POLICE INVESTIGATE INTERNET SCAM

Grammar The big picture

Speculation about the past, present and future

1 Choose the correct answers.

1 The photographers **must / may** be waiting for somebody important to appear. That much is certain.
2 I have no idea who they're waiting for. It **must / might** be a politician, I suppose.
3 The person they're waiting for **must / could** have done something newsworthy. Otherwise, why would they be there?
4 It **might not / can't** be easy to face up to all those photographers. I'd hate to be in that situation.
5 They **could / must** be standing outside a restaurant where a major film star is eating. That's one possibility, at least.
6 Whoever they're hoping to photograph **has to / may** be worth the wait. Look at all that equipment!

2 Complete each gap with the correct form of a modal verb and verb below. You can use the modal verbs more than once.

▪ must ▪ can't ▪ might ▪ may not

▪ see ▪ worry ▪ know ▪ stand ▪ shout ▪ attack

Interviewer: I'm chatting to Jerry Clark. You ¹_____ who Jerry is. He isn't a household name. However, his photographs of celebrities are a familiar sight in our tabloid newspapers. Just about everybody in the country ²_____ one of Jerry's photographs in a newspaper at one time or another during the past ten years. So, what's the secret to being a paparazzi photographer?
Jerry: Well, patience, first of all. It's possible that you ³_____ outside someone's house for weeks on end, waiting for that all-important photo.
Interviewer: And you need bravery, too, right? I'm sure you ⁴_____ at by a celebrity's bodyguard more than once in your career. Do you worry that someone ⁵_____ you and beat you up?
Jerry: Well, I have had my share of insults, but I've never been beaten up, yet. To be honest, you ⁶_____ about that sort of thing if you want to photograph celebrities.

3 Complete the text with the words below. Use each word once.

▪ safe ▪ like ▪ probably ▪ bound to ▪ must ▪ seems ▪ may

Andy Carvin – the one-man news bureau

The social networking site Twitter is already incredibly popular, and, without doubt, its popularity is ¹_____ grow even more in the coming years. The site has changed the face of news journalism in recent years. In fact, it's ²_____ to say that our understanding of recent wars, uprisings and major social disruptions across the world has been influenced by the website to a remarkable degree, and it ³_____ likely that this influence will continue. So, who's behind the revolution? Somebody ⁴_____ be out there, tweeting and retweeting, sorting the interesting tweets from the dull ones and verifying sources, that's for sure. Meet Andy Carvin. You have most ⁵_____ never heard of him before, but it is people like Andy who are behind this revolution in spreading the news. Without him, it's possible that our understanding of what happened during the Arab Spring in 2012, for example, ⁶_____ have been very different. Andy works on the Social Media Desk at National Public Radio in the US and he spends his days tweeting and retweeting messages. When a major news story looks ⁷_____ it's going to break on Twitter, Andy gets to work. He's the man behind many of the stories we read and it's almost certain that we will increasingly rely on people like Andy for our news in the future.

4 CHALLENGE! Look at the photo. Speculate about the questions below.

1 Who took the photo? Where, when and how was it taken?
2 Why did the photographer take this photo? What is the story behind it?
3 How did the man feel and react?

The media and the message **45**

Listening, speaking and vocabulary Making the headlines

V | insight | Idioms with *in* and *out*

1 Complete idioms 1–6 with *in* or *out*. Then match them to sentences a–f which show their meaning.

1 Andy is .... of his depth in his new job at the news agency. ....
2 Jane's reporting is .... step with the policy of the news agency. ....
3 Dan went .... on a limb when he reported on government corruption. ....
4 Eddie's report on crime in schools was .... of character. ....
5 Charlie loves being .... the limelight, so she's working on a TV news channel. ....
6 Ben hopes that a promotion to news editor is .... the offing. ....

a He doesn't usually write in that way.
b It's something that may happen soon.
c It's too difficult and he doesn't know what to do.
d She enjoys getting a lot of interest and attention.
e It is no different from what everybody else does.
f He risked his career because nobody would support him.

Choosing news photos

2 Look at the two photos of snow sculptures and answer the questions.

1 How and why do you think these snow sculptures might have been constructed?
2 Would you consider uploading one of these photos to your own website or blog? If so, which one would you choose and why? How do you think your friends would react to the photo?

3 🔊 3.06 Claire, Tom and Michael run a website called *Weird photos*. Every day, they choose funny, strange or fascinating photos from around the world and post them on their website. Listen to the dialogue and answer the questions.

1 Which photo in exercise 2 do they each prefer?
  Tom: .... Claire: .... Michael: ....
2 Which photo do they decide to use on their website? ....

4 🔊 3.06 Look at the phrases from the dialogue. Tick the ones that Claire uses. Listen again and check.

1 We might as well ... .
2 Let's go with it.
3 So, do we all agree ... ?
4 In other words ... .
5 I'm just saying that ... .
6 Hang on a minute, are you saying that ... ?
7 It ticks lots of boxes.
8 I didn't mean that exactly ... .
9 We could include ... .

5 Put phrases 1–11 in exercise 4 in the correct category, A–C.

A Using modals to comment and suggest: ...., ...
B Agreeing on a choice: ...., ..., ...
C Restating a point of view: ...., ..., ..., ...

6 Look at the three photos of sand sculptures. Decide which photo you would upload to *Weird photos* and which two you would not use. Give reasons for your choices using the phrases in exercise 4.

46 **The media and the message**

Vocabulary and grammar Truth or lies?

V Documentaries

1 Choose the correct answers.

1 In the 1920s, some documentary makers used .... scenes. They filmed their own versions of real events using actors.
   a staged   b acted   c presented
2 In a fly-on-the-.................... style documentary, you never see the camera crew or a presenter.
   a floor   b stage   c wall
3 Docu-.................... is a kind of film which tries to manipulate the viewer's opinion.
   a soap   b scene   c ganda
4 When a documentary is financed by ordinary members of the public, it's called .... funding.
   a people   b crowd   c society
5 .... scores can make documentaries more dramatic and interesting.
   a Musical   b Final   c Adventure
6 In making a film about the Vietnam War, the documentary maker used .... footage – scenes that were filmed during the war in the 1960s.
   a old-time   b archival   c presented

V Film-making

2 Match the sentence halves.

1 A scriptwriter produces
2 A voice-over is
3 A stuntman or stuntwomen performs
4 A costume designer makes
5 A storyboard artist produces
6 An audio engineer records

a actors' voices, sound effects and music.
b drawings that show the plot of a film.
c a film's screenplay.
d all the dangerous actions in a film.
e clothes and props for the film.
f a commentary spoken by someone you don't see on the screen.

Emphasis and inversion

3 Complete the second sentence so that it has a similar meaning to the first sentence. Use no more than three words.

1 Anna uploaded her news to her website.
   All she .... her news to her website.
2 Dan watched a documentary last Sunday.
   Last Sunday, what he .... a documentary.
3 Paul took the photograph.
   It .... took the photograph.
4 Walter only ever talked about himself.
   All he ever did .... himself.
5 The documentary revealed that the government was corrupt.
   It .... that revealed the government's corruption.
6 Sarah took lots of photographs at the crime scene.
   What she .... lots of photographs at the crime scene.

4 Rewrite the second sentence so that it has a similar meaning to the first sentence.

1 I have rarely seen such a fascinating documentary.
   Seldom ....
2 Hollywood director James Cameron has made movies and he has also made documentaries.
   Not only ....
3 We haven't heard such awful news before.
   Never ....
4 We had only just sat down when they announced the news.
   Hardly ....
5 The newsroom has hardly ever been as busy as it is today.
   Rarely ....

5 Choose the correct answers.

Newsreels

¹**Not only / Hardly / Seldom / How often** did people go to the cinema to watch films in the first half of the twentieth century, but they also went there to catch up with the news. ²**That / What / It / Often** they went to see were newsreels, which were short, informative news programmes on the big screen. ³**What / All / That / It** was newsreel cinema that reported on the great historical events of the 1920s and 1930s and on the major battles of the two World Wars. Many of the reports were shot ⁴**in / at / on / over** location, some were in colour and they often included a lively musical ⁵**sound / score / tuning / noise** and a voice-⁶**over / through / under / above** which was witty and entertaining. A lot of the archival ⁷**screening / footage / view / showings** that we have of everyday life in the early twentieth century comes from cinema newsreels. ⁸**What / All / That / It** was television that finally put an end to their use. In the 1960s, when people started watching the news regularly on TV, cinemas stopped screening newsreels.

6 CHALLENGE! Imagine that you are going to prepare a news bulletin about events at your school in the past week. Decide on three stories to include in your bulletin. What will be your lead story? Why?

The media and the message 47

Reading The life of a war photographer

1 Read the article about the life and work of a famous war photographer. Match headings 1–6 to paragraphs A–F.

1 Opportunity
2 Motivation
3 Legacy
4 Guilt
5 Background
6 Risk

2 Read the article again. Choose the correct answers.

1 According to the article, Don McCullin
  a has only ever been a war photographer.
  b took most of his photographs in the 1960s and 1970s.
  c has taken photographs both at home and abroad.
  d began his career at the time of the Vietnam War.
2 When he was a boy, Don
  a hung out with a gang of thugs on London's rough streets.
  b found it hard to get on with other kids in his neighbourhood.
  c was encouraged to be objective and hard-working.
  d learned to be a strong and resilient person.
3 Dan took the photo of the gang of young thugs
  a soon after they had murdered a police officer.
  b but didn't sell it until one of the photo's subjects committed a crime.
  c as part of his first assignment for a major national newspaper.
  d in order to highlight their deprived background.
4 During his career, Don
  a was wounded by a sniper.
  b narrowly avoided death more than once.
  c was wounded in Cambodia.
  d felt depressed whilst away on demanding photo shoots.
5 According to his interviews, Don McCullin is
  a keen to take photographs that tell the truth about suffering.
  b proud of the artistic quality of his war photography.
  c trying hard to develop his own moral sense of purpose.
  d unmoved by the images of horror he has seen.

The life of a war photographer

'Looking at what others cannot bear to see is what my life has been about.' Don McCullin

A ....

Known as one of the greatest war photographers in history, Don McCullin has spent the last sixty years taking photographs of devastation and suffering in war zones all over the planet. His prolific output includes haunting photographs of the Vietnam War in the 1960s, of civil war in Cyprus, of massacres in the Congo, of famine in Sudan and Bangladesh, and, most recently, of the invasion of Iraq in 2003. Often at great personal risk, he has been to the most horrific places on earth in search of photographs that bear witness to the tragedy and heartbreak of war, disaster and poverty. His work will always remind people of the suffering endured by so many people during the second half of the twentieth century.

B ....

McCullin started out, not as a war photographer, but as a photojournalist of poverty and crime in his native country, England. In what must have been a difficult childhood, young Don was brought up in a one-bedroom basement flat in a rough and violent part of London. He shared a bed with his brother and the bedroom with his parents, and he grew up streetwise and tough. His childhood was good preparation for his career. Like the people he has photographed, Don experienced hunger, violence and poverty in his life. He understood what it was like to experience extreme hardship, which enabled him to really observe people's suffering. He could look at hard reality when most people would have just looked away.

C ....

Young Don's big break as a photographer came as a direct result of his deprived childhood. He snapped a gang of young thugs from his neighbourhood and, soon after he took the photo, one of the gang members stabbed and killed a policeman. As a result, a national newspaper bought and published Don's photo and offered him a contract to take more photographs. This was the start of his career as a photographer.

48 The media and the message

D

Don McCullin was fearless and reckless in his search for the perfect photograph. He would just walk into the houses of people who had had a death in the family, and point his camera at their faces, and he would go up to starving children or injured soldiers and snap their portraits. In many ways, he was a 'war junkie'. He found the adrenalin-rush of living in a war-zone so exciting that he felt depressed and useless whenever he was back home in peaceful England. On several occasions, he was very nearly killed. In Uganda he was captured by soldiers, imprisoned for four days and threatened with execution, and, in Cambodia, a sniper shot at him just as he was lifting his camera to his face to take a photo. By pure luck, the bullet struck the camera and bounced away.

E

Despite the risks, McCullin was driven throughout his career not just by his personal need to experience danger and excitement, but by a sense of moral purpose. He wanted to reveal the true face of war and famine and to tell the stories of those who have no voice. In interviews, he stresses that he wants his photographs to provide evidence of what is really happening in the world. 'You have to bear witness,' he says. 'You cannot just look away.'

F

In later life, McCullin has spoken about how he felt remorse for being so intrusive during his career. However, he is also haunted by the people he photographed. 'Sometimes,' McCullin said, 'it felt like I was carrying pieces of human flesh back home with me, not negatives. It's as if you are carrying the suffering of the people you have photographed.' In his quest to photograph the truth of war and struggle, he has paid a high personal price.

3 Read the statements about Don McCullin. Match the highlighted words in the article to the statements.

1 He was highly motivated to do what he did. (an adjective) ....
2 He interfered in people's lives in an unwelcome way. (an adjective) ....
3 He produced an enormous number of photographs. (an adjective) ....
4 He was clever and quick-thinking in an urban environment. (an adjective) ....
5 His work is beautiful, but makes you feel sad and thoughtful. (an adjective) ....
6 In his work, he observes and records the dramatic and terrible events of the twentieth century so that they won't be forgotten. (a verb + noun phrase) ....
7 When he was young, his family had no money and not enough food. (an adjective) ....
8 In his life, he went on an inner personal journey to achieve something important. (a noun) ....

4 CHALLENGE! Look at these famous news photos. Choose one photo and answer the questions.

1 What does the photo show?
2 When do you think it was taken?
3 In what way is it memorable or powerful?

The media and the message 49

Writing An article

Discourse markers

1 Complete the article with the words above each paragraph.

A ■ worryingly ■ undoubtedly

To tweet or not to tweet?

The social networking site Twitter has over 500 million registered users, and, on a positive note, is, ¹_____, one of the most significant methods that young people use to keep up with news and gossip. However, ²_____, the site seems to spend more time 'in the news' than it does commenting on the news. It is sometimes used to spread false or vicious rumours and to make personal and hurtful verbal attacks on other people. Personally, I really do think it's preferable not to tweet than to tweet.

B ■ in reality ■ theoretically

³_____, tweeting allows users to shape and control the news. ⁴_____, however, this doesn't happen. Tweets aren't often much more than a means of gossiping with a group of often ill-informed strangers. The claim that it is a way of keeping up with breaking news has no validity whatsoever. When a story breaks – whether it's a car bomb in the Middle East or a relationship break-up between two celebrities – enthusiastic tweeters immediately start commenting. Most of what they say is pointless and silly and the volume of traffic on the Twitter feed can overwhelm any user. The best way of keeping up with the news is to use a reliable news website.

C ■ presumably ■ distressingly ■ in all honesty

⁵_____, the anonymity that users have on Twitter allows many people to be abusive. It brings out the worst in people. Twitter gives them licence to tweet things they would never say in real life. Who knows why? ⁶_____, they think it's clever to be rude to people they don't know. ⁷_____, I would not want myself or anyone I know to be subjected to any abuse. In short, Twitter is a place for ignorant playground bullies with little of value to say – so let's go elsewhere.

2 Read the text again. Does the writer support or oppose using Twitter to follow the news?

Creating emphasis

3 Rewrite the second sentence so that it has a similar meaning to the first sentence.

1 In the days before social networking, people only read news stories that newspaper owners wanted them to read.
   All _____.

2 Many people follow what their favourite commentators or celebrities have to say about breaking news.
   What _____.

3 You can watch a breaking news story on TV and follow comments about the event online.
   Not only _____.

4 Ordinary people haven't been able to instantly share their views on current events before.
   Never _____.

5 In my opinion, the best thing about Twitter is that it allows you to hear the views of real people as they experience events.
   By far _____.

6 You can hear about news that isn't covered in newspapers or on TV.
   What _____.

WRITING GUIDE

■ **Task** Write an opinion piece article in favour of using social networking sites as a way of keeping up with breaking news.

■ **Ideas** Brainstorm ideas and then select the main points you want to make. Use the ideas in exercise 3 and your own arguments. Try to include unusual angles on the topic, or facts and opinions that the reader may not have considered.

■ **Plan** Follow the plan:
   Paragraph 1: State the topic and main purpose of your article. Outline your main ideas.
   Paragraph 2: Present your first point.
   Paragraph 3: Present your second point.
   Paragraph 4: Restate the main points you have covered.

■ **Write** Write your article. Use the paragraph plan to help you.

■ **Check** Check the following points.
   ■ Is the topic clearly stated?
   ■ Have you used emphasis to underline your main ideas?
   ■ Have you checked grammar, vocabulary, spelling and punctuation?

Progress check Unit 6

Read 1–12 and evaluate your learning in Unit 6. Give yourself a mark from 1 to 3. How can you improve?
1 I can't do this.   2 I have some problems with this.   3 I can do this well.

A Who controls the news?	Mark (1–3)	How can I improve?
1 In what way are citizen journalists different from professional journalists?		
I can understand an article about citizen journalism.		

2 Choose the correct answers.
    a set / put the agenda   b go / do viral
    c do / make headlines		

I can use collocations about journalism.		
3 Which of the adjectives below means *in a powerless position*? a devastated b vulnerable c scrambled d armed		
I can analyse words in a text.		

B The big picture	Mark (1–3)	How can I improve?
4 Which modal verbs can you use to express certainty in the present and the past? Which modal verbs can you use to express possibility in the present and the future?		
I can speculate about the past, present and future.		

5 Which sentence is least certain?
    a John is bound to win.   b John looks as if he's going to win.
    c It's safe to say that John will win.		

I can use phrases to express certainty and possibility.		

C Making the headlines	Mark (1–3)	How can I improve?
6 Give a strategy for adapting to authentic listening situations.		
I can adapt to authentic listening situations.		

7 Complete the idioms with *in* or *out*.
    a Paul is .... of his depth.
    b Claire is .... her element.		

I can use idioms with *in* or *out*.		
8 Give one way of using modals to comment and suggest, one way of agreeing on a choice and one way of restating a point of view.		
I can use modals to comment and suggest, agree on a choice and restate a point of view.		

D Truth or lies?	Mark (1–3)	How can I improve?
9 Name one fly-on-the-wall style film of the 1970s and one docu-ganda of the last twenty years.		
I can understand a text about documentaries.		
10 Explain the meaning of the words below. a voice-over b crowd funding c docu-ganda		
I can use words and phrases to do with documentaries.		

11 Rewrite the sentence below in three ways.
    Susie wrote a critical review of the documentary.
    a What ....
    b All ....
    c It		

I can use emphasis and inversion.		

E An article	Mark (1–3)	How can I improve?
12 Which of the discourse markers below means that you acknowledge a point despite not really wanting to? a undoubtedly b presumably c admittedly d hypothetically		
I can use discourse markers.		

7 That's life

Vocabulary Before I die …

V insight Phrasal verbs with *off*

1 Complete the sentences with the correct form of the verbs below. There is one verb that you do not need.

■ cross ■ put ■ fight ■ set ■ laugh ■ wear ■ call ■ make

1 Our bodies won't be able to …………………… off new viruses which will eventually kill us.
2 Drugs that keep us alive will …………………… off and then our bodies will stop working.
3 Everyone has a list of things to do in life. Once we've …………………… off everything on that list, what is the point of living?
4 When we …………………… off on our journey through life, we feel positive, but over time we will become tired of life.
5 We won't be able to …………………… off the inevitability of death forever. We will eventually die!
6 Some people think that the idea of immortality is a joke, but you can't …………………… off the advances in medical science which may make much longer lifespans possible in the future.
7 Thieves have …………………… off with secret scientific data which is worth millions of dollars.

V Phrases with *life*

2 Rewrite the parts of the sentences in bold using an idiom which contains the word in brackets.

1 Tinned products often **last a very long time**.
Tinned products often have …………………………………………………. (shelf)
2 People at the festival came from **many different backgrounds**.
People at the festival came from ………………………………………. (walk)
3 In the 1990s, Melanie was **at an age when she felt at her best**.
In the 1990s, Melanie was ……………………………………………. (prime)
4 Taking up mountain climbing gave Harry **an opportunity to really start enjoying himself again**.
Taking up mountain climbing gave Harry …………………………………………. (lease)
5 Staying warm in Arctic regions is **a very urgent and important issue**.
Staying warm in Arctic regions is ………………………………………. (matter)
6 People who do stunts in movies, and avoid serious injuries, are **being very lucky and fortunate**.
People who do stunts in movies, and avoid serious injuries, are ……………………………………. (living)

V Phrases with *time*

3 Choose the correct answers.

1 I don't remember the fall of the Berlin Wall. I'm only sixteen, so it was **before my time / behind the times / at one time**.
2 I'm generally happy with the age I am, but, **in the course of time / from time to time / ahead of time**, I wish I were a bit older.
3 I'm not very fit or fast **in the nick of time / at the best of times / at the same time**. Yesterday, after a big lunch, I was really slow!
4 One of my friends criticizes me **all the time / in the course of time / before my time**. He never stops!
5 Let's keep playing **at one time / from time to time / for the time being**. If the rains gets much heavier, we'll stop.
6 Our holiday will be over **in next to no time / at the best of times / at the same time**. We'll be back at school before we know it.

4 Complete the text with one word in each gap.

Struldbrugs

In the classic story *Gulliver's Travels*, written in 1726, the hero, Lemuel Gulliver, escapes in the ¹…………………… of time from tiny people who want to kill him, and uses his sword to ²…………………… off giant animals which attack him. He also visits Luggnagg, a place inhabited by the Struldbrugs, a group of people who live forever. Gulliver learns that, although they are immortal, they don't stop ageing. At ³…………………… time, when they were under the age of eighty, many of the ancient Struldbrugs had meaningful lives. They enjoyed reaching the ⁴…………………… in life, such as getting married and getting important jobs. But, in the ⁵…………………… of time, these people have aged, lost their hair, their teeth and their memories. Hundreds of years old, they are now ⁶…………………… off from society, with no friends and no home. They are so behind the ⁷…………………… that they have no understanding of what modern life is like. In the end, Gulliver learns that eternal life without eternal youth is a life not worth living.

5 CHALLENGE! Think of an example for each of the things below. Then describe what you remember about them.

1 something you managed to do in the nick of time
2 a problem that you recently shrugged off
3 a place that you used to visit from time to time
4 an important milestone in your life

Grammar Lucky break or lucky escape?

Conditionals

1 Complete the sentences with the correct form of the words in brackets. Use the second or third conditional forms.

1 We've won a car in a prize draw! If we ………………… (not buy) a ticket, we ………………… (not win) anything!
2 Sally doesn't have a mobile phone because she hasn't got much money. She ………………… (get) one if she ………………… (have) more money.
3 I felt exhausted after the race. I ………………… (not feel) so tired if I ………………… (not finish) first.
4 Penny had a lucky escape when she was hit by a car. She ………………… (be) hurt if she ………………… (not wear) her bicycle helmet.
5 I'm going to the beach later today. I ………………… (stay) at home if it ………………… (not be) so sunny.
6 We won last night's match! We ………………… (lose) if our goalkeeper Emma ………………… (not save) a penalty in the last minute.
7 I'm sorry, but Jill can't help organize the party later. If she ………………… (not be) busy, she ………………… (help).
8 Andy knocked over an expensive vase. He was lucky. It ………………… (smash) to pieces if it ………………… (not land) on the soft carpet.

Mixed conditionals

2 Rewrite the second sentence so that it has a similar meaning to the first sentence. Use mixed conditionals.

1 I can't pay the bill because I didn't get paid last week.
   If I ………………………………………………………… .
2 Sally is only here because you invited her.
   If you ………………………………………………………… .
3 Louise is a great tennis player; that's why she won the tournament last week.
   If Louise ………………………………………………………… .
4 We are late because the train left earlier than expected.
   We ………………………………………………………… .
5 We're not lucky, so we've never won anything in our lives.
   If we ………………………………………………………… .
6 Sam won a thousand euros at the race course. That's why he's so happy.
   If Sam ………………………………………………………… .

3 Complete the text with the most suitable conditional form of the verbs in brackets.

Paul Newman – a lucky life

If Paul Newman (1925–2008) ¹………………… (become) a shopkeeper like his dad, we ²………………… (never hear) of him. Instead, he took up acting and became one of Hollywood's most famous and prolific film stars, appearing in numerous films, notably *Butch Cassidy and the Sundance Kid*, *The Sting* and *The Color of Money*. They are all classic films, but they ³………………… (not be) so well-known now if Newman ⁴………………… (not star) in them.

As well as being talented, Paul Newman was also one of the luckiest actors in Hollywood history. In fact, he ⁵………………… (could / die) before his acting career began if fortune ⁶………………… (not smile) on him. During the Second World War, he was a gunner on a bomber aircraft and he served in the war in the Pacific. One day, all the planes in his squadron were ordered to fly to an aircraft carrier out at sea. All the planes flew except Newman's, which was grounded because the pilot was ill. If Newman's plane ⁷………………… (fly) to the carrier, the actor ⁸………………… (die), as the aircraft carrier was attacked by the Japanese and every other serviceman in his squadron was killed.

4 **CHALLENGE!** Read two news extracts about lucky breaks. What would have happened if the people hadn't been so lucky? What would you have done in these situations?

Lucky survivors

Balloonists survived when their balloon started to deflate. Strong winds blew them away from the mountains and out to sea, and their experienced pilot was able to crash-land just off the coast.

Lucky mountaineers

Mountaineers who got trapped in the mountains for six days stayed alive because they found a small cave where climbers on a previous expedition had left supplies of food and drink.

Listening, speaking and vocabulary The golden years

V The old and the young

1 Circle two words in each list that could be used to describe the person in the sentence.

1. William is only fifteen, but he's very grown-up for his age and is able to deal with things without much help.
   - a self-reliant
   - b vulnerable
   - c adolescent
   - d infantile

2. Tom is almost ninety, but he still does his own shopping and cooking and likes trying out new things.
   - a set in his ways
   - b long in the tooth
   - c over the hill
   - d independent

3. Although he's nineteen, my brother behaves like someone half his age.
   - a mature
   - b wise
   - c adolescent
   - d infantile

4. Agnes is fifty-eight, but she still likes going out to nightclubs on a Friday.
   - a mature
   - b elderly
   - c youthful
   - d juvenile

5. My grandfather is full of clever advice and always helps us out. He's full of life and likes travelling.
   - a wise
   - b dependent
   - c supportive
   - d childish

6. Sally has just left school and moved out of her parents' home, and is about to start her first job. She's not sure what to do, but she's very excited.
   - a inexperienced
   - b independent
   - c supportive
   - d juvenile

V Generation gap

2 Complete the sentences with the missing words in the correct form.

1. Now that he has a good job, Michael has left home and is .... on his own two feet at last.
2. If you're lazy, you'll .... away with doing nothing for a while, but eventually you'll have to start working.
3. My grandfather is very .... in his ways. He always has lunch at twelve and he always eats fish on Fridays.
4. Stop .... on about your weekend. I'm bored! You never ask me what I've been doing.
5. My aunt Amy's so friendly that I always .... at ease in her company.
6. Will you .... me alone? I'm trying to do my homework and you keep asking me questions!
7. Sally is a very spoilt child. Her parents aren't strict. She always .... her own way.
8. Tom has left school and has no job or money. He is .... off his parents.

Discussing old age

3 Read the statement below. Do you agree? Why / why not?

'Young people are generally more selfish than their parents.'

4 3.07 Listen to three people, Jenny, Simon and David, discussing the statement in exercise 3. Answer the questions.

1. Which speakers generally agree with the statement in exercise 3?
2. What do the speakers think are the main reasons why teenagers today are selfish?

5 3.07 Listen again. Which speakers, Jenny (J), Simon (S) or David (D), make the following points or suggestions?

1. Teenagers are more independent than their parents were at the same age. ....
2. Teenagers don't do jobs around the house in the way they once did. ....
3. Teenagers can't avoid being influenced by society and the media. ....
4. Teenagers are constantly using computers and mobile phones. ....
5. Teenagers rarely find time to socialize with older family members. ....
6. Although teenagers are selfish, it's not their fault. ....

6 3.07 Write who uses each phrase, Jenny (J), Simon (S) or David (D). Listen again and check.

1. I totally support that idea. ....
2. What if … ? ....
3. The main benefit that … . ...
4. The most obvious reason for this is … . ...
5. Even if … . ...
6. My main worry is … . ...
7. What bothers me … . ...

7 Put phrases 1–7 in exercise 6 in the correct category, A–C.

A Supporting a statement: ...., ..., ...
B Opposing a statement: ...., ...
C Discussing hypothetical situations: ...., ...

8 Read the statement below. Decide whether you agree or disagree with it. Think of ways of expressing your view.

'Parents shouldn't finance their children after they are eighteen.'

Vocabulary and grammar The Road Not Taken

V insight Analysing meaning

1 Look at the phrases from Robert Frost's poem *The Road Not Taken*. Refer back to the poem on page 88 of the Student's Book and write answers to the questions about the phrases.

1 *… long I stood …*
What does this mean? What does it tell us about the poet's state of mind?

2 *In leaves no step had trodden black*
What does this tell the reader about the path that the poet decides to take?

3 *… that has made all the difference.*
What does *that* refer to? What has it made *all the difference* to?

Unreal situations

2 Choose the correct answers.

1 Imagine you **passed / had passed** all your exams last summer. What would you be doing now?
2 Jason looks very bored. Perhaps he'd sooner there **wasn't / hadn't been** so much homework to do.
3 I'd rather we **didn't go / hadn't gone out** later. It's raining and I'm tired.
4 Supposing we all **helped / had helped**. I feel terrible leaving her to do everything. She already looks tired.
5 Dan didn't seem upset when he lost. It was as if he **knew / had known** what the result was going to be.
6 Suppose tomorrow's party **ended / had ended** late, would we be able to get home?
7 I know you want to go out, but I'd sooner you **stayed / had stayed** at home this evening.
8 Supposing it **snowed / had snowed** in the mountains later. The climbers could get into difficulties.

3 Complete the sentences with the correct form of the verbs in brackets.

1 Harry is refusing to talk to me. Perhaps he'd rather he .... (not be) here with me.
2 Amy was very angry when we got back. It was as if she .... (wait) for us all day.
3 Suppose we .... (buy) a house last year. Would the house prices have been lower then?
4 Imagine you .... (not go) on holiday last summer. You'd be so tired now!
5 Simon is very outgoing and fun, but imagine he .... (be) here, living with us all the time. It would be a nightmare!
6 Supposing Karen .... (not tell) the truth that day. How would you have felt about that?

4 Read the letter from a parent to a child. Complete the gaps with the correct form of the verbs in brackets.

Dear Child (now grown-up)
Imagine you ¹................... (listen) to all the advice I gave you when you were a child and suppose you ²................... (act) on all that advice. Where ³................... (you / be) now? Well, if you ⁴................... (do) what I told you to do then, you ⁵................... (fulfill) all my wishes. And today you ⁶................... (have) more wealth than a king and more wisdom than a judge. In life, however, it is not only children who should listen and learn. I have learned that everybody should make their own way in life, choosing the advice that makes sense and learning from experience. If you ⁷................... (do) everything I said, you ⁸................... (not learn) from your own mistakes, and you ⁹................... (not be) the person you are now. In truth, I'd rather you ¹⁰................... (be) the strong-minded, independent adult I see before me now than the person I wanted to make.

Your loving parent

5 CHALLENGE! Read the biographical details of Mark Wahlberg's life. Then speculate about his life choices.

Six things you didn't know about superstar actor Mark Wahlberg

* He left school without passing his High School Diploma.
* He joined a street gang when he was in his teens.
* He went to prison when he was sixteen after he assaulted a man.
* He joined the boy band *New Kids on the Block*, but left before they became world famous.
* Film critics praised him for his role in *The Basketball Diaries* in 1995 and many offers of parts in films followed.
* He founded his charity, the Mark Wahlberg Youth Foundation, in 2001. It helps young people from deprived backgrounds like Mark's.

Reading Serendipity – how we make our own luck

1 Read the quotes by famous Americans. Decide which of them you agree with and why.

1. *Diligence is the mother of good luck.*
   Benjamin Franklin (18th-century politician)
2. *Shallow men believe in luck. Strong men believe in cause and effect.*
   Ralph Waldo Emerson (19th-century poet)
3. *The best luck of all is the luck you make for yourself.*
   Douglas MacArthur (World War II general)
4. *Everything in life is luck.*
   Donald Trump (billionaire businessman)

2 Read the article and match missing opening sentences A–E to paragraphs 1–5.

A A world without luck would be a world without many of the great scientific breakthroughs that have been made in history.
B The psychologist Professor Richard Wiseman, who wrote the book *The Luck Factor*, goes further.
C Imagine a world in which there was no such thing as luck or chance.
D As we have seen, everybody has lucky breaks, but not everybody spots them.
E Psychologists are fascinated by these stories of outrageous good fortune.

3 Read the article again. Are the statements true (T) or false (F)?

1. We're lucky to live in a world where luck plays a part.
2. Fleming's discovery of penicillin was mostly down to good fortune.
3. Both Percy Spencer and Spencer Silver invented something whilst working on something else.
4. Researchers at University College London analysed their own experiences and found patterns that suggested human beings respond differently to luck.
5. In Wiseman's newspaper experiment, unlucky people usually spent longer counting pictures.
6. There is a link between sociability and good fortune, according to Wiseman.
7. It's better to trust the judgement of experienced others rather than rely on your own feelings if you want to be lucky in life.
8. In Wiseman's opinion, sometimes, what might seem to be unlucky may actually not be so bad.

Serendipity
– how we make our own luck

serendipity: a chance encounter or accident that leads to a happy – sometimes life-changing – conclusion

1 .... It would be a world in which nothing unexpected ever happened. In truth, of course, we live in a world of lucky accidents, and it's fortunate that we do so. Without the flukes, coincidences and accidents that make up our daily lives, the world would be dull and predictable. Suppose, also, that we lived in a world in which you could not make your own luck, a world in which we had to accept the hand dealt to us by chance. That would be a frightening and chaotic world. Fortunately, as we shall see, that isn't true either. We live in a world of luck, but one that we can shape and change if we have the right mindset.

2 .... That's because lucky accidents, or moments of 'serendipity', have given us hundreds of inventions and discoveries. If Alexander Fleming hadn't accidentally allowed mould to grow in a dish in his laboratory, he wouldn't have discovered penicillin, a cure for bacterial diseases. If Percy Spencer hadn't noticed that a chocolate bar in his pocket melted when he stood next to a radar transmitter, he would have never invented the microwave oven. And if Dr Spencer Silver hadn't failed to make the super strong glue he was trying to make, he wouldn't have accidentally made the weak glue that was perfect for his invention – Post-it notes.

3 .... Consequently, they have been carrying out research into why some people seem to live charmed lives while others are unhappy with their lot in life. A research team at University College London recently asked people to post their own good luck stories on the team's website, which they then investigated to find patterns amongst the stories. What they found was that while most of us experience moments of good fortune, not all of us recognize and act on the opportunities they give us. Lucky people, who always seem to be in the right place at the right time, are really good at seizing the moment. So, while Fleming, Spencer and Silver were lucky that accidents gave them ideas, what was important was that they took advantage of those ideas and turned them into important discoveries and inventions.

4 .... His studies show that luck is as much a state of mind as an uncontrollable quality. In other words, if we think we're lucky, we are lucky. In one experiment, Professor Wiseman asked people to say whether they thought they were lucky or not. Then he asked them to count the number of photographs in a newspaper. About halfway through, an advertisement read: *Stop counting. There are 43 photographs in this newspaper!* Remarkably, people who thought they were lucky were much more likely to spot the advertisement and stop counting. What this revealed was that 'lucky' people have a different mindset from 'unlucky' people. In his book, Professor Wiseman argues that lucky people are very relaxed and open to new ideas whereas unlucky people are often stressed and concerned with failure. The personal attributes that lucky people have make them lucky. That's because it's only by trying new things and noticing the unexpected that luck comes your way, and it's only by being outgoing and being optimistic that you find yourself in situations where lucky things happen.

5 .... So what should we do if we want to maximize our luck? Professor Wiseman suggests that we should, first of all, be open to new experiences; secondly, we should listen to our own hunches, as it is often our own intuition that tells us whether an opportunity is a good one or not; and thirdly, we should be positive and optimistic at all times. He also encourages people to make the best of their luck, good or bad. The power of positive thinking can transform the way we see our luck and our lives. So, be lucky, and remember that luck is everywhere, and you have the power to shape it.

4 Study the highlighted words in the article. Then use the correct form of the highlighted words to complete the sentences below.
1 Amelia's most positive .... is her optimism.
2 I had a .... that Paul would be a good person to go on holiday with. And we had a great time!
3 There is a clear .... to the way young children develop. It follows a regular path.
4 Life didn't deal Tom a great .... However, he made the most of the opportunities he had.
5 I didn't intend to score a goal when I kicked the ball. It was a ....
6 Emily was never satisfied with her .... in life. She wanted something better.
7 If you have a positive ...., you can achieve anything! Just think positive!

5 Complete the text with the singular or plural form of six of the nouns in exercise 4.

Prize-winning photo was taken by chance!

The personal [1].................. required for nature photographers are perseverance and also a patient [2].................. in order to prepare for the rare moments when spectacular things happen. Sometimes, however, all they need is to be in the right place at the right time. For example, amateur photographer Robert Bass was taking photos with his smartphone when he heard thunder. He pointed his smartphone at the sky, but couldn't believe it when he realized he had captured a rainbow and a bolt of lightning together. Bass said that he had had a [3].................. that the weather was going to be dramatic that day and that's why he was outside. But it's not every photographer's [4].................. in life to capture such a memorable photo. Luck dealt him an amazing [5].................., especially as he hadn't noticed the lightning at the time. 'I was concentrating on the rainbow,' he said. 'Capturing both was a complete [6]................... I suppose it will be the best photo I'll ever take.'

6 CHALLENGE! Read the quote below and discuss the questions.

'If you want more luck, take more chances.'
Brian Tracy (motivational speaker and author)

1 To what extent does Tracy's quote reflect the view of the writer in the article about serendipity?
2 In your opinion, what factors affect whether a person is lucky in life or not?

Writing An opinion essay

Making comparisons

1 Rewrite the sentences. Use the phrases in brackets.

1. If you can buy lots of things, you are going to be happier. (The more … , the happier …)
2. Good health and good friends are much more important than money. (far less)
3. I've never met a wealthier man than Howard Hughes. (such … as)
4. Very rich people are less motivated to work hard than people who aren't rich. (not as … as)
5. As you get older, having a good standard of living is of increasing importance. (more and more)
6. People who aren't well-off get exactly the same amount of fun out of life as the super-rich. (just as much)

2 Read the four opinion essay topics and decide whether you agree or disagree with them and why. Then read the opinion essay and decide which topic it is answering.

1. The lives of lucky people are no more interesting than anybody else's. Do you agree?
2. The harder you work, the luckier you get. Do you agree?
3. Being lucky in life is more important than working hard. Do you agree?
4. High achievers are just luckier than the rest of us. Do you agree?

Some people seem to be luckier than others. ¹They get much better qualifications, jobs and opportunities. They also do more exciting things in their lives. In my opinion, however, successful people are not just lucky. Working hard and showing a lot of perseverance plays a large part in doing well in life.

Firstly, I think that the more effort you put into doing something, the more you get out of it. ²It takes effort to play a musical instrument, be good at sport and even make friends. But all that hard work can lead to opportunities. For example, it can lead to being in a band, or playing for a team. Rock stars and sports stars aren't just lucky. I suspect that nobody at Cristiano Ronaldo's school practised their soccer skills as much as Ronaldo himself did.

Secondly, working harder and harder to learn a new skill makes you feel lucky. ³It makes you feel good about yourself and your life. You become a confident and optimistic person and research shows that positive people feel luckier.

⁴They are less likely to miss opportunities in life, feel negative when things go wrong, or give up when something is difficult to do.

In conclusion, although everybody needs breaks in life, the chances of enjoying that luck are far higher when you put in time, effort and perseverance. Working hard does not guarantee luck in life, but it makes your chances of being lucky much greater than those who are lazy or demotivated.

3 Follow the instructions below to rewrite the underlined sentences in the essay in a more persuasive way.

1. Use the repetition of key words and ideas to create emphasis in this sentence.
2. Put information you want to emphasize at the beginning of the sentence.
3. Use the repetition of key words and ideas to create emphasis in the sentence.
4. Use three sentences instead of one to create emphasis.

WRITING GUIDE

- **Task** Write an opinion essay on the topic below.

  'The more money you have, the happier you are.' Do you agree?

- **Ideas** Use the ideas in exercise 1 to help you. Decide whether you agree or disagree with the ideas and think of other ideas to support your opinion.

- **Plan** Follow the plan:

  Paragraph 1: State the topic of the essay and give your point of view.
  Paragraph 2: Introduce the first argument to support your opinion.
  Paragraph 3: Introduce a second argument to support your opinion.
  Paragraph 4: Sum up any arguments against your opinion.
  Paragraph 5: Summarize and restate your opinion.

- **Write** Write your essay. Use the paragraph plan to help you.

- **Check** Check the following points.
  - Have you stated your opinion in the introduction and the conclusion?
  - Have you used persuasive language?
  - Have you made comparisons to illustrate your point of view?
  - Have you checked grammar, vocabulary, spelling and punctuation?

Progress check Unit 7

Read 1–12 and evaluate your learning in Unit 7. Give yourself a mark from 1 to 3. How can you improve?
1 I can't do this.   2 I have some problems with this.   3 I can do this well.

A Before I die …	Mark (1–3)	How can I improve?
1 What are the disadvantages of being immortal?		
I can understand a text about immortality projects.		
2 Write phrasal verbs with *off* that have the same meaning as the words below. a become less b run away c cancel		
I can use phrasal verbs with *off*.		

3 Complete the phrases with *life* using one word.
  a People came from every .... of life. There were young and old, rich and poor.
  b Danny lives a .... life. I don't know how he is so lucky and never gets into trouble.		

I can use phrases with *life*.		

B Lucky break or lucky escape?	Mark (1–3)	How can I improve?
4 When do you use the second and third conditional form?		
I can use conditionals.		

5 Choose the correct answers.
  a If Janice hadn't travelled in Peru, she **wouldn't know** / **wouldn't have known** so much about Peruvian culture now.
  b If Jake was rich, he **would travel** / **would have travelled** to Mexico last year.		

I can use mixed conditionals.		

C The golden years	Mark (1–3)	How can I improve?

6 Complete the phrases with one word. Do these phrases usually describe old or young people?
  a Terry is .... in the tooth.   b Frank is .... the hill.
  c Margaret is .... in her ways.		

I can use adjectives and phrases to describe the old and the young.		
7 Give one way of supporting a statement, one way of opposing a statement and one way of discussing a hypothetical situation.		
I can support and oppose statements, and discuss hypothetical situations.		

D The Road Not Taken	Mark (1–3)	How can I improve?
8 What decision did the writer have to make in the poem?		
I can understand a poem about life-changing decisions.		
9 In the poem, what is the road a metaphor for?		
I can analyse meaning.		

10 Choose the correct answers.
  a Imagine you **missed** / **had missed** the bus. You would have missed the party, too.
  b Supposing we **left** / **had left** now. Do you think Sarah would mind?		

I can talk about unreal situations.		

E An opinion essay	Mark (1–3)	How can I improve?

11 Complete the sentences with one word.
  a Money isn't .... important as having friends.
  b The film got more and .... interesting as it went on.		

I can make comparisons.		
12 Give two techniques of persuasive writing.		
I can recognize and use persuasive writing.		

8 Food and ethics

Vocabulary A right to eat

V insight Synonyms: intensity

1 Read the campaign leaflet from the Organization Against Battery Farming. Match the intense adjectives below to the phrases in italics 1–7 with a similar meaning.

- critical ■ countless ■ outlawed ■ agonizing
- distressing ■ cold-blooded

Battery chickens are kept in small cages where they live out their lives under artificial lights with very little space. It is ¹*incredibly upsetting* for any bird to be prevented from nesting, moving around or cleaning itself. The only thing that battery chickens are allowed to do is lay ²*a huge number of* eggs. Many organizations, such as Compassion in World Farming, believe that this is a ³*very cruel* crime and have campaigned against the use of battery cages for many years. Since 2012, many types of battery cages have been ⁴*made illegal* by EU laws which state that birds may only be kept in cages which have 750 cm² or more of space for the chicken to move around in. However, Compassion in World Farming has criticized this legislation, saying that chickens continue to suffer and die in ⁵*very painful* ways on battery farms. They say that this terrible practice should be stopped and that it is ⁶*really important* that action is taken now.

V insight Prepositions

2 Choose the correct answers.

1. The rise **in** / **of** / **with** population means that we need to find new ways of producing more food.
2. Farmers who treat animals in inhumane ways should be threatened **of** / **with** / **at** prison terms.
3. Dairy products are key ingredients **at** / **in** / **with** most European diets.
4. The development of genetically modified crops is based **on** / **at** / **in** decades of scientific research.
5. The survival of the rainforest will depend **at** / **of** / **on** how we manage our resources in the future.
6. A lot of farmers think we'd be better off **on** / **over** / **without** large numbers of wild animals.
7. Thanks **for** / **at** / **to** recent research, we are able to grow crops which are less likely to get diseases.
8. Current research may result **in** / **of** / **at** the creation of an artificial form of meat.

V The environment

3 Choose the correct answers.

1. It's important that we **conserve** / **reduce** emissions from cars. If we can lower them, it will reduce climate change.
2. The authorities have introduced measures to **prevent** / **protect** fires from starting in areas where it is hot and dry.
3. If we **maintain** / **overexploit** natural resources, they will run out.
4. Loss of habitat **threatens** / **causes** numerous species with extinction. If we aren't careful, they will die out.
5. Factories **maintain** / **produce** a lot of toxic waste which we have to find ways of dealing with.
6. At last, governments are trying to **conserve** / **produce** nature by financing wetland schemes and other wildlife programmes.

4 Choose the correct answers.

The Irish potato famine

The potato was introduced to Ireland in the 17th century, and soon became the country's main crop. By the 19th century, most of the country's poor people ¹........ potatoes as their only food source. Then, in 1845, the potato crop in Ireland was completely ²........ by disease, which ³........ the starvation of over a million people. It was ⁴........ for families whose children were starving and there was a huge ⁵........ in the number of young people leaving the country to build new lives in England, America or Australia. Nowadays, specialists continue to be concerned ⁶........ populations who live on only one type of food, because if the crop fails, they will go hungry. Any one type of food should only make up a small fraction ⁷........ our diet and it is important that we grow a variety of crops.

1	a depended on	b based on	
	c rose in	d thanks to	
2	a wiped out	b slaughtered	
	c outlawed	d threatened	
3	a based on	b concerned about	
	c threatened with	d resulted in	
4	a critical	b cold-blooded	
	c agonizing	d awe-inspiring	
5	a ingredient	b rise	
	c result	d impact	
6	a of	b in	
	c about	d against	
7	a on	b for	
	c from	d of	

5 CHALLENGE! Describe how you choose which eggs to buy. What factors do you consider?

Grammar Wet wealth

The passive

1 Read the facts about super-trawlers. Complete the sentences with the correct passive form of the verbs in brackets.

THE FRIGHTENING TRUTH ABOUT SUPER-TRAWLERS

1 Trawlers are fishing boats that pull a large net along the sea bed. Fish .... (catch) in the net and pulled on board.
2 The first trawlers .... (design) by the British and Dutch in the 17th century.
3 Currently, new super-trawlers .... (build) that are over 140 m long!
4 One super-trawler, the *Margiris*, is currently at sea. In the next few weeks, over 6,000 tonnes of fish .... (process) on board the ship!
5 In the last fifteen years, over 1,500 endangered turtles .... (kill) by super-trawlers and the situation is getting worse.
6 About ten years ago, scientists realized that the number of mackerel in the South Pacific .... (reduce) by 90% because of over fishing.
7 West African waters .... (over fish) by super-trawlers until the fishermen realized there were almost no fish left.
8 A lot of jobs in Scotland's fishing villages .... (lose) recently because small fishing boats can't compete with big trawlers.

2 Rewrite the end of each sentence using the modal verb in brackets and the passive form.

1 If we stopped trawling, it would be possible to protect a lot of endangered fish.
   If we stopped trawling, a lot of endangered fish .... (could)
2 It is essential that we stop hunting elephants for their ivory.
   Hunting elephants for their ivory .... (must)
3 If we increase the size of cages in zoos, it is possible that we will improve the lives of many zoo animals.
   If we increase the size of cages in zoos, the lives of many zoo animals .... (might)
4 Using some powerful insecticides is harmful, so it is advisable to ban them.
   Using some powerful insecticides is harmful, so they .... (should)
5 It is necessary to take action to protect the rainforests now.
   Action to protect the rainforests .... (have to)
6 We should catch and imprison people who dump their waste in the countryside.
   People who dump their waste in the countryside .... (have to)

More passive structures

3 Complete the sentences with *be*, *to be* or *being*.

1 In the developed world, we all expect .... served food whenever we want it.
2 Thirteen per cent of the world's population suffers from not .... given enough to eat.
3 A child's development can .... seriously affected by malnutrition.
4 We don't want children .... held back because they are poor.
5 We can help to stop malnutrition .... a major cause of death in developing countries.
6 If we care about children .... fed properly in the developing world, we should take action.

4 Complete the text with one word in each gap.

Disposable chopsticks

China's forests are [1] .... devastated to produce chopsticks. Every year, over 20 million trees [2] .... cut down in the country just to make the long, thin pieces of wood that people use for eating, and people in China get through about 80 billion chopsticks a year. That's an extremely high figure when you consider that each one of these implements [3] .... thrown away after barely fifteen minutes of use. So, why isn't anything [4] .... done to address the problem? Well, a lot of Chinese people are concerned about their disappearing forests, but it's unlikely that the widespread use of disposable chopsticks [5] .... be stopped any time soon. China is a rapidly expanding economy, with lots of new factories and cities, so why, in the face of all this growth, should people there [6] .... worried about saving a few trees, all of which have [7] .... grown with the express purpose of producing cheap wood anyway? The truth is that, currently, the overwhelming majority of people in China, and many other parts of Asia, like disposable chopsticks and don't see any reason why such a long-standing habit should [8] .... changed.

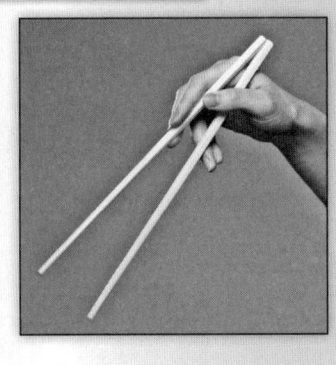

5 **CHALLENGE!** Choose one of the campaigns below and make suggestions for what could be done to improve the situation. Use passive structures.

- Stop plastic polluting our seas and killing marine animals!
- Stop the hunting of elephants!
- Make oil companies clean up oil spills in the sea!

Food and ethics 61

Listening, speaking and vocabulary Feeding the world

V Phrases with *face*

1 Choose the correct answers.

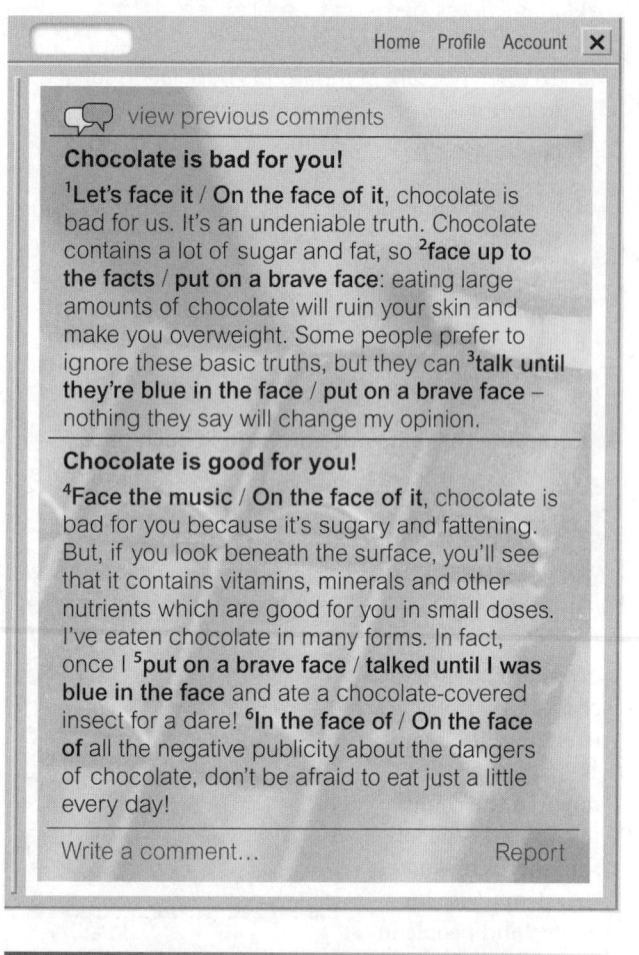

> Home Profile Account ✕
>
> view previous comments
>
> **Chocolate is bad for you!**
> ¹**Let's face it / On the face of it**, chocolate is bad for us. It's an undeniable truth. Chocolate contains a lot of sugar and fat, so ²**face up to the facts / put on a brave face**: eating large amounts of chocolate will ruin your skin and make you overweight. Some people prefer to ignore these basic truths, but they can ³**talk until they're blue in the face / put on a brave face** – nothing they say will change my opinion.
>
> **Chocolate is good for you!**
> ⁴**Face the music / On the face of it**, chocolate is bad for you because it's sugary and fattening. But, if you look beneath the surface, you'll see that it contains vitamins, minerals and other nutrients which are good for you in small doses. I've eaten chocolate in many forms. In fact, once I ⁵**put on a brave face / talked until I was blue in the face** and ate a chocolate-covered insect for a dare! ⁶**In the face of / On the face of** all the negative publicity about the dangers of chocolate, don't be afraid to eat just a little every day!
>
> Write a comment...   Report

Talking about photos

2 Look at photos A–C and answer the questions.
1 Where are the people in each photo? What are they doing?
2 What is the relationship between the people in the photos?
3 Describe the place, the food and the implements the people are using to eat with.

3 🔊 **3.08** Listen to a dialogue between Tom and Susie. Which of the photos in exercise 2 are they talking about?

4 🔊 **3.08** Listen again. Are the sentences true (T) or false (F)?
1 Tom likes eating in the sort of place in the photo more than most other places. ....
2 Susie thinks that the people in the photo all know each other. ....
3 Like Tom, Susie thinks that the people could be at a birthday party. ....
4 Both Tom and Susie agree that the photo was taken towards the end of the meal. ....
5 Tom has eaten similar food to what is shown in the photo. ....
6 Susie thinks that the place in the photo looks like a pricey place to eat. ....
7 At the end, Susie offers to drive Tom to the restaurant on Saturday. ....

5 🔊 **3.08** Complete the phrases from the dialogue. Then listen again and check.
1 I .... if they know each other.
2 Well- .... I didn't really .... that.
3 What I .... is ....
4 It looks .... though it might be someone's birthday or something.
5 It's .... to say.
6 .... by the amount of food that's still going round, ...
7 That's an interesting ....
8 It doesn't look .... an expensive place.

6 Put phrases 1–8 in exercise 5 in the correct category, A–C.
A Speculating and reflecting: ...1..., ..., ..., ..., ..., ...
B Conceding a point: ....
C Clarifying an opinion: ....

7 Choose one of the other photos in exercise 2. Write a dialogue between you and a friend in which you speculate about the photo. Use the questions below to help you.
1 Where are the people and why? What is the relationship between them?
2 What are they eating? What can you guess about the food and the place?
3 Have you ever tried eating in this way? What do you think of it? Why? Would you like to try it? Why / why not?

62 Food and ethics

Vocabulary and grammar The origins of food

V insight Adjective + noun collocations: food

1 Complete the text with the words below.

■ snack ■ portion ■ takeaway ■ order ■ ration ■ fare

In my great-grandparents' time, the only
¹ .... restaurants in the UK were fish and chip shops. The wartime ² .... book generally only permitted small amounts of food to be bought, so eating fish and chips was a big treat. Today, of course, times have changed. We eat fast food from all over the world, so a slice of Italian pizza is considered a lunchtime ³ .... by busy working people with no time to go out for a proper meal, and a burrito in a local Mexican café is a popular ⁴ .... for busy executives. Sometimes, they'll even have the food delivered to their desks because they have no time to leave the office. Varieties of food that my great-grandparents probably never knew about, such as kebabs from Turkey or Lebanon, are standard ⁵ .... on the streets of London nowadays. They're served with chips, of course, and, if you're really hungry, you can always order a double ⁶ .... Now, *that's* the sort of food my great-grandad would have loved!

V Ways of cooking

2 Label the photos with the words below. You can use more than one word for each photo.

■ bake ■ barbecue ■ boil ■ fry ■ grill ■ poach ■ roast
■ scramble ■ steam ■ stew ■ stir-fry ■ toast

1 ....

2 ....

3 ....

4 ....

5 ....

The passive: verbs with two objects

3 Jenny has just returned from Thailand. Her friend Amy is asking her about the food there. Rewrite Amy's questions in another way, using the passive.

1 When were you served Thai food for the first time?
....

2 Have you been taught the secrets of Thai cooking?
....

3 How much money were you paid for working in the restaurant?
....

4 Are you sometimes sent advice by your Thai cookery teacher?
....

5 Have you had a Thai recipe book bought for you?
....

4 Complete Jenny's answers using appropriate verbs in the passive form. Then match answers a–e to questions 1–5 in exercise 3.

a Oh, no money .... to me! I got a free room and free meals. I did it for the experience.
b Yes, I am. Twenty emails .... to me by Nok since I got back to England! She thinks I don't use enough spices!
c Well, it was on my first day in Bangkok. I .... green curry and steamed rice, and it was delicious!
d Funny you should ask that! I .... three recipe books for my birthday last week by friends and family!
e Of course. I took a course in the city of Chiang Mai and I .... how to make tom yam, pad Thai and all the different curries. Then I got a job in a restaurant as a cook!

5 CHALLENGE! Fast food is often unhealthy. Think of five fast food snacks that are quick, cheap and easy to prepare and that are also healthy. Describe how they are made and in what ways they are healthy.

Food and ethics

Reading Designer shoes and the Amazon rainforest

1 **Read the questions and guess the answers.**
   1 Why is the Amazon rainforest important to us all and how is it threatened by the production of leather products?
   2 Which European country is the main producer of designer leather shoes?
   3 How can Western consumers influence whether the Amazon rainforest is cut down or not?
   4 Why do leather producers continue to ignore environmental concerns?

2 **Read the article and compare your ideas. Which paragraph A–E provides the best answer to each of the questions in exercise 1?**

3 **Read the article again and choose the correct answers.**
   1 According to the text,
      a Italy produces no leather of its own.
      b most of the leather used in Italy is Brazilian.
      c Italy's leather industry depends on foreign imports.
      d Italy possesses much of the world's leather.
   2 In Mato Grosso in Brazil,
      a almost all of the land is suitable for breeding cows.
      b only part of the land is flat plains.
      c cattle ranches are largely in the north.
      d only a small fraction of the land is rainforest.
   3 The cattle in Mato Grosso
      a bring in a great amount of money for the country.
      b amount to almost two million.
      c are greater in number than elsewhere in Brazil.
      d are different from those in the rest of the nation.
   4 The text says that in the future
      a the number of cows in Brazil will increase to about two hundred million.
      b there will be twice as many cattle ranches.
      c it will be easier for cattle ranchers to take more land from the rainforest.
      d a Forest Code will be introduced to protect the rainforest.
   5 According to government figures,
      a almost half the deforestation in Brazil since 2005 has taken place in Mato Grosso.
      b a significant amount of deforestation is taking place in the west of Brazil.
      c the rate of deforestation in Mato Grosso has grown since 2003.
      d there has been a 48% rise in the amount of deforestation in Brazil.
   6 One advantage of having rainforest which the text does not mention is
      a the protection it provides against natural disasters.
      b the opportunities it may offer to find new treatments for illness.
      c the way it stops harmful chemicals from entering the atmosphere.
      d the environment it provides for animals to breed and diversify.

Designer shoes and the Amazon rainforest

A Last year, over 11 billion pairs of leather shoes were produced in Italy and sold around the world. It's a remarkably large number and one which, on the face of it, suggests that Italy must be covered in enormous herds of cows. How else could the country possess so much leather? Well, the answer, of course, is that much of the leather that goes into producing all those shoes is imported from overseas. Unsurprisingly, one of Italy's most significant sources of tanned leather is Brazil, a country with vast cattle ranches and countless herds of cows.

B The bulk of Brazil's cows can be found in the state of Mato Grosso, where, on a clear day, you can look out on an awe-inspiring panorama of grazing cattle. Located in the west of Brazil, the southern half of Mato Grosso is composed largely of flat plains which are perfect for breeding cows. However, the northern half of the state is completely made up of Amazon rainforest, and its rich biodiversity is threatened with destruction by the encroaching demands of the cattle ranchers. The animals are a major resource generating a huge income. Indeed, in the country as a whole, there are close to two hundred million cattle and in order to increase revenue, there are plans to double that number. Recent legislation in Brazil's parliament has changed the Forest Code, a law that protected the rainforest. It seems likely that, in the future, there will be fewer legal barriers to preventing cattle owners from cutting down the rainforest to make space for their ranches.

C In 2005, the Brazilian government admitted that 48% of the deforestation that had taken place in the country in 2003 and 2004 had been perpetrated in the state of Mato Grosso. Vast expanses of land are being cleared every day across many other Brazilian states as well in order to make room for more cattle ranches. This is a major concern. Trees in the rainforest absorb carbon dioxide, which, in turn, prevents this gas from entering the atmosphere and causing the greenhouse effect. The trees also absorb heavy rainfall, preventing floods and mudslides which might otherwise pour down the valleys and destroy coastal towns. And not all the animals and plants of the rainforest have been discovered yet – many scientists believe that there may be plants there that contain medicines that we don't know about. In short, losing large amounts of rainforest is an ecological disaster for all of us.

D So, is there a solution? Let's face it, Brazilian cattle ranchers are hard-headed businessmen who run big businesses. They are hardly going to listen to liberal-minded ecologists from Europe and North America if protecting the rainforest will affect their profit margins, or, worse still, force them into bankruptcy. Ecologists can talk until they're blue in the face, but unless a case can be made that sustainability is a more profitable option than exploitation then no agreement will be reached, and more and more square kilometres of rainforest will be lost to cattle ranching. Can anything be done to protect the rainforest? There is, perhaps, one last hope.

E Increasingly, Italian leather goods manufacturers and also big retailers selling beef are under pressure from environmental campaigners to use leather and beef whose source can be traced. As a result, some companies are refusing to buy from Brazilian producers who are cutting down rainforest and they are labelling their products in such a way that consumers can see at a glance that what they are buying has not had a detrimental effect on the environment. Already, retailers are keen to stock and be associated with these more ethical products, and consumers are being asked to pay just a little bit more for their beef and luxury leather. It is a small step, but a step in the right direction and one that may help make the case that there is more money in sustaining Brazil's biodiversity than in destroying it.

7 The text says that ordinary consumers should buy ethically-produced products, which
   a may be more costly.
   b may be difficult to find.
   c may result in most Brazilian ranches closing.
   d may mean avoiding the most expensive brands.

4 Find the verbs in the article that collocate with nouns 1–6. Then match the phrases to the correct definition, a or b.
   1 .... carbon dioxide
      a keep carbon dioxide and stop it spreading
      b force carbon dioxide to spread wider
   2 .... the greenhouse effect
      a create the greenhouse effect
      b prevent the greenhouse effect
   3 .... a business
      a purchase a business
      b manage a business
   4 .... an agreement
      a fail to agree
      b finally agree
   5 .... the source
      a find where something came from
      b hide where something came from
   6 .... a case
      a present an argument
      b lose an argument

5 Complete the sentences with the correct form of the collocations in exercise 4.
   1 Representatives of cattle ranchers in Brazil have failed to .... for continuing to exploit the rainforest. Since they've lost the argument, deforestation must stop.
   2 At first, the managers of the companies argued, but eventually they .... and signed the contract.
   3 People who .... often have to manage staff and do the accounts.
   4 The explorers followed the river into the jungle. They wanted to .... to find out where the river began.
   5 Scientists agree that human activity is .... to get worse.
   6 Trees .... This is a good thing as it is a harmful gas that is bad for the environment.

6 CHALLENGE! How important is product labelling? Consider the questions below.
   1 What information can you find on a product label?
   2 When you are shopping, do you consider the source of the products and how they were grown or made? Why / why not?
   3 Do you know any shops with a good or bad reputation for selling ethical products?

Food and ethics 65

Writing A for and against essay

The passive with reporting verbs

1 Rewrite the sentences to make them more impersonal. Use the passive and the verbs in brackets.

1 The number of local markets across Europe is declining.
   It .... (believe)
2 Local markets have started selling a wider range of products.
   Local markets .... (know)
3 Local markets are losing a lot of their trade to supermarkets.
   Local markets .... (think)
4 According to a 2012 report, the number of stalls in Portobello Market in London went down by 20% between 2004 and 2009.
   In 2012, it .... (report)
5 These days, shoppers don't want to go to outdoor markets on cold, wintry days.
   It .... (say)

2 Choose the <u>two</u> linking words or phrases that can be used in each of the sentences below.

1 .... the fact that the produce hasn't been transported very far, it is more environmentally friendly.
   a Owing to   b Leading to   c Due to
2 .... the quality of produce they offer, and the support to local farmers they provide, they deserve our support.
   a Because of   b As   c Due to
3 There are strong arguments on both sides. ...., it is important to examine the case thoroughly.
   a Consequently   b As a result   c Since
4 Everything has been picked recently, ... it is almost certainly going to be fresh and in season.
   a which leads   b and hence   c which means
5 .... the produce isn't local, it doesn't help local farmers financially.
   a On account   b Since   c As
6 Supermarkets can also buy in bulk .... their size.
   a because of   b resulting in   c on account of

3 Read the for and against essay. Complete gaps A–F with missing sentences 1–6 in exercise 2.

4 Look at the three for and against essay titles below. Think of three pros and three cons for each essay title.

A It is better to use tap water than bottled water. Discuss.
B It is better to choose fair-trade coffee than ordinary supermarket coffee. Discuss.
C It is better to buy fast food from local restaurants than from international chains. Discuss.

<u>It is better to buy our food from local markets than from supermarkets. Discuss.</u>

It has been argued that we should all do our food shopping in local markets, since this would benefit the environment, the local economy, and also our health, as local food is fresh and free from additives. On the other hand, supermarkets offer variety, value and reliability, and have the power to put pressure on suppliers to ensure that products are produced hygienically and in an environmentally-friendly way. **A** ....

An advantage of buying, for example, fruit at a market is that you know that it has come straight from local farms. **B** .... This is an important consideration as fresh food contains more vitamins. Furthermore, consumers who buy locally-produced food are supporting the local economy. In contrast, the fruit you buy in a supermarket is likely to have come from half way round the world. **C** .... On the other hand, supermarket food is of a reliable quality, and the larger supermarkets sell almost any type of fruit or vegetable you can think of. **D** .... Consequently, they can offer large quantities of food at a lower price than many markets.

That said, there is a further advantage to shopping at a local market. **E** .... On the other hand, a lot of supermarkets are very good at putting pressure on suppliers to provide food from sources where workers have been well-treated or where the environment has been protected. In recent years, supermarkets have been promoting organic and fair-trade produce, so it is unfair to suggest that they do not care about the environment or the welfare of workers in the food industry.

In conclusion, the advantages of shopping in local markets are considerable. **F** .... However, it also needs to be said that supermarkets offer advantages, too, in terms of value, range and reliability. I see no reason why we should not continue to do our weekly shop at the supermarket, but we should support markets, too, by buying fresh food, such as fruit, vegetables and meat, from their stalls whenever we can.

WRITING GUIDE

- **Task** Choose one of the essay titles in exercise 4 and write a for and against essay.

- **Ideas** Look at your list of pros and cons in exercise 4. Add more pros and cons to the list that you have made. Decide which ideas you are going to use and make notes for each paragraph.

- **Plan** Follow the plan:

  Paragraph 1: Introduction: state the subject of the essay, summarize the main areas you want to cover and state your purpose.
  Paragraph 2: Present your first argument for or against and any counterarguments.
  Paragraph 3: Present your second argument for or against and any counterarguments.
  Paragraph 4: Conclusion: sum up the main arguments and restate your opinion.

- **Write** Write your for and against essay. Use the paragraph plan to help you.

- **Check** Check the following points.
  - Have you presented a balanced argument?
  - Have you used impersonal language?
  - Have you checked grammar, vocabulary, spelling and punctuation?

Progress check Unit 8

Read 1–12 and evaluate your learning in Unit 8. Give yourself a mark from 1 to 3. How could you improve?

1 I can't do this.   **2** I have some problems with this.   **3** I can do this well.

A A right to eat	Mark (1–3)	How can I improve?
1 Give two reasons why people kill sharks for their fins.		
I can understand a text about hunting sharks for their fins.		
2 Write adjectives that are more intense synonyms of the adjectives below. a numerous b painful c cruel		
I can use intense synonyms.		

3 Write the prepositions needed to complete these sentences.
   a It depends .... what we do.   b It resulted .... a disaster.
   c It's threatened .... extinction.		

I can understand and use prepositions.		

B Wet wealth	Mark (1–3)	How can I improve?

4 Which of these sentences is in the past continuous passive form?
   a What was being taught at the school?
   b Who were they chatting to outside?		

I can understand and use passive forms.		

C Feeding the world	Mark (1–3)	How can I improve?

5 Complete the following phrases.
   a They talked until they were blue ....
   b He was caught cheating – now he has to face the		

I can use phrases with *face*.		
6 Name one advantage and one disadvantage of meat grown in a lab.		
I can understand a talk about feeding the world.		
7 Name one thing you should pay attention to when taking notes.		
I can apply the strategy for taking notes.		
8 Give one way of speculating, one way of conceding a point and one way of clarifying an opinion.		
I can speculate, concede a point and clarify an opinion.		

D The origins of food	Mark (1–3)	How can I improve?
9 Where did fish and chips originally come from?		
I can understand a text about the origins of fish and chips.		
10 When talking about food, which words collocate with the adjectives below? a standard b six-course c side		
I can use adjective and noun collocations to talk about food.		
11 Rewrite the sentence in two different ways using the passive. She offered me a cup of tea.		
I can use the passive with verbs with two objects.		

E A for and against essay	Mark (1–3)	How can I improve?
12 Give two words or phrases to express a cause and two words or phrases to express an effect.		
I can express cause and effect.		

9 Technology

Vocabulary What's new?

V insight Word analysis

1 Choose the correct meaning of the word in bold in each sentence.

1 If your business is **sinking**, you need to cut every possible expense.
   a literally going underwater
   b failing
2 I think you'll need **dedicated** software for that job.
   a specifically for one purpose
   b hardworking and caring
3 His behaviour has all the **hallmarks** of someone losing control.
   a typical characteristics
   b signs of excellence
4 Sam's jokes are **groan-inducing**.
   a physically painful
   b not amusing or entertaining
5 I think your business could **have legs**.
   a potentially be very successful
   b fail easily
6 The doctor **murmured reassurances** after he told her the name of her illness.
   a said how sorry he was
   b quietly told her not to worry
7 Jenny will need to **get you up to speed with** the project.
   a tell you how quickly the project is going
   b help you catch up with the project

V Technology nouns

2 Complete the text with the words below. There are two words that you do not need.

■ emerging technologies ■ an early adopter
■ tech start-up ■ handset ■ cord ■ keypad ■ headset
■ earbuds

The new Iona smartphone is expensive, but if you consider yourself ¹............., you'll be glad you invested in it. The ²............. is incredibly light, especially considering there's a pull out ³............. for those of you that don't like tapping on a screen. Battery life is good, but perhaps the best things are the ⁴............. for listening to music or other downloads. They work using Bluetooth technology, so you won't get in a tangle with the ⁵............. . But, if you do want a proper ⁶............. with earphones and microphone, this can be purchased separately.

V Describing gadgets

3 Write synonyms of the words below.

1 exorbitant   ....
2 resilient   ....
3 cutting-edge   ....
4 cumbersome   ....
5 convenient   ....
6 elegant   ....

4 Complete the text with the correct form of the words and phrases below. There are two words that you do not need.

■ launch with fanfare ■ fragile ■ bring up to speed
■ tech start-up ■ cutting-edge ■ pricey ■ reasonable
■ emerging technologies ■ headset ■ lightweight
■ cord ■ early adopter

Ever since Google Glass was ¹............., I've wanted to try it. I'm interested in all sorts of ²............., but this seems really amazing. It's basically a computer that you wear like a pair of glasses, though apparently it weighs less than the average pair of sunglasses, so it's incredibly ³............. . It looks quite ⁴............., but I'm told that the ⁵............. is actually pretty tough. To operate it, you just give simple voice commands. It can do all sorts of things, such as take a photo instantly, show you a map of where you're going, translate for you and so on. But what about the cost? Won't it be very ⁶.............? Apparently not. They say it will only cost as much as the average smartphone, which is very ⁷............. considering how ⁸............. the technology is. As a keen ⁹............. I will certainly be getting one as soon as it comes out. I just wish my own ¹⁰............. company had had the idea first!

5 CHALLENGE! Speak or write about a piece of technology that you either have now and love, or that you would like to have. Use the questions below to help you.

■ What do you / would you use the technology for?
■ What do you / would you particularly like about it?
■ What are the product's disadvantages?

Grammar Young minds

Reported speech

1 Rewrite the well-known quotes about science in reported speech. Change the tenses and pronouns as appropriate.

1. 'Science is a wonderful thing if one does not have to earn one's living at it.'
   Albert Einstein said that ....

2. 'An expert is a person who has made all the mistakes that can be made in a very narrow field ....'
   Nils Bohr said that ....

3. 'I learned very early the difference between knowing the name of something and knowing something.'
   Richard P. Feynman said that ....

4. 'You cannot teach a man anything; you can only help him discover it in himself.'
   Galileo said that ....

5. 'I think that a particle must have a separate reality independent of the measurements. I like to think that the moon is there even if I am not looking at it.'
   Albert Einstein said that ....

2 Read the text. Then complete the reported version with the correct modal verbs.

Will we ever discover aliens?

'Well, there almost certainly must be alien life on other planets, but no one knows if we will ever discover it. You know, some scientists from the SETI Institute in California have to stay up every night, just looking for radio or light beams that could only come from an intelligent civilization. They think they may discover alien life within the next twenty years, based on how quickly astronomers are discovering new planets these days. The scientists assume that if there are intelligent life forms, they will try to make contact with us. But you shouldn't worry: they'll probably be very peaceful.'

The girl's father explained that there almost certainly ¹............ be alien life on other planets, but no one knew if we ² .... ever discover it. He told her that some scientists from the SETI Institute in California ³............ stay up every night looking for radio or light beams that ⁴............ only come from an intelligent civilization. He said these scientists thought they ⁵............ discover alien life within the next twenty years, based on how quickly astronomers were discovering new planets. He added that the scientists assumed that if there were intelligent life forms, they ⁶............ try to make contact with us. Finally, he said that the girl ⁷............ worry: the aliens ⁸............ probably be very peaceful.

3 Choose the correct answers.

According to a recent survey, less than half of scientists in New Zealand would recommend science as a career to young people. Scientists were asked ¹......... about pay levels, and ² .... recommend science as a career. Almost three quarters of the scientists surveyed ³......... the pay was not sufficient and nearly half said that they ⁴......... recommend it as a career.

The number of women employed in science has risen to around one in three since 1996 from less than a quarter in 1996 and many scientists ⁵......... that they ⁶......... there were plenty of opportunities for women. In fact, four-fifths of scientists under thirty-five are female, so more and more women are joining the profession.

When interviewed, the Minister for Health and Science said that although this ⁷......... cause for celebration, she thought perhaps the increased number of female scientists ⁸......... to the rate of pay having dropped over time.

1. a how did they feel
   b how they had felt
   c how they felt
2. a if they would
   b they would
   c would they
3. a told that
   b told
   c said that
4. a cannot
   b could not have
   c could not
5. a said
   b told
   c told to
6. a believed
   b believe
   c had believed
7. a should have been
   b shall be
   c should be
8. a leads
   b had led
   c has led

4 **CHALLENGE!** Imagine that you are going to interview someone about the technologies they use and the ones they think they will use in the future. Make a list of six questions you could ask them. Then interview another student, your teacher or parent. Write a short report of your interview, saying what you asked and what the answers were.

I recently interviewed ...

Technology

Listening, speaking and vocabulary Digital footprints

V Phrases with *under*

1 Rewrite the underlined part of each sentence with an idiom below. There is one idiom that you do not need.

- under attack ■ under the radar ■ under pressure
- under the weather ■ under age ■ under your belt
- under control ■ under scrutiny

1 Are you feeling <u>a bit unwell</u>? You don't look good.

2 It's important to have some computer skills <u>mastered</u> before you start working.

3 I'm <u>really stressed</u> – there's just too much to do and too little time!

4 Britain's internet networks are <u>being targeted</u> by hackers.

5 It's very hard to keep a room of excited children <u>doing what you tell them to do</u>.

6 He couldn't go into the nightclub because he was <u>too young</u>.

7 If you're applying for a new job, keep it <u>secret</u> so the boss doesn't notice.

V Problems with technology

2 Choose the correct answers.

1 It's very important to set up a **firewall / backup** to protect your computer from attack.
2 The latest version of the software seems to have a few **cookies / bugs**. It isn't working properly.
3 You need a new memory stick; this one can't fit much more **data / spam** on it.
4 I thought it was a useful piece of software, but it turned out to be a **Trojan / firewall**.
5 Nowadays, a lot of websites ask you to agree to accept their **cookies / viruses**.
6 Don't ignore the messages about new **bugs / updates** to your anti-virus system; they're important to stay protected.
7 **Spyware / Spam** can track your keyboard strokes to discover your secret passwords.

Giving a presentation

3 3.09 You are going to listen to a short student presentation answering the question 'Which invention has had the greatest impact on society?' Listen and put the topics in the order they are mentioned.

a Campaigning ....
b Social life ....
c How and what we learn ....
d The role of experts ....
e Buying things ....

4 3.09 Listen again and compare statements 1–7 with what the speaker says. Which statements are different (D) from what the speaker says?

1 The internet has completely changed the way we interact with friends and family. ....
2 Internet shopping is having a positive effect on the high streets. ....
3 People who provide expertise may suffer because of the internet. ....
4 The value of traditional teachers in the classroom is undeniable. ....
5 Not having to memorize information will have a massive impact on education. ....
6 The internet is only really affecting richer countries. ....
7 The internet allows people across the world to campaign together. ....

5 3.09 Match phrases 1–12 to categories A–D. Then listen again and tick the phrases you hear.

A Stating the purpose of a presentation: .... , ... , ...
B Describing the structure of a presentation: ..1.. , ...
C Moving between points: .... , ... , ... , ...
D Concluding a presentation: .... , ... , ...

1 First, I'm going to … ; then I'll … , followed by … .
2 I hope my arguments have convinced you that … .
3 I'm here today to tell you about … .
4 I've got one final point to make, and it regards … .
5 I've just told you about … . Now I'm going to move on to … .
6 In today's presentation, I'm going to talk about … .
7 OK, that's all about … . I'd now like to look at … .
8 Please feel free to ask any questions and I'll do my best to answer them.
9 That's what I'm going to talk about now.
10 The aim of my presentation is to … .
11 There'll be some time for questions and answers once I've finished, so please hold any queries that you have until the end.
12 To sum up, … .

6 Think about other great inventions, such as electricity, the wheel, the printing press, plastic and so on. Choose one and write (and give) your own presentation answering the question 'Which invention has had the greatest impact on society?'

Vocabulary and grammar First?

V | insight Adverbs with two forms

1 Choose the correct answers.

In 1876, Alexander Graham Bell, a Scottish inventor, designed and patented his device to transmit speech electrically. However, he was very **¹close / closely** followed by the American, Elisha Gray, who submitted his patent for a telephone just *hours* later. So who actually invented the telephone first? It **²hard / hardly** seems fair to make a decision based on who reached the Patents' Office first. In fact, Alexander Graham Bell only **³just / justly** won the title of inventor after a fierce legal battle.

But Gray is not the only other inventor with a claim. What about Antonio Meucci? He has **⁴late / lately** received more recognition for his claim that he first came up with the idea in 1871. An Italian-American Congressman, Vito Fossella, introduced a Congressional Resolution to recognize that Meucci came very **⁵close / closely** to beating Bell and that he should be just as **⁶high / highly** regarded.

The truth of the matter is that with many inventions, several inventors are working **⁷hard / hardly** on similar ideas at the same time and it can simply be a matter of luck who makes – or just records – the final breakthrough first.

2 Complete the sentences with the adverbs below. There are two adverbs that you do not need.

■ hard ■ hardly ■ just ■ justly ■ high ■ highly ■ close
■ closely ■ late ■ lately

1 Have you seen Sarah ....? I haven't seen her for ages.
2 The speaker was so quiet, I could .... hear him.
3 He stood too .... to me, making me feel a bit uncomfortable.
4 That's an excellent report; your teacher obviously thinks very .... of you.
5 I had to run, but I .... managed to catch the bus!
6 Meucci is .... considered a great inventor, whether he was the first to invent the telephone or not.
7 Prices have got too .... for many people to afford their own home.
8 I'm afraid you're too .... to go in now – the performance has already started.

Verb patterns in reported speech

3 Choose the correct answers.

1 She apologized .... upsetting him.
　a for　　　　b of　　　　c about
2 The man accused the girl .... stealing his wallet.
　a to　　　　b of　　　　c on
3 The teacher congratulated me .... my excellent results.
　a about　　　b for　　　c on
4 I warned you .... getting involved with him, didn't I?
　a on　　　　b about　　c before
5 The man confessed .... committing fraud.
　a about　　　b to　　　　c for
6 She criticized him .... not being ambitious enough.
　a for　　　　b against　　c of
7 I didn't like it when he boasted .... winning the tennis tournament.
　a to　　　　b about　　c for
8 She insisted .... paying for dinner.
　a about　　　b of　　　　c on

4 Complete the second sentence so that it has a similar meaning to the first. Use the correct form of the word in brackets.

1 'I didn't take the money!' (deny)
　He ....
2 'You should definitely enter the competition, John.' (encourage)
　She ....
3 'Don't forget to take your key, Julie.' (remind)
　He ....
4 'You are not allowed to go out after midnight!' (forbid)
　Sarah's father ....
5 'Please, please don't forget me, Olivia!' (beg)
　He ....
6 'I'll help you, Simon, I promise.' (promise)
　She ....
7 'It'll be very icy on the roads.' (warn)
　He ....
8 'We're getting married!' (announce)
　She ....
9 'OK, we forgot to take the dog for a walk.' (admit)
　They ....
10 'I can run faster than anyone else in school.' (boast)
　He ....

5 CHALLENGE! Think of an inventor you know something about. Answer the following questions about him or her.

1 What did they invent?
2 Why was this invention important?
3 Were they justly rewarded for their work? How? (Or why not?)
4 Are they still highly regarded or well-known today? Why / why not?

Technology 71

Reading Living without technology

1 Read the article and match opinions 1–7 to the person that expresses them.

1 Being on the internet means you can miss out on real life.
2 It's possible to find a middle way in terms of our relationship with technology.
3 Young people need access to computers.
4 Products and services are often cheaper on the internet.
5 People waste huge amounts of time on using technology.
6 Not using mobiles makes life a bit harder, but there are definite benefits.
7 People are more addicted to technology than they would like to admit.

a Sarah Walker ....
b Donovan Corliss ....
c Tiffany Shlain ....
d SandyR67 ....
e HHHannah ....
f Mashup ....
g Sencam7 ....

2 Decide if the following statements are probably true (T) or probably false (F), by making inferences from the article. Underline the part of the article which helps you to decide.

1 Sarah Walker assumes the reader is still in education. ....
2 The Wegman-Corliss family have no electricity in their home. ....
3 Tiffany Shlain doesn't enjoy meeting up with people at the weekend. ....
4 SandyR67 doesn't have any children. ....
5 HHHannah is for the use of technology. ....
6 Mashup thinks the Wegman-Corliss family has got the right idea. ....
7 Sencam7 has a busy life. ....

3 Match sentences a–g to gaps 1–6 in the article. There is one sentence that you do not need.

a He goes on to explain how much more time they have now.
b The experience refreshes your brain and your body and you remember what it feels like to feel happy!
c It's important to catch up with what's happening in your social group, after all.
d It's a bit extreme to cut yourself off from technology altogether.
e Which is not so bizarre – after all, it's the way people used to do things!
f This involves making a concerted effort to remove all technological devices from their lives.
g I really think technology is destroying our memory, our attention and our relationships.

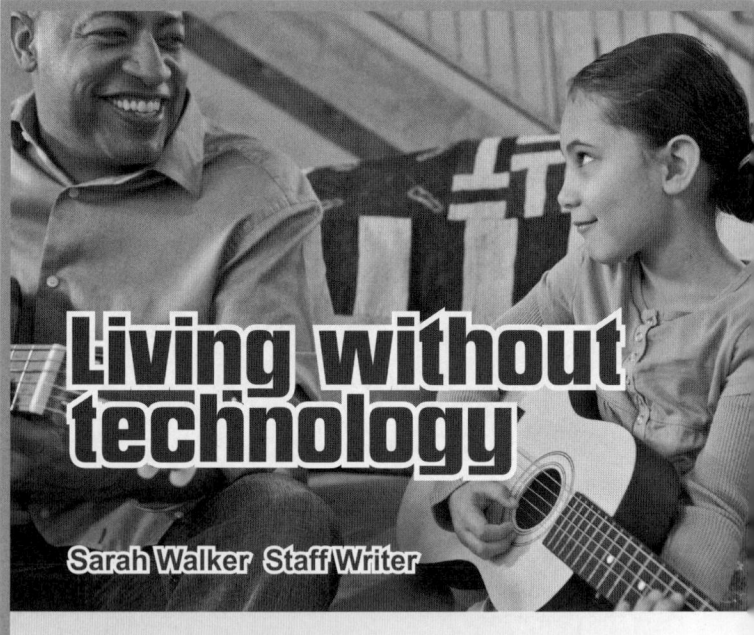

Living without technology

Sarah Walker Staff Writer

Are you addicted to technology? You probably think you aren't, but just take a minute to look more closely at your daily life. Your mobile phone alarm wakes you up, and the first thing you do is check if you have any new email messages, maybe even check the weather forecast so you can decide what to put on.

On the way to college, you pop in your MP3 player earbuds and listen to some music you downloaded the previous night. You might also take a look at your Facebook page on your smartphone. [1].......... Your friend Mike has posted some groan-inducing jokes on his page.

Once at college, your teacher is using an interactive whiteboard. Some students are using tablets to take notes. When the class has finished, you look at your mobile to see that your friend Lucy has texted to tell you where everyone's meeting for lunch … . Are you still so sure you could relinquish technology?

Increasing numbers of people, however, are taking the decision to go technology free. [2].......... Take Laura Jo Wegman and Donovan Corliss. Not only have they got rid of the obvious technology, such as computers and TVs, they have also modified their cooker to remove the LED display and have a rotary dial telephone. 'I think TV and internet and phones become such a time suck that people feel they don't have time for anything else,' explains Corliss. [3].......... The family now play musical instruments, make bread and even talk to each other! They say it's revolutionized their lives.

And this family isn't alone. The 'unplugging' movement is growing fast. Not everyone takes it as seriously as Wegman and Corliss, but more and more people are adopting new approaches to technology. For example, Tiffany Shlain pioneered the idea of having a technology-free day once a week, usually on a Saturday. Shlain says that 'It's definitely harder to make plans,' as, instead of sending lots of texts, she needs to make an arrangement and stick to it. [4].......... And as Shlain points out, the quality of interaction with people who aren't constantly checking their mobiles is much better.

Another popular activity is to take a digital detox retreat, a long weekend hiking out in the countryside with no gadgets. It allows you to develop the skill of finding your way without Google Maps, and seeing the beauty of nature without having to take a digital photograph of it. ⁵......... So why not try reverting back to a tech-free world, even if just for a while? And, if you can't even imagine kicking the habit, ask yourself if you really aren't addicted.

Comments

SandyR67

There's nothing wrong with technology in itself, the problem comes when we overuse it. We just need to find a balance. We have technology in the house and the kids still manage to read books and play musical instruments. And it's ridiculous to say that having an old-fashioned telephone is going to transform the quality of your life!

HHHannah

I'm sorry, but this movement is not only silly and unnecessary, it's also positively dangerous. Whether we like it or not, the world is run by technology and to bring up your kids without access to technology is likely to turn them into unemployable adults. We have to adapt our behaviour to fit in with the world as it is, not try to turn back the clock.

Mashup

I can't understand why more comments aren't supporting this family. I can't bear watching people connecting to the internet on their smartphones and completely failing to connect with each other or with the world around them. ⁶.........

Sencam7

I think we could all live without TV pretty easily, but living without the internet is a different matter. The fact is, we need to be connected these days to pay bills, book tickets, shop and talk to each other, etc. Anyone who can't do these things will end up paying more and wasting an awful lot of precious time!

4 Choose <u>two</u> of the highlighted phrases in the article to match with each meaning.

1 To make something completely different:
....
....

2 To change back to what was happening before:
....
....

3 To change something slightly, especially in order to improve it or make it more suitable for a new use or situation:
....
....

4 To change by stopping doing something you previously did often:
....
....

5 Choose the correct answers.

1 The newly decorated room was completely .... It looked terrific.
  a transformed   b modified
2 I really need to .... checking my mobile every few minutes.
  a modify   b kick the habit of
3 I'm fed up with technology. I want to .... to a simpler life.
  a relinquish   b revert back
4 We .... the bathroom to make it suitable for wheelchair use.
  a transformed   b adapted
5 I decided against .... my computer; I really do need it.
  a relinquishing   b turning the clock back on
6 Instead of replacing the windows, we .... them slightly to make them easier to open.
  a modified   b transformed
7 My father would love to .... He thinks modern life is rubbish.
  a kick the habit   b turn back the clock
8 Jogging has .... my life. I have so much more energy.
  a adapted   b revolutionized

6 **CHALLENGE!** Speak or write about five ways in which your life would change if you gave up technology.

Writing A report

1 Read the report. What advantages of sending texts are mentioned?

The purpose of this report is to ¹**examine / suggest** how young people in Poland use text messaging to keep in touch with friends and family, and ²**testify / assess** the benefits and drawbacks of doing so. The report uses data from interviews, surveys and focus groups, and concludes by making some recommendations about whether texting should be permitted in schools.

According to a recent online report by the British organization Ofcom, the average UK consumer now sends over fifty texts a week. Ofcom ³**suggests / examines** that, particularly among sixteen-to-twenty-four-year-olds, texting is more popular than speaking on the phone or face-to-face. Amongst those surveyed for our report, 95% said that they used texting as a means of communication, testifying to the fact that Ofcom's findings are likely to be true of more countries than just Britain.

When discussing the issue, a group of students pointed out that texting is usually considerably cheaper than paying for phone calls. Our survey also found that 75% of respondents said that when someone does not want to speak or be overheard, such as in the library, or on public transport, it is easier to send a text message than make a phone call.

Nevertheless, in conclusion, the vast majority of those interviewed or surveyed felt that texting had many benefits, and few, if any drawbacks. I would recommend that unless it can be ⁴**proved / assessed** that texting negatively affects society, it is a useful tool and there is no need to ban texting in schools. However, we should also try to make face-to-face contact whenever possible.

2 The paragraph below is missing from the report. Decide where it should go.

However, according to one of our interviewees, the fact that texting is seen as being easier than calling ⁵**examines / suggests** that people do not enjoy communicating face-to-face. He felt that the figures produced by Ofcom ⁶**demonstrated / assessed** that the use of technology was having a negative effect on society.

V Evidence verbs

3 Choose the correct evidence verbs to complete the report and the paragraph in exercise 2.

4 Look at extracts a–d from the report. What different way of conducting research does each extract refer to? Name one other way of collecting information which is not mentioned in the report.

a However, according to one of our interviewees, the fact that … .
b According to a recent online report by the British organization Ofcom, the average UK consumer … .
c When discussing the issue, a group of students pointed out that texting … .
d Our survey also found that 75% of respondents said that … .

WRITING GUIDE

■ **Task** Research the use of smartphones as opposed to mobile phones without an internet connection and write a report on your findings.

■ **Ideas** Think about your research:
- Think about what information you will need. For example, levels of smartphone use, age groups using smartphones, advantages and disadvantages of smartphones.
- What desk research could you do into the topic?
- What other forms of research could you use?
- Who could you interview or survey about the topic?

■ **Plan** Follow the plan:
- Prepare your research questions.
- Conduct your research.
- Analyse your data.
- Make notes under the following headings:
  1 Introduction
  2 Current usage
  3 Benefits
  4 Drawbacks
  5 Conclusions and recommendations

■ **Write** Write your report. Use the plan to help you.

■ **Check** Check the following points.
- Have you explained the purpose of the report?
- Have you included researched facts and figures?
- Have you used a variety of evidence verbs?
- Have you written a conclusion and a recommendation for the future?
- Have you checked grammar, vocabulary, spelling and punctuation?

Progress check Unit 9

Read 1–13 and evaluate your learning in Unit 9. Give yourself a mark from 1 to 3. How could you improve?
1 I can't do this.   2 I have some problems with this.   3 I can do this well.

A What's new?	Mark (1–3)	How can I improve?
1 Give two examples of technology that the writer's mum was using before most other people.		
I can understand some of the main points of a text about new technologies.		
2 Complete the following sentence. An inference can be made by putting together information from the .... and our own		
I can make inferences while reading texts.		
3 Explain the meaning of the phrase *to have legs*.		
I can understand meaning from context.		
4 Explain the difference between a *headset* and a *handset*.		
I can use a variety of technology-related words.		

B Young minds	Mark (1–3)	How can I improve?
5 Rewrite the sentences in reported speech. a 'I lived in the UK for five years.' He said .... b 'I've never been to Scotland.' He said .... c 'Where do you come from?' She asked .... d 'I can't speak Chinese.' She said		
I can use reported speech.		

C Digital footprints	Mark (1–3)	How can I improve?
6 Give a phrase with *under* which means a not feeling very well. b being looked at very carefully.		
I can use a variety of phrases with *under*.		
7 What is a digital footprint?		
I can understand a radio discussion about digital footprints.		
8 Give a phrase for each of the following stages of a presentation. a Stating the purpose of a presentation b Describing the structure of a presentation c Moving between points d Concluding a presentation		
I can structure a presentation.		

D First?	Mark (1–3)	How can I improve?
9 What evidence is there that the Wright Brothers may not have been the first people to invent a successful plane?		
I can understand an article about inventions.		
10 Choose the correct adverb in each sentence. a The aeroplane flew very **high** / **highly** above the ground. b He spoke very **high** / **highly** of you.		
I can use adverbs with two different forms.		
11 Rewrite the sentence as reported speech in two different ways. 'Don't walk across the road on a red light,' he said.		
I can use different verb patterns in reported speech.		

E A report	Mark (1–3)	How can I improve?
12 Give two evidence verbs used to say something is true.		
I can use different evidence verbs in a report.		
13 Give four ways of conducting research.		
I can collect information for a report in a variety of ways.		

10 Power

Vocabulary Utopia?

insight Word analysis

1 Choose the correct answers.

1 In our society, we live together and share all our food, clothes and living space. It is a .... lifestyle.
 a communal   b together   c self-centred

2 I dislike people who expect to get food and housing without doing any work. They're just ....
 a money-makers   b freeloaders   c penny-pinchers

3 In a successful society, it's important to .... our leadership. We should have leaders of all sexes and ages, and from different backgrounds.
 a maintain   b accept   c diversify

4 In our family, it's always been the women who wear the .... They've always been the decision-makers.
 a boots   b trousers   c skirts

5 You can't take out a loan without having .... You need to have savings.
 a power   b family   c collateral

6 At first, there were lots of social changes, but then they slowed down and lost .... Now, we see little change.
 a power   b momentum   c movement

Society and citizenship

2 Match the sentence halves to make statements about a utopian society.

1 We believe in the **distribution of** ....
2 All members of the community will work in the fields for **the common** ....
3 We will have regular votes on issues and will accept **majority** ....
4 People from all races will be welcome here, as we believe that **ethnic** ....
5 Both men and women shall have **equal** ....
6 Elected officials will be responsible for **law** ....

a **rule** in our community. We will do what most people vote for.
b **opportunities** to do the same work and take up the same leadership positions.
c **wealth** so that all men and women have enough money to live on.
d **enforcement**. They will act as police officers in the community.
e **good**. We must all help each other.
f **diversity** makes for a varied and happy society.

Politics and society

3 Match the words below to the political statements.

■ mainstream ■ communal ■ spiritual ■ egalitarian
■ alternative ■ secular

1 We believe in equality and fairness for all!
 ....
2 Our society should not be based on religious values.
 ....
3 Everybody should live together on large farms and share everything. ....
4 We support the government's policy and what the majority of people believe. ....
5 The teachings of the great religions are what we follow. ....
6 Our new society will have different and better values from societies today – we will think differently.
 ....

4 Complete the text with the words below.

■ engagement ■ extreme ■ opportunities ■ ethnic
■ wealth ■ communal ■ social ■ moderate

Fruitlands

Fruitlands was founded in 1843 by Charles Lane and Bronson Alcott, two idealistic men who wanted to create a self-sufficient utopian farming community in which work and possessions would be shared in a(n) [1]......... way. The two men were no strangers to civic [2]......... and [3]......... responsibility – Alcott was an educational reformer who wrote frequently on the subject. However, neither man had any aptitude for farming. They believed strongly in the distribution of [4]......... and in [5]......... diversity, to the point that they banned wearing cotton because it was produced by exploiting poor rural black people. They were strict vegetarians, and refused to use animals on the farm because they saw this as exploitation. Many of their views were [6]......... rather than [7]......... and mainstream. The two men claimed to believe in gender equality and equal [8]........., but because they spent most of their time making rules, it was left to the women on the farm to do most of the work. After seven months, when winter set in, the community failed and most people left. One of Bronson Alcott's daughters was Louisa May Alcott, who grew up to be one of America's best-known novelists. She wrote a very critical account of her life at Fruitlands.

5 CHALLENGE! Imagine you grew up at Fruitlands like Louisa May Alcott. What was your life like? What was good about your life there? What was bad or difficult about it?

Grammar Dirty sport

Defining and non-defining relative clauses

1 Read the text about the famous cricketer Hansie Cronje. Join each pair of sentences using a defining or non-defining relative clause, and a relative pronoun only if necessary.

¹Hansie Cronje became captain of the South African national team in 1994. He was one of the most talented cricketers of his generation. / ²However, he will be remembered not for his cricketing ability, but for a scandal. It shocked the world of cricket. / ³In April 2000, a recording of a conversation about match fixing was revealed to be in the possession of the Indian police. Hansie Cronje had held the conversation with the head of a betting organization. / ⁴Cronje eventually admitted accepting thousands of dollars to fix the results of matches. He had a lot of power to influence the score in a match because of his position as captain. / ⁵As a result, the King Commission banned Cronje from playing or coaching the game. He had devoted his life to cricket. / ⁶In 2001 Cronje challenged the life ban, but he was unsuccessful. The King Commission had imposed the life ban. / ⁷There was no happy ending for Hansie Cronje. His death was announced following a plane crash in June 2002 when he was only thirty-two.

1 ....
2 ....
3 ....
4 ....
5 ....
6 ....
7 ....

Participle clauses

2 Rewrite the three sports scandal stories below. In each story, replace two relative clauses with participle clauses using present or past participles.

1 An agent who is known in sporting circles for his high-profile clients was arrested last night for stealing money from some of his young players, who include at least two English Under-21 stars.

   ....

2 Two golfers who were playing in an international tournament which was broadcast on TV in Europe and America have been accused of cheating.

   ....

3 When they arrived at the stadium, 800 fans who supported the away team were not permitted entry, despite holding tickets which were purchased for £100.

   ....

3 Complete the text with the correct form of the words in brackets. Add any other words where necessary. Use defining or non-defining relative clauses or particle clauses. Sometimes more than one answer is possible.

The Black Sox Scandal

The greatest scandal ¹................................ (confront / baseball) took place in 1919 when eight star players of the Chicago White Sox, ² .... (include / legendary figure) of Shoeless Joe Jackson, were banned for life. The players, ³ .... (lead) by the first baseman Chick Gandil, ⁴ .... (have) a long-standing association with gangsters, conspired to deliberately play badly during the World Series of 1919 in return for bribes. New York gangster Arnold Rothstein, ⁵ .... (be / one of) the most notorious figures in the American underworld at the time, provided the money to pay the bribes. The White Sox lost the World Series to the Cincinnati Reds.

In 1921, a grand jury, ⁶ .... (set up) to investigate the bribery scandal, acquitted the players, but the Commissioner of Baseball, Kenesaw Mountain Landis, ⁷ .... (reputation) as a tough, uncompromising judge was well-known, banned the players anyway. They never played professional baseball again. Journalists ⁸ .... (cover) the case soon nicknamed it the Black Sox Scandal and that's how it is remembered today.

4 **CHALLENGE!** Decide what you think is an appropriate punishment for the following cheating sportspeople. Remember to use relative and participle clauses in your sentences.

1 A football player who accepts money from gamblers to deliberately play badly in an important match.
2 A basketball player who places a bet on his team to lose even though he intends to play in the match and do his best.
3 A tennis player who pretends to be injured in order to miss a tournament because she wants to be fully fit for a more important tournament later in the month.

Listening, speaking and vocabulary Have your voice heard

V The electoral system

1 Complete the sentences with one word in each gap.
1 Socialists and communists are involved in left-................................ politics.
2 In an election, you choose who to vote for by ticking a name or political party on the list on your .... paper.
3 In the .... election, which takes place every five years, people vote for the next government of their country.
4 During an election, schools and town halls become .... stations where people can go to vote.
5 Nationalism and fascism are considered to be right-................................ political movements.
6 Politicians are elected to represent a town or district in a .... election.
7 A political party's views and key issues are set out in their ....
8 The .... is the number of people who vote at an election.

A debate

2 Read the three opinions on the debate topic below. Decide which opinion you agree with.

'Should students have a vote on issues and decisions which affect them at school?'

A I think that students should have a say on school issues in a school council. School administrators should listen to students' views, but I don't think they should have to do what the council decides.

B I don't think there is any point in letting students have a say on school issues in a school council. School administrators are there to make decisions. Students are there to learn, not to decide how to run the school.

C I think that students should have a say on school issues in a school council, and I also think that school administrators should listen and act on what the council decides.

3 🔊 **3.10** Listen to a debate on the topic in exercise 2. Joe is chairing the debate, and Simon, Amelia, Molly and Tom are expressing their views. Match the speakers to the opinions A–C in exercise 2 that they agree with.
1 Simon: ....
2 Amelia: ....
3 Molly: ....
4 Tom: ....

4 🔊 **3.10** Listen again. Write the first letter of the names of the speakers, Simon (S), Amelia (A), Molly (M) and Tom (T), who express each of the opinions below. Sometimes more than one speaker expresses the opinion.
1 Under-eighteens are not treated as fairly as adults.
....
2 Head teachers don't take any notice of what school councils say. ....
3 Making head teachers act on what students decide is not a practical way of running a school.
....
4 Being involved in the decision-making process helps students to become more responsible adults.
....
5 It's important to respect the fact that head teachers are experts in how to manage schools. ....
6 If students express a strong view on something, head teachers should have no choice but to accept and act on that view. ....

5 🔊 **3.10** Choose the phrase, a or b, that a speaker uses in the debate. Then listen again and check.

A Chairing a debate
1 a Who would like to start us off?
  b I'd like to move on now to … .
2 a Does anyone else have anything they'd like to add?
  b Let's have some other views on this.

B Interrupting
3 a Can I just come in here?
  b Excuse me, can I just say … ?

C Dealing with interruptions
4 a Sorry, but could you just hear me out?
  b If you could just let me finish, please, … .

D Getting your point across
5 a The main issue here is … .
  b The other important question is whether … .

6 Read the debate topic and make some notes. Appoint one person as the chair and have a debate.

'Should the age at which you can vote in national elections be lowered from eighteen to sixteen?'

78 Power

Vocabulary and grammar The power of words

V insight Synonyms: global politics

1 Replace the words in italics with the synonyms below.

- humanity ■ abolish ■ liberty ■ swore ■ adversary ■ nation

1 William Wilberforce campaigned to *eradicate* .... the slave trade. As a result, slavery ended throughout the British Empire in 1833.
2 Kenya became an independent *country* .... in 1963.
3 In 1988, American presidential candidate George Bush *pledged* .... that he wouldn't raise taxes. In 1990, when he was president, he raised taxes.
4 During the American War of Independence in the 1770s and 1780s, African Americans fought for their own *freedom* .... from slavery.
5 During the Cold War in the late twentieth century, the United States' most significant *enemy* .... was the Soviet Union.
6 Over 15% of the world population died during the Mongol conquests of the 13th and 14th centuries. That's the largest percentage of deaths in war in the history of *mankind* ....

V Idioms: politics

2 Complete the idioms in the sentences with two words.

1 When we asked how much it would cost, the politician just plucked a figure .... of the .... He had no idea if it was correct or not.
2 I'd like to .... the record .... I did not make an illegal deal with anyone.
3 I feel that the government has been quick .... the .... in dealing with this crisis. They have reacted rapidly and successfully.
4 The minister was economical .... the .... She did not tell us all the facts.
5 Success in the election boils .... being honest with the electorate.
6 The minister came .... for not revealing all the facts to parliament.

Relative clauses: other structures

3 Complete the sentences with *which* or *whom* and the prepositions below.

- for ■ with ■ without ■ at ■ in ■ about

1 I'd like to thank all the people .... this event wouldn't have been possible.
2 This is the room .... the president made his most important speech.
3 He was a politician .... we now know very little.
4 They weren't the audience .... my words were intended.
5 It was an important conference .... many world leaders were present.
6 Let's deal with the issues .... all of us are concerned.

4 Complete the text with *whom* or *which* and a preposition, or with *everyone, many, those, whatever* or *whenever*.

Tear down this WALL

¹................... historians think of Berlin, famous speeches and American presidents, two great events come to mind. Firstly, there is the speech ²................... John F. Kennedy pledged to support the people of Berlin at a time of great need. Without exception, ³................... who were there will always remember it. It was 1963 and the people of capitalist West Berlin were being blockaded by communist East Germany and the Soviet Union. The food ⁴................... the people of the city depended for survival was being flown in from America and Western Europe. In his speech, Kennedy famously announced 'Ich bin ein Berliner' (*I am a Berliner*), thus showing solidarity with the citizens of Berlin.

Twenty-five years later, in June 1987, President Ronald Reagan was in Berlin to make a speech. Reagan chose to issue a challenge to the reformist leader of the Soviet Union, Mikhail Gorbachev, a man ⁵................... the hopes of many people were resting at the time. ⁶................... who was listening was stunned when he said: 'Tear down this wall!' ⁷................... who were there felt inspired by the speech, although others present felt it was not realistic. Three years later, the Berlin Wall was pulled down. ⁸................... the impact of the speech may have been, history was quick to give Reagan his wish.

5 CHALLENGE! Imagine that you are standing as a representative for the student council at your school. Prepare a speech in which you outline your strengths and your pledges. Include three of the phrases below in your speech.

- Whatever challenges lie ahead, ...
- I am someone on whom you can rely.
- Those who doubt me only need to look at my ... .
- Anyone who places trust in me will find that ... .
- I will speak up for all of you, no matter how difficult the issue.

Reading Making the case for the monarchy

1 **Read the statements. Decide which ones you agree with and explain why.**
  1 Modern-day European monarchs have a positive influence on democracy.
  2 Kings and queens are unacceptable in a nation with values of equality for all.
  3 Royal families make use of the media to promote their image and popularity.
  4 The monarchy is an institution that brings a nation together with a communal sense of identity.

2 **Read the two articles. Which of the statements in exercise 1 does Lionel Toady agree with? Which ones does Ivor Scorn agree with?**

3 **Read the first article again. Are the sentences true (T) or false (F)?**
  1 The writer remarks on how the monarchy has survived despite so many changes in society. ……….
  2 The popularity of Queen Elizabeth II has risen since she became Queen in the 1950s. ……….
  3 The writer says that democracy itself might well collapse if the monarchy were to be abolished. ……….
  4 The British nation lacks the sense of identity that other nations have. ……….
  5 The experience felt by many British people during the Diamond Jubilee exemplified the unifying nature of the institution of monarchy. ……….

4 **Read the second article again and match sentences A–G to gaps 1–5. There are two sentences that you do not need.**
  A In truth, it is a form of manipulation.
  B Nevertheless, she remains a central figure to this day.
  C She cannot be representative if she is unelected.
  D However, this is misleading.
  E It is the qualifications, qualities or capabilities of a person that should be important, not the pedigree of their parents.
  F Its powers cannot be challenged in a British court, for instance.
  G It is about how the nation wishes to define itself as a modern democracy.

Making the case for the ♛ monarchy

Long live the monarchy! by Lionel Toady

Given the enormous number of social changes that have taken place in Europe over the last sixty years, it seems remarkable that an institution such as the monarchy, where power and privilege are inherited, should continue to be popular. Yet, in the UK at least, that is the case. Since Queen Elizabeth II ascended the throne in 1953, opinion polls have fairly consistently shown that over three quarters of the British population support the royal family. They enjoy a high level of popularity and, whatever republicans might think, there are excellent reasons why the Brits love their royals.

Many people argue that Britain's democracy would be weaker without the monarch as the head of state. In a modern Europe, in which freedoms and human rights are protected, the suggestion that Britain could not get rid of the monarchy and become a republic without seriously undermining its democracy is certainly unfounded. However, it is surely the case that if the institution of monarchy were lost, the nation's identity would be undermined. The monarchy is an age-old institution which has shaped the destiny of the nation for over a thousand years and its existence helps to unify the country and its people.

More than any other country in Europe, Britain has come to be defined by its monarchy. On important ceremonial occasions and at times of crisis or national mourning, the monarch is there to support and uphold the traditional and moral values which define Britain. This is the real power of a monarch. When, in 2012, the British had street parties on the occasion of Queen Elizabeth's Diamond Jubilee (celebrating her sixty years on the throne), and when, in 2013, everybody was excited about the birth of Prince George, the Queen's great-grandchild, what people were really celebrating was their shared experience of being British, of feeling a part of the fabric of British national life.

80 Power

5 Match the words below to definitions 1–8. Check your answers in the articles.

■ undermining ■ ascended the throne ■ lobbying
■ wields ■ uphold ■ privilege ■ ornamental ■ relevance

1 trying to influence politicians in order to persuade them to change policy or introduce a law
....
2 an advantage that has not been earned
....
3 making something less successful or effective
....
4 direct connection with or importance to something else ....
5 looking attractive but having no practical use
....
6 has something and uses it (for example: power and influence) ....
7 became king or queen ....
8 support (for example: an idea, a value, a claim)
....

6 Complete the text with the corect form of six of the words in exercise 5.

Norway's monarchy

In Norway, the present monarch is King Harald V, who has been king since he [1]............................ in 1991. Like most monarchs, he lives a life of [2]............................ in a fabulous house and with many amazing events to attend. The Norwegian parliament [3]............................ the real power in the country and the King's role is largely ceremonial. However, he is not merely [4]............................. The king plays a role as head of the church in Norway and supreme commander of the army, and he works hard to [5]............................ traditional values and aspects of Norway's culture. He is extremely popular with the people of Norway and the institution of monarchy still has [6]............................ in Norwegian society.

7 CHALLENGE! If you live in a monarchy, discuss the pros and cons of having a king or queen. If your nation does not have a monarch, discuss the pros and cons of introducing one.

Down with the monarchy! by Ivor Scorn

The monarchy has no place in a modern European democracy such as Britain. Nations are defined by their values, and a democratic country which is supposed to believe in equal opportunities, an egalitarian distribution of wealth, and an elected government, should have no place for a head of state whose position and power are purely a result of their birth. [1].......... Monarchists argue that a king or queen is somehow good for our democracy because he or she is a 'figurehead', with no powers, who allows the government of the day to go about its business, relieving it from the necessity of taking care of the symbolic duties of a head of state. [2].......... The idea that the monarch is powerless and merely ornamental is a myth.

The British monarchy has more influence on British politics than any other pressure group. It defends its own privilege and wealth fiercely, lobbying ministers to act in its interests. The monarchy is, in many ways, above the law. [3].......... The monarch has a private weekly meeting with the Prime Minister, and, therefore, a unique opportunity to express the royal family's views and influence the government. Nobody can argue that the British monarch has no power.

There are other ways in which the monarchy wields power. Its ability to promote itself in a positive light through the media, using celebrations such as the Jubilee or carefully choreographed photo sessions, is actually a means of preventing debate about its function and relevance. By linking itself to flag-waving ceremonies, it makes people feel that the monarchy is the nation, and that republicans are unpatriotic. [4]..........

The debate about whether Britain should have a monarchy is not about whether the Queen or King is popular, or hard-working, or good value, or whether the royal family attracts American tourists. [5].......... Currently, that point is not being addressed.

Writing A for and against essay

V Giving examples and explanations

1 Choose the correct answers.

1. Several North European countries, ... Sweden, the Netherlands and the UK, still have a monarchy.
   a such as   b a case in point   c to illustrate this
2. There are many forums that allow young people to engage in politics. .... is the youth parliament which takes place annually in the UK.
   a In particular   b As an illustration
   c An example of this
3. Dictators .... Hitler and Stalin ruled their countries without listening to the views of the people.
   a for example   b like   c this can be illustrated by
4. Decisions made by the European Parliament in Brussels affect the whole of the EU. .... the common agricultural policy, which has changed farming in Europe.
   a Such as   b A case in point is   c Particularly
5. A lot of politicians work hard. My local MP .... is always available to deal with issues.
   a in particular   b such as
   c this can be illustrated by

2 Read the four paragraphs of a for and against essay. Then put them in the correct order by labelling each paragraph with one of the aims below.

1. to introduce the topic
2. to present arguments in favour of the statement
3. to present arguments against the statement
4. to draw a conclusion

'We should fund political parties with taxpayers' money.' Discuss.

A ....   On the other hand, there is a strong argument to be made against public funding. Firstly, it is very difficult to allocate money on a fair basis. If money is given depending on the size of a party, then that gives an unfair advantage to the most powerful parties. [1] ...., it favours the party or parties in government. If public money is given to all parties equally, then minority parties, or undesirable movements, [2] .... fascist groups, may be given more money and support than they deserve. Moreover, most taxpayers don't want their taxes to go on politics.

B ....   In the last US presidential election, over $6 billion was spent on campaigning. In the UK, the figure in the 2010 general election was £31.1 million (just under $50 million). The problem, however, is where the money comes from. Many people feel that political parties should be publicly funded. This essay assesses whether the taxpayer should provide the majority of income for political parties or whether political parties should find private sources of income.

C ....   In conclusion, there are strong arguments to be made for both sides of the debate about public funding in politics. On balance, however, I feel that there should be some public funding so that all parties can fight for power on an equal and fair basis.

D ....   On the one hand, supporters of public funding argue that it makes politics fairer. No party can dominate an election by outspending its opponents on advertising. Public funding means that parties don't have to rely on money from sponsors who want something in return. [3] ...., a Spanish political party recently accepted millions of dollars from a construction company, in return for which they gave the firm major building contracts after they won the election – a clear abuse of democratic principles.

---

3 Answer the questions.

In which paragraph of the essay can we find:
1. the personal opinion of the writer? ....
2. a thought-provoking fact to get the reader interested in the subject? ....
3. an example of how private funding can influence politics in a negative way? ....
4. an argument about how public funding may help some parties too much? ....

4 Complete gaps 1–3 in the essay with phrases for giving examples and explanations.

WRITING GUIDE

■ **Task** Write a for and against essay on the topic below.

'We should pay MPs (members of parliament) more.' Discuss.

■ **Ideas** Make notes about:
1. arguments in favour of the statement.
2. arguments against the statement.
3. examples to back up both sets of arguments.

■ **Plan** Follow the plan:

Paragraph 1: Write an introduction, including a definition if necessary, a hook and a thesis statement.
Paragraph 2: Present the arguments in favour of the statement.
Paragraph 3: Present the arguments against the statement.
Paragraph 4: Write a balanced conclusion, giving your own opinion.

■ **Write** Write your essay. Use the paragraph plan to help you.

■ **Check** Check the following points.
- Have you written a clear, concise thesis statement?
- Have you used a range of suitable linking words?
- Have you checked spelling, grammar, vocabulary and punctuation?

Progress check Unit 10

Read 1–13 and evaluate your learning in Unit 10. Give yourself a mark from 1 to 3. How can you improve?
1 I can't do this.   2 I have some problems with this.   3 I can do this well.

A Utopia?	Mark (1–3)	How can I improve?
1 What are the differences between the Twin Oaks Community and the community of Meghalaya?		
I can understand a text about different communities.		

2 Complete the sentences.
  a We have .... diversity in our state. There are people of many different races and cultures.
  b There should be .... opportunities at work for men and women.		

I can talk about society and citizenship.		

B Dirty sport	Mark (1–3)	How can I improve?
3 What is the difference between a defining and a non-defining relative clause?		
I can use relative clauses.		
4 When do we use present participles and past participles?		
I can use participle clauses.		

C Have your voice heard	Mark (1–3)	How can I improve?
5 Give two things to listen out for in order to identify attitude.		
I can identify attitude when listening.		

6 What is the difference between the pairs of words or phrases below?
  a general election / local election
  b electorate / turnout		

I can use words and phrases to describe the electoral system.		
7 Give a phrase used when chairing a debate, interrupting, dealing with an interruption and getting your point across.		
I can chair a debate, interrupt, deal with an interruption and get my point across.		

D The power of words	Mark (1–3)	How can I improve?
8 Give one promise or request Kennedy made in his 1961 speech.		
I can understand a speech.		
9 Give an example of alliteration.		
I can understand the use of language devices in speeches.		
10 Give a synonym of *enemy*.		
I can use global politics synonyms.		
11 Complete the sentence with a preposition and a relative pronoun. It is a peace treaty .... the future of this region depends.		
I can use other relative clauses.		

E A for and against essay	Mark (1–3)	How can I improve?
12 Which of the phrases below are used in the same way as *for example*? ■ specifically ■ like ■ for instance ■ in particular		
I can give examples and explanations.		
13 Name one thing to include in the opening paragraph of a for and against essay to motivate the reader.		
I can write introductions.		

Literature insight 1 *Jane Eyre* – Charlotte Brontë

BEFORE YOU READ

1 Read about Charlotte Brontë. In which literary works did the Brontë sisters create imaginary worlds?
2 Read the background to the story on page 85. Why is Jane afraid of being locked in the red room?

About the author
Charlotte Brontë (pen name Currer Bell)
Born: 1816 in Thornton, Yorkshire, England
Died: 1855
Important works: *Jane Eyre* (1847), *Shirley* (1849), *Villette* (1853), *Poems of Currer, Ellis and Acton Bell* (1846)
Did you know? Charlotte and her sisters Emily and Anne spent their short lives living in isolation on the edge of the Yorkshire Moors. They were mostly self-educated and together they created their own imaginary worlds called Angria and Gondal which became the settings for many of their poems. The Brontë sisters came from a new generation of socially aware female novelists who felt that they had to adopt male pen names if they were to be considered serious writers. Their work had a profound impact on the English novel. *Jane Eyre* was controversial in its criticism of Victorian society's treatment of impoverished women, and Charlotte created a character in Jane with the power to make her own decisions. The novel was a great success, but also received criticism on social and moral grounds.

READ ON

Spring arrives and the weather, combined with the lack of care that the students receive, leads to half of the girls in the school becoming ill with typhus. Later, Jane is shocked to learn that Helen Burns is also seriously ill with tuberculosis. One evening Jane falls asleep with her friend in her arms and in the morning, Helen is dead.
Under Miss Temple's guidance, Jane does very well at school. After six years of study she becomes a teacher at Lowood, but when Miss Temple leaves to get married, Jane places an advertisement in a newspaper and accepts the position of governess at Thornfield Hall. Jane is warmly welcomed to her new home by Mrs Fairfax, the housekeeper, but she learns that Mr Rochester, who owns the manor house, is a strange man who often travels abroad. He is also responsible for a little French girl called Adèle.
One winter's day, Jane startles a horse and rider on a country lane. The rider falls and Jane helps him back onto his horse. She does not know until she returns to Thornfield that the man is Mr Rochester. He is keen to talk to the new governess and to discover what Jane's impressions of him are.

---

1 Read the extract on page 85. What benefit does Mr Brocklehurst think that physical punishment can have?

2 Read the extract again. Put the events a–h in the correct order.
  a He tells the students that this seemingly ordinary girl is evil.
  b Jane is afraid that it will no longer be possible to start a new life at Lowood.
  c The girls are not allowed to speak to her that day.
  d Jane fears that Miss Temple's good feelings towards her will change when her true character is revealed. (1)
  e Mrs Reed believes that Jane was having an evil influence on her children.
  f Mr Brocklehurst says that Jane is a liar.
  g Helen Burns looks at Jane and calms her feelings of anger and shame.
  h Jane is placed on a chair close to Mr Brocklehurst's nose.

3 **SPEAKING** Work in pairs. Answer the questions.
  1 Do you think the other girls believe Mr Brocklehurst? Why / why not?
  2 Do you think that Jane is right to feel anger and shame? Why / why not?

4 Read what happens next. Why do many of the girls become ill?

5 🔊 3.11 Listen to the next part of the story. What does Mr Rochester think about Jane's character?

6 🔊 3.11 Listen again. Are these sentences true (T) or false (F)? Correct the false ones.
  1 Mr Rochester asks if Jane considers herself handsome.
  2 Jane's first response is that beauty doesn't matter.
  3 Jane asks Mr Rochester if he is good as well as intelligent.
  4 Mr Rochester commands Jane to speak.
  5 Mr Rochester made good decisions when he was younger.
  6 Mr Rochester feels that he can confide in Jane.

7 **SPEAKING** Work in pairs. Answer the questions.
  1 In this scene Mr Rochester and Jane discuss beauty and goodness. Which do you think is more important? Why?
  2 What do you think happened to Mr Rochester when he was twenty-one years old?
  3 Who do you tell your problems and secrets to? Can you keep a secret? Why / why not?

Writing

8 Imagine you are Jane Eyre. Write a letter to Bessie, a maid who was kind to you at Gateshead. Include this information:
  ▪ why you left Lowood School and what you are doing now
  ▪ a description of Mr Rochester
  ▪ your memories of your life at Gateshead

BACKGROUND TO THE STORY

Jane Eyre is a ten-year-old orphan who is sent to live with her aunt, Mrs Reed, and her cousins at Gateshead Hall. Jane is neither beautiful nor meek, and her aunt, who makes no attempt to conceal her dislike of Jane, allows her son John to bully and torment her. One day, as punishment for fighting with John, Jane is locked in the red room, the room where her uncle died. Jane is terrified and believes that she can see the ghost of Mr Reed. She faints and when Dr Lloyd comes to check if she is well, he suggests that she be sent away to school.

Jane is pleased to leave her cruel aunt and cousins, but life at Lowood is bleak and the girls suffer from cold and hunger. Jane's teacher, Miss Temple, is kind and protective towards her and Helen Burns becomes a good friend. However, the school manager, Mr Brocklehurst, is a cruel and hypocritical man. One day when he is visiting the school, Jane drops her slate on the floor and it breaks. Mr Brocklehurst met Jane once at her aunt's house and he remembers her.

Jane Eyre

'Come here, child.'

I was too frightened to move, but two big girls pushed me towards him. Miss Temple whispered kindly in my ear,

'Don't be afraid Jane. I saw it was an accident.' Her kindness touched me, but I knew that soon she would hear the lies about me, and then she would hate me!

'Put the child on that chair,' said Mr Brocklehurst. Someone lifted me up on a high chair, so that I was close to his nose. Frightened and shaking, I felt everyone's eyes on me.

'You see this girl?' began the black marble column. 'She is young, she looks like an ordinary child. Nothing about her tells you she is evil. But she is all wickedness! Children, don't talk to her, stay away from her. Teachers, watch her, punish her body to save her soul – if indeed she has a soul, because this child … I can hardly say it … this child is a liar!'

'How shocking!' said the two Brocklehurst daughters, each wiping a tear or two from their eyes.

'I learned this fact,' continued the great man, 'from Mrs Reed, the kind lady who took care of her after her parents' death and brought her up as a member of the family. In the end Mrs Reed was so afraid of this child's evil influence on her own children that she had to send her here. Teachers, watch her carefully!'

The Brocklehurst family stood up and moved slowly out of the schoolroom. At the door, my judge turned and said,

'She must stand half an hour longer on that chair, and nobody may speak to her for the rest of the day.'

So there I was, high up on the chair, publicly displayed as an ugly example of evil. Feelings of shame and anger boiled up inside me, but just as I felt I could not bear it any longer, Helen Burns walked past me and lifted her eyes to mine. Her look calmed me. What a smile she had! It was an intelligent, brave smile, lighting up her thin face and her tired grey eyes.

When all the girls left the classroom at five o'clock, I climbed down from the chair and sat on the floor. I no longer felt strong or calm, and I began to cry bitterly. I had wanted so much to make friends at Lowood, to be good, to deserve praise. Now nobody would believe me or perhaps even speak to me. Could I ever start a new life after this?

From *Jane Eyre*, Oxford Bookworms. Text adaptation by Clare West.

Literature insight 2 *The Great Gatsby* – F. Scott Fitzgerald

BEFORE YOU READ

1 Read about F. Scott Fitzgerald. What is his connection with the US national anthem?
2 Read the background to the story on page 87. What is the difference between East Egg and West Egg?

About the author
Francis Scott Fitzgerald
Born: 1896 in Minnesota, USA
Died: 1940
Important works: *This Side of Paradise* (1920), *The Beautiful and Damned* (1922), *Tender is the Night* (1934)
Did you know? His full name was Francis Scott Key Fitzgerald and he was named after a distant relative (Francis Scott Key) who wrote the words to the US national anthem 'The Star Spangled Banner'. Although he was from an upper-middle-class background, Fitzgerald didn't feel wealthy. It was at Princeton University in 1913 that Fitzgerald mixed with rich young men, possibly inspiring the themes in his first novel about loss and emptiness, money and materialism. He later described his experience as being 'a poor boy in a rich town; a poor boy in a rich boy's school; a poor boy in a rich man's club at Princeton'.

This Side of Paradise was a great success and the financial rewards that came with this first novel enabled him to ask the beautiful Zelda Sayre to marry him. The couple moved to a rented house in Westport, next door to an eccentric millionaire who was famous for having lavish Gatsby-style parties. They lived a glamorous lifestyle and Francis had to write film scripts to pay their debts. He became an alcoholic, his wife suffered from mental illness and his novel *The Last Tycoon* was left unfinished. He suffered a heart attack and, like many great authors, died thinking he was a failure.

1 Read the extract on page 87. Where does Gatsby want to take Nick the next morning?

2 Read the extract again. Answer the questions.
   1 Where has Gatsby seen Nick before?
   2 Why does Nick think that the party is unusual?
   3 Why is the situation awkward when Gatsby introduces himself?
   4 What does Gatsby's smile tell Nick?
   5 What makes Nick even more curious?
   6 How does Gatsby appear different to everyone else?

3 SPEAKING Work in pairs. Answer the questions.
   1 Why do you think people are curious about Gatsby?
   2 If you had a large mansion, would you have parties for people you did not know? Why / why not?
   3 Do you think that Gatsby has a dark secret? What could it be?

4 Read what happens next. Why has Gatsby moved to West Egg?

READ ON

There are many rumours about Gatsby's past and he speaks to Nick one day in an attempt to reveal the truth. Gatsby says that he was born into a wealthy family from San Francisco and educated at Oxford, which was a family tradition. He was sent to France as an army officer and received medals for bravery. At first, Nick doesn't believe him, but then Gatsby shows him a medal and a photograph of himself standing in the doorway of an Oxford college with six young men.
Later that afternoon, Nick meets Jordan for tea and she tells him that when Daisy was eighteen, she fell in love with a young officer. His name was Jay Gatsby. Her family did not approve of the match and when Gatsby left to fight in the war, she married Tom Buchanan, a wealthy, but brutal man. Jordan says that it is no coincidence that Gatsby has moved to West Egg. He can see Daisy's house across the bay. Gatsby wants to ask a favour of Nick. He wants him to invite Daisy for tea one afternoon so he can meet her as if by accident.

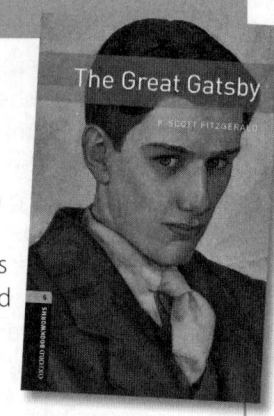

5 **3.12** Listen to the next part of the story. How does Daisy feel about seeing Gatsby again?

6 **3.12** Listen again. Complete the sentences with one word.
   1 Gatsby's demeanour has changed and he shines with ....
   2 He wants to .... Daisy around his house and asks Nick to come, too.
   3 Nick tells Gatsby that his house is very ....
   4 It took Gatsby three years to .... the money to buy the mansion.
   5 Nick is sure that there are .... hiding behind the furniture.
   6 Gatsby stares around the apartment in a confused way at his .... possessions.

7 SPEAKING Work in pairs. Answer the questions.
   1 Why do you think Daisy cried when she met Gatsby again?
   2 Do you think that Gatsby has told Nick the truth about his inherited wealth? Why / why not?
   3 Do you think it's possible to fall in love with an ex-boyfriend / girlfriend again?

Writing

8 What do you think is going to happen between Daisy and Gatsby? Write an ending for the story. Include this information and your own ideas:
   - where and when they see each other again
   - Daisy's husband's reaction
   - the final conclusion

BACKGROUND TO THE STORY

Nick Carraway is a young stockbroker from Minnesota who was educated at Yale. He has come to New York to enter the bond business and he rents a house in West Egg in the summer of 1922. West Egg is a wealthy, but unfashionable area where members of New York society who have recently acquired money live. Those who were born into wealthy and well-connected families live in East Egg.

Nick's cousin Daisy and her husband Tom live in East Egg and one evening when Nick is there for dinner, he meets Jordan Baker, a beautiful, but cynical girl. Over dinner Jordan speaks about Nick's neighbour. He is the mysterious Jay Gatsby who lives in a mansion and throws extravagant parties every Saturday night.

The summer continues and Nick receives an invitation to a party where he finally meets the great Gatsby.

THE GREAT GATSBY

We were sitting at a table with a man of about my age, and during a pause in the music he looked at me and smiled.

'I've seen you somewhere before,' he said politely. 'Weren't you in the army during the war?'

'Why, yes. I was in the First Infantry Division.'

'So was I, until June 1918. I knew I recognized you.'

We talked for a moment about some wet, gray little villages in France. Then he told me he had just bought a new motorboat and was going to try it out the next morning.

'Want to go with me, old sport?' he asked. 'Just off the beach near here. Any time that suits you best.'

'I'd like that,' I replied and added, 'This is an unusual party for me. I haven't even seen the host. I live next door, and this man Gatsby sent his driver over with an invitation.'

For a moment he didn't seem to know what I meant. Then he said suddenly, 'I'm Gatsby.'

'What!' I cried. 'Oh, I'm so sorry!'

'I thought you knew, old sport. I'm afraid I'm not a very good host.' He smiled understandingly. It was one of those smiles that you see only four or five times in your life. It showed you that he understood you, believed in you, and had the best possible opinion of you. Suddenly it disappeared – and I was looking at a fashionably dressed young man, a year or two over thirty, who seemed to choose his words with great care.

The butler appeared, with the information that Chicago was calling Gatsby on the telephone.

'Excuse me,' he said, standing up. 'I have to go. If you want anything, just ask for it, old sport.'

When he was gone, I turned to Jordan impatiently. 'Who *is* he?' I demanded. 'Where is he from? And what does he do?'

'Now you're just like everyone else,' she replied, smiling. 'He told me once he was an Oxford man. But I don't believe it.'

'Why not?'

'I don't know. I just don't think he went there.'

This made me even more curious than before. After a few minutes I caught sight of him. He had come out of the house and was standing there, looking in a pleased way at his guests. I could see nothing darkly mysterious about him at all. I wondered if the fact that he was not drinking made him appear different from the rest of us. It seemed to me that he grew more formal as everyone else behaved more wildly. There was no girl in his arms, or glass in his hand, or song on his lips.

From *The Great Gatsby*, Oxford Bookworms. Text adaptation by Clare West.

Literature insight 3 *The Legacy* – Virginia Woolf

BEFORE YOU READ

1 Read about Virginia Woolf. Why was she not satisfied with her education?
2 Read the background to the story on page 89. What is a 'legacy'?

About the author

Adeline Virginia Woolf
Born: 1882 in Kensington, London
Died: 1941
Important works: *Jacob's Room* (1922), *Mrs Dalloway* (1925), *To the Lighthouse* (1927)
Did you know? Virginia was born into a privileged family and grew up in a literary and intellectual atmosphere, mixing with Thomas Hardy, William Thackeray and Henry James, who were her father's friends. At the age of eleven, she started a newspaper called *The Hyde Park Gate*. Virginia was educated at home, but although she studied Greek and English literature and had access to her father's extensive library, she felt that her education was incomplete without a university degree.
When she was only thirteen, her mother died suddenly, and after her half-sister's death two years later, she suffered her first nervous breakdown. Virginia married Leonard Woolf in 1912. She began to suffer mood swings and spent periods of time in nursing homes.
The outbreak of the Second World War increased her anxiety and she drowned herself in the river Ouse. She once said that her death would be 'the one experience I shall never describe'.

1 Read the extract on page 89. What does Gilbert understand from the look in Sissy Miller's eyes?

2 Read the extract again. Choose the correct answers.
  1 The .... tells Gilbert that he is still a good-looking man.
    a window   b mirror   c diary
  2 Gilbert had often thought when dining with his wife that she was ....
    a beautiful   b proud   c jolly
  3 When they toured Gilbert's constituency, the audience .... and sang.
    a stood up   b sat down   c cheered
  4 Gilbert remembers how she had .... at him during the election.
    a stared   b looked   c glared
  5 Gilbert loved travelling with Angela because she was .... to learn.
    a keen   b reluctant   c nervous

3 **SPEAKING** Work in pairs. Answer the questions.
  1 What is your impression of Gilbert?
  2 Do you think it's dangerous to read someone's diary even once they have died? Why / why not?

4 Read what happens next. Why is Gilbert's vanity offended?

READ ON

Gilbert continues reading the diaries, scanning over many of the entries that do not interest him. He looks for what his wife has written about him, but as the years go by, Angela mentions him less and less. The diaries show how their lives completely revolve around Gilbert's career and social obligations. Angela is childless and feels there is nothing meaningful in her life, so she turns to charity work. Gilbert slowly begins to see how little he knew about his wife and his vanity is offended when he realizes that she felt unfulfilled in their marriage. Soon there are references to someone called B.M. and as he reads on he discovers that B.M. is a man. Gilbert turns the pages and picks out every entry that refers to B.M. He begins to feel a growing dislike for this man, who is a radical Marxist, when he lends Angela books on the coming revolution and says disagreeable things about Gilbert.

5 🔊 3.13 Listen to the next part of the story. What does the use of initials in the diary tell Gilbert?

6 🔊 3.13 Listen again. Answer the questions.
  1 Where was Gilbert when B.M. came to their house?
  2 What can Gilbert remember about that night?
  3 What do you think Angela and B.M.'s relationship was like when Angela started writing her final diary?
  4 What is Gilbert's interpretation of the page that has been scored out?
  5 What does Gilbert do with the last diary? Why do you think he does this?
  6 What do you think Gilbert imagines has happened to Angela?

7 **SPEAKING** Work in pairs. Answer the questions.
  1 Why do you think *Egypt* is written across an entire page? Why do you think that Angela didn't leave Gilbert and run away with B.M.?
  2 Do you keep a diary? What do / would you write in your diary?

Writing

8 Write a description of what you think B.M. is like. Include this information:
  - a physical description
  - his character
  - his political views
  - where he and Angela met
  - how their relationship grew

88 Literature insight 3

BACKGROUND TO THE STORY

Angela Clandon, the wife of a prominent politician, has died in a tragic accident. She has left a list of things – legacies – to people who were important to her. Gilbert considers that this thoughtfulness is as if Angela had foreseen her own death, yet she had been in good health when she stepped into the road and was struck down by a car.

Angela's legacy to her husband is fifteen leather-bound diaries. She had kept a diary since the day they were married, but Gilbert was not allowed to read it, until now.

Angela's secretary, Sissy Miller, arrives and Gilbert gives her the legacy that Angela left for her – a small brooch. Gilbert wonders what Sissy's plans are and if she will be able to cope financially. As she is leaving, he tells her that he will help her in any way that he can.

The Legacy

For a moment, on the threshold, as if a sudden thought had struck her, she stopped.

'Mr Clandon,' she said, looking straight at him for the first time, and for the first time he was struck by the expression, sympathetic yet searching, in her eyes. 'If at any time,' she continued, 'there's anything I can do to help you, remember, I shall feel it, for your wife's sake, a pleasure …'

With that she was gone. Her words and the look that went with them were unexpected. It was almost as if she believed, or hoped, that he would need her. A curious, perhaps a fantastic idea occurred to him as he returned to his chair. Could it be, that during all those years when he had scarcely noticed her, she, as the novelists say, had entertained a passion for him? He caught his own reflection in the glass as he passed. He was over fifty; but he could not help admitting that he was still, as the looking-glass showed him, a very distinguished-looking man.

'Poor Sissy Miller!' he said, half laughing. How he would have liked to share that joke with his wife! He turned instinctively to her diary. 'Gilbert,' he read, opening it at random, 'looked so wonderful …' It was as if she had answered his question. Of course, she seemed to say, you're very attractive to women.

Of course Sissy Miller felt that, too. He read on. 'How proud I am to be his wife!' And he had always been very proud to be her husband. How often, when they dined out somewhere, he had looked at her across the table and said to himself, She's the loveliest woman here! He read on. That first year he had been standing for Parliament. They had toured his constituency. 'When Gilbert sat down the applause was terrific. The whole audience rose and sang: "For he's a jolly good fellow." I was quite overcome.' He remembered that, too. She had been sitting on the platform beside him. He could still see the glance she cast at him, and how she had tears in her eyes. And then? He turned the pages. They had gone to Venice. He recalled that happy holiday after the election. 'We had ices at Florians.' He smiled – she was still such a child; she loved ices. 'Gilbert gave me a most interesting account of the history of Venice. He told me that the Doges …' she had written it all out in her schoolgirl hand. One of the delights of travelling with Angela had been that she was so eager to learn. She was so terribly ignorant, she used to say, as if that were not one of her charms. And then – he opened the next volume – they had come back to London.

From *And All for Love* … edited by Diane Mowat and Jennifer Bassett.

Literature insight 4 *Oliver Twist* – Charles Dickens

BEFORE YOU READ

1. Read about Charles Dickens. What did the new Poor Law of 1834 mean for working class people?
2. Read the background to the story on page 91. Why did Oliver have to ask for more food?

About the author
Charles Dickens (nickname Boz)
Born: 1812 in Portsmouth, England
Died: 1870
Important works: *Oliver Twist* (1839), *A Christmas Carol* (1843), *David Copperfield* (1849–1850), *Little Dorrit* (1855–57)
Did you know? Charles Dickens had an unhappy childhood. His father was bad at managing money and in 1824, he was arrested for being in debt and sent to prison. Charles, who was twelve years old, was sent to work in a factory where he pasted labels on bottles for six shillings a week. The horrific conditions in the factory haunted him for the rest of his life, and for a time he knew what it was like to be an orphan.
Working-class children suffered in Victorian times and many had to work from the age of eight. Orphans like Oliver in *Oliver Twist* had an even harder time in the workhouses. A new Poor Law had been passed in 1834 which allowed the poor to receive public money only if they lived and worked in workhouses. Families were split up and living conditions were deliberately terrible. Charles Dickens exposed this reality in his novels. His grim and realistic descriptions shocked his readers, with the result that the wealthier classes began to learn about the conditions that poor people were forced to live in for the first time.

1. Read the extract on page 91. What prevented Oliver from begging when he reached some villages?

2. Read the extract again. Match sentences A–G to gaps 1–7 in the extract.
   A "The magistrate? What's that?"
   B If they had not given him some food, he surely would have died like his mother.
   C Meat, bread and beer were placed before Oliver,
   D He slept the first night in a field, feeling lonely, tired, cold, and hungry.
   E "I'm very tired and hungry," answered Oliver, almost crying. "I've been walking for a week."
   F He was short for his age and had little, sharp, ugly eyes.
   G After a long time the boy crossed the road and said to Oliver,

3. **SPEAKING** Work in pairs. Answer the questions.
   1. What does the description of Dodger, the boy that Oliver meets, tell you about him?
   2. What do you think Dickens is trying to show the readers in this section of the book?

4. Read what happens next. What kind of work do the boys do?

READ ON

The boy, whose name is The Artful Dodger, tells Oliver that he will take him to a kind old gentleman who will help him. Dodger takes Oliver to a London neighbourhood where a gang of pickpockets live. The boys, who are Dodger's age, are smoking pipes and drinking liquor. The gentleman in charge of them is called Fagin. One day, Fagin sends Oliver out 'to work' with Dodger and Charley. Oliver is shocked when his friends steal a handkerchief from a wealthy gentleman's pocket and when the gentleman turns round, he thinks that Oliver is the thief. Oliver is taken before the magistrate, who sentences him to three months' hard labour. Oliver faints, but the owner of a bookstall, Mr Brownlow, arrives to say that two other boys and not Oliver were the thieves.
Mr Brownlow takes Oliver home with him, but Fagin is furious when he learns what has happened. He is terrified that Oliver will tell the police where the gang lives.

5. **3.14** Listen to the next part of the story. When does Oliver feel rather confused?

6. **3.14** Listen again. Complete sentences 1–7 with characters A–C.
   A Oliver **B** Mr Brownlow **C** Mr Grimwig
   1. .... offers to help around the house.
   2. .... doesn't believe that Oliver is a criminal.
   3. .... wants to hear all about Oliver's life.
   4. .... is an argumentative elderly gentleman who appears to know about Oliver.
   5. .... whispers to Mr Brownlow.
   6. .... suggests that Oliver returns some books.
   7. .... thinks that Oliver will disappear with the money and return to the thieves.

7. **SPEAKING** Work in pairs. Answer the questions.
   1. Why does Mr Grimwig stare at Oliver?
   2. Should Mr Brownlow have sent Oliver out alone? Why / why not?
   3. What do you think will happen to Oliver?

Writing

8. It is dark and Oliver has not returned to Mr Brownlow's house. Write a dialogue between Mr Brownlow and Mr Grimwig. Include this information:
   - Mr Grimwig is triumphant. He knew this would happen.
   - Mr Brownlow is angry with himself for sending Oliver out alone. He is afraid that the thieves have snatched him.
   - Mr Grimwig wants to call the police.
   - Mr Brownlow wants to go out looking for the boy.

BACKGROUND TO THE STORY

Oliver Twist is born in a workhouse, but sadly his mother dies soon after his birth. The doctor learns that Oliver's mother, who had been found lying in the street, was not wearing a wedding ring and, from the state of her shoes, had walked a great distance. Oliver is placed in a badly-run home for young orphans and on his ninth birthday is taken to the workhouse. The boys are given very little food, so they discuss who will ask for some more. They decide that Oliver should be the one to ask. No boy has ever asked for more food and Mr Bumble, who is in charge of the workhouse, is furious. He offers five pounds to anyone who will take the boy and Oliver is apprenticed to Mr Sowerberry, a local undertaker. They make him sleep in the room where they keep the coffins. One day Noah, another apprentice, makes horrible comments about Oliver's mother and there is a fight. Mr Sowerberry beats Oliver and at dawn the next day, Oliver runs away and travels towards London.

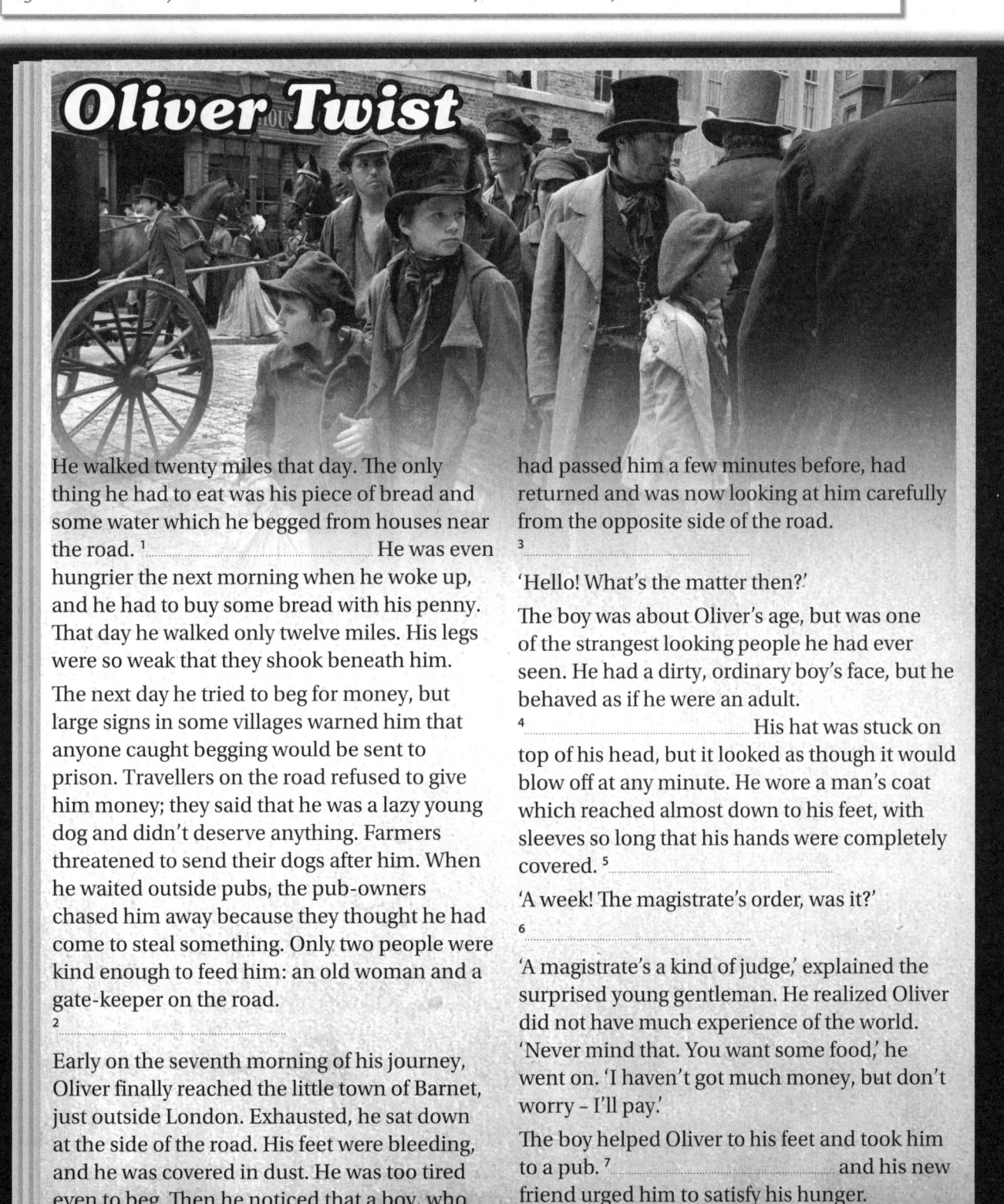

Oliver Twist

He walked twenty miles that day. The only thing he had to eat was his piece of bread and some water which he begged from houses near the road. **1** _____ He was even hungrier the next morning when he woke up, and he had to buy some bread with his penny. That day he walked only twelve miles. His legs were so weak that they shook beneath him.

The next day he tried to beg for money, but large signs in some villages warned him that anyone caught begging would be sent to prison. Travellers on the road refused to give him money; they said that he was a lazy young dog and didn't deserve anything. Farmers threatened to send their dogs after him. When he waited outside pubs, the pub-owners chased him away because they thought he had come to steal something. Only two people were kind enough to feed him: an old woman and a gate-keeper on the road.
2 _____

Early on the seventh morning of his journey, Oliver finally reached the little town of Barnet, just outside London. Exhausted, he sat down at the side of the road. His feet were bleeding, and he was covered in dust. He was too tired even to beg. Then he noticed that a boy, who had passed him a few minutes before, had returned and was now looking at him carefully from the opposite side of the road.
3 _____

'Hello! What's the matter then?'

The boy was about Oliver's age, but was one of the strangest looking people he had ever seen. He had a dirty, ordinary boy's face, but he behaved as if he were an adult.
4 _____ His hat was stuck on top of his head, but it looked as though it would blow off at any minute. He wore a man's coat which reached almost down to his feet, with sleeves so long that his hands were completely covered. **5** _____

'A week! The magistrate's order, was it?'
6 _____

'A magistrate's a kind of judge,' explained the surprised young gentleman. He realized Oliver did not have much experience of the world. 'Never mind that. You want some food,' he went on. 'I haven't got much money, but don't worry – I'll pay.'

The boy helped Oliver to his feet and took him to a pub. **7** _____ and his new friend urged him to satisfy his hunger.

From *Oliver Twist*, Oxford Bookworms. Text adaptation by Richard Rogers.

Literature insight 5 *Great Expectations* – Charles Dickens

BEFORE YOU READ

1. Read about Charles Dickens. What obsessions did Dickens suffer from?
2. Read the background to the story on page 93. Who is Estella?

About the author

Charles Dickens (called himself The Sparkler of Albion)
Born: 1812 in Portsmouth, England
Died: 1870
Important works: *Nicholas Nickleby* (1838–1839), *Bleak House* (1852–1853), *Hard Times* (1854), *Great Expectations* (1860–1861)
Did you know? Charles Dickens loved names. He named two of his sons after his favourite authors and he gave each of his ten children nicknames like Skittles and Chicken Stalker. He used the diminutive 'Pip' for Philip in *Great Expectations* and he liked to give many of his characters endearing nicknames.
Because Dickens' stories were often serialized in magazines, they reached a wider audience than any writer before him. He published fifteen novels, wrote hundreds of short stories and non-fiction pieces and lectured both in England and the United States. However, some people have said that he was an obsessive and compulsive man. He frequently looked in the mirror and combed his hair, and if the furniture in his house wasn't in the correct position, then he couldn't work. Dickens was obsessed with magnetic fields and every bed he slept in had to be positioned so that it was aligned north to south.
Many critics think that *Great Expectations* was Dickens' most accurate self-portrait and his attempt to come to terms with the painful facts of his childhood.

1. Read the extract on page 93. What does Pip notice about the clocks in Satis House?

2. Read the extract again. Are the sentences true (T) or false (F)? Correct the false ones.
   1. Miss Havisham's house is full of daylight.
   2. The dress she is wearing has yellowed with age.
   3. Pip tells Miss Havisham that he is scared of her.
   4. Pip tells her that his heart has been broken.
   5. Pip feels at ease in Satis House.
   6. One day Miss Havisham will leave her jewellery to Estella.

3. **SPEAKING** Work in pairs. Answer the questions.
   1. Characters and relationships are central in *Great Expectations*. What is Dickens showing the reader about the relationship between Pip and Miss Havisham?
   2. Why do you think Pip says that the house is sad?
   3. Do you think that Miss Havisham is an interesting character? Why / why not?

4. Read what happens next. How is Pip's background different from Estella's?

READ ON

Estella makes fun of Pip's coarse hands and thick boots, and when Miss Havisham asks Pip what he thinks of Estella, he says that she is proud and rude, but very pretty. Pip realizes that he is a common working boy and he wishes he were different.
Pip desperately wants to be accepted by Estella and the next time he visits Satis House, it is Miss Havisham's birthday and her relatives are there. As Pip is leaving, he meets a pale young gentleman who picks a fight with him. Pip knocks him down, punches him and wins the fight. When he reaches the gate, Estella is waiting for him.

5. 3.15 Listen to the next part of the story. What are the expectations of Pip's sister and Mr Pumblechook?

6. 3.15 Listen again. Complete the sentences with the words below.

   ■ apprenticed ■ cruel ■ warns ■ break ■ directly
   ■ worthless ■ endlessly

   1. Pip feels that the kiss is ....
   2. Miss Havisham wants Estella to be .... to Pip and to learn how to .... men's hearts.
   3. Pip's sister and Mr Pumblechook talk .... about Miss Havisham's wealth.
   4. It is Miss Havisham who decides that Pip should be .... to Joe.
   5. Rather than speaking .... to Miss Havisham, Joe talks through Pip.
   6. Miss Havisham .... Joe that he won't receive more money from her.

7. **SPEAKING** Work in pairs. Answer the questions.
   1. Dickens uses a lot of symbols (objects which represent abstract ideas) in his writing. Which symbols have you noticed in these extracts?
   2. Miss Havisham has a certain power over Pip and Estella. How does she shape their lives? Have you met anyone who has shaped your life?

Writing

8. Imagine you are Pip. Miss Havisham has just died and you are writing an obituary for a newspaper. Include this information:

   ■ what your life was like before you met Miss Havisham
   ■ your first visit to Satis House and your first impression of her
   ■ her relationship with Estella
   ■ her meeting with you and Joe
   ■ her influence on your life

BACKGROUND TO THE STORY

Pip, a young orphan, lives with his uncaring older sister and her kind, gentle husband at their blacksmith's forge in the Kent marshlands. One day, when Pip is in the cemetery looking at his parents' tombstones, a coarse and frightening man grabs him. His name is Magwitch, an escaped convict, and he orders Pip to bring him food and a file so he can remove the chains on his legs. Pip takes a pork pie, some brandy and a file from the forge to Magwitch, but he learns soon after that the convict has been caught and put on a prison ship bound for Australia.

Miss Havisham, a wealthy spinster, sits, still wearing her wedding dress, in her dilapidated mansion, Satis House. She asks Pip's uncle, Mr Pumblechook, to find a boy to play with her adopted daughter Estella. Years before, Miss Havisham was jilted on her wedding day and now she is training the beautiful Estella to break men's hearts.

Great Expectations

I knocked at the door and was told to enter. I found myself in a large room, where the curtains were closed to allow no daylight in, and the candles were lit. In the centre of the room, sitting at a table, was the strangest lady I have ever seen, or shall ever see. She was wearing a wedding dress made of rich material. She had a bride's flowers in her hair, but her hair was white. There were suitcases full of dresses and jewels around her, ready for a journey. She only had one white shoe on. Then I realized that over the years the white wedding dress had become yellow, and the flowers in her hair had died, and the bride inside the dress had grown old. Everything in the room was ancient and dying. The only brightness in the room was in her dark old eyes, that stared at me.

'Who are you?' said the lady at the table.

'Pip, madam. Mr Pumblechook's boy. Come – to play.'

'Come close. Let me look at you.' As I stood in front of her, I noticed that her watch and a clock in the room had both stopped at twenty minutes to nine.

'You aren't afraid of a woman who has never seen the sun since you were born?' asked Miss Havisham.

I am sorry to say I told a huge lie by saying, 'No.'

'Do you know what this is? she asked, putting her hand on her left side.

'Yes, madam.' It made me think of my convict's travelling companion. 'Your heart, madam,' I added.

'My heart! Broken!' she cried almost proudly, with a strange smile. Then she said, 'I am tired. I want to see something different. Play.'

No order could be more difficult to obey in that house and that room. I was desperate enough to consider rushing round the table pretending to be Pumblechook's carriage, but I could not make myself do it, and just stood there helplessly.

'I'm very sorry, madam,' I said, 'my sister will be very angry with me if you complain, but I can't play just now. Everything is so strange, and new, and sad …' I stopped, afraid to say more. Miss Havisham looked down at her dress, and then at her face in the mirror on the table.

'So strange to him, so well-known to me,' she whispered. 'So new to him, so old to me. And so sad to us both! Call Estella!'

When Estella finally came, with her candle, along the dark passage, Miss Havisham picked up a jewel from her table and put it in Estella's hair. 'Very pretty, my dear. It will be yours one day. Now let me see you play cards with this boy!'

From *Great Expectations*, Oxford Bookworms. Text adaptation by Clare West.

Exam insight 1

Reading

EXAM STRATEGY

Working out what types of texts you are dealing with will help you to understand them better.

1 Read quickly through the three texts. Decide where you might find each text. Use the list to help you.

- in an autobiography ■ on a newspaper TV page
- on a CD cover ■ on a noticeboard ■ on a website
- in a health magazine

2 **EXAM TASK** Read the texts and answer the questions.

In which text
1 does someone find it difficult to relax?
2 is it stressed that preparation is essential?
3 is a change of plan mentioned?
4 does the weather become a concern?
5 is there evidence of a lack of preparation?
6 can the reader find useful advice?

A

9.00 p.m. *A Life of Travel*

Robert Attwood looks at the life of Geoffrey Moorhouse, travel writer and journalist, who in 1972, at the age of forty, with no experience of either the desert or camels, or indeed navigation, set off to attempt the first solo crossing of the Sahara desert from west to east. With numerous obstacles to overcome, Moorhouse eventually employed local people to help him meet the challenge. However, they proved as much of a problem as the desert itself. They stole food, carelessly wasted water and accidentally broke his navigation equipment. Moorhouse's account of his extraordinary journey retells how he came to face his own fears and to explore the extremes of human experience. Attwood's documentary includes interviews with Moorhouse himself and his friends and colleagues, and rare video footage of the start of his amazing trip.

B

So ... Britain's best cycling challenge is on your radar: around 1,500 kilometres from Land's End in the far south-west of the country to John O'Groats in the far north-east. Well, this is your knowledge base for the trip. I've been there, done that and got the T-shirt. Believe me, doing the groundwork before you set off is vital. It really will enhance your experience. The key word is TREK. Four things to remember: Training, Route, Enjoyment and Kit.

Training (click here for more information)
Don't skimp on physical preparation. It's a 10–14-day journey. Ignore fitness, and the first week will seem like an endurance test.

Route (click here for more information)
Advance planning is strongly recommended. Take in as much of the magnificent scenery along the way as you can!

Enjoyment (click here for more information)
Enjoyment is everything. If you are a challenge-oriented individual, then go for it. If you want something gentler, steep hills and long days in the saddle can be sensibly avoided.

Kit (click here for more information)
As little as possible. Give your bike a good overhaul. Take essential tools only. Pack as few clothes as you can. Remember you will need to carry water.

C

As I drew close to the coast of Antigua, the wind picked up and the waves grew more threatening. The clouds darkened and I became apprehensive about spending another night at sea. Negotiating a route into English Harbour was not an option to be undertaken at night in heavy seas.

I had made good progress during the night, but the whole forty-day trip had taken its toll. I was exhausted. I had slept badly throughout that time. Not only was I physically exhausted, but sleepless nights worrying that a huge container ship might crash into me – despite the wonderful technology – meant I was close to breaking point.

Then, as suddenly as the sky had grown dark, it started to clear. I could make out Fort Berkeley in the entrance to the harbour and realized that my dream, my goal, would be achieved that afternoon. My spirits lifted. New energy and enthusiasm coursed through my veins. I bent my back to the task ahead.

Listening

EXAM STRATEGY

Before you listen, think about the words you are likely to hear. Being prepared in this way will make the listening easier to understand.

3 You are going to hear a radio programme about the Royal Flying Doctor Service in Australia. Tick (✔) the words below that you think you will hear.

■ aircraft ■ mechanic ■ medicine ■ healthcare
■ emergency ■ unskilled ■ radio ■ nurse ■ travellers
■ dentist ■ preventative ■ fuel ■ first-class ■ community
■ four-wheel drive

4 **EXAM TASK** 3.16 Listen to the radio programme and choose the correct answers.

1 When do flights involve a doctor?
   a When moving patients to a hospital.
   b When a health clinic is being held.
   c When the situation requires it.
   d When putting a medicine chest in place.
2 What is the main purpose of the Royal Flying Doctor Service?
   a To provide an emergency service for people in outback Australia.
   b To provide all-round health care for people in outback Australia.
   c To make medicine available in remote areas.
   d To persuade people to live in a healthier way.
3 What does the speaker say about the Healthy Living Program?
   a It has reduced demand for the emergency services.
   b It has been around for many years.
   c It is an idea that will be developed in the future.
   d It is a fairly recent development by the RFDS.
4 How does the speaker feel about the Royal Flying Doctor Service?
   a He thinks it is an excellent organization.
   b He thinks it concentrates too much on preventative health care.
   c He thinks it costs too much money.
   d He thinks the government should fund it completely.
5 How would you describe the tone of the speaker?
   a Serious and persuasive.
   b Casual and friendly.
   c Overconfident and arrogant.
   d Tired and uninterested.
6 What is the main purpose of the radio broadcast?
   a To inform the listener about the Royal Flying Doctor Service.
   b To appeal for donations to the Royal Flying Doctor Service.
   c To advertise jobs at the Royal Flying Doctor Service.
   d To praise the Royal Flying Doctor Service.

Use of English

EXAM STRATEGY

First, read the text quickly to get a general understanding of what it is about. This will help you when you start to choose the right words. Then, before you look at the options given, read the text again and see if you can work out what words might be missing. Check if the words you guessed are among the options.

5 Read the text and answer the questions.
1 Why did the man call at Jack Whiting's house?
2 Why did Jack race to the scene?
3 Why did he climb onto the lorry?
4 Why did the police chief say his behaviour was awesome?

6 **EXAM TASK** Read the text again. Choose the correct answers.

One evening, seventeen-year-old Jack Whiting was in his family's home, just a few hundred metres from the Wharton Gorge, a deep narrow valley through ¹_____ the Wharton River runs. Suddenly there was a loud and urgent knocking at the door. Whiting opened the door to a panic-stricken man who told him that a huge lorry had come off the road and was ²_____ on the edge of the gorge, and about to plunge down into it.

Whiting did not ³_____ stop to put on his shoes. He shouted to his family to call the police and raced to the scene as fast as he could. The front of the lorry was already half ⁴_____ the edge and the driver was still in the cab. Whiting realized that the most sensible thing to do ⁵_____ be to call the fire service and wait. ⁶_____, he could hear strange noises coming from the lorry and decided that he needed to act fast. Quickly he climbed onto the lorry and miraculously was able to break the rear window of the cab. He helped the ⁷_____ driver out of the cab and back to safety, just seconds before the lorry plummeted eighty metres into the river.

'Awesome' is how police chief, Julia Jackson, ⁸_____ Whiting's behaviour. 'He risked his own life to save another. At seventeen, that takes some courage.'

1	a	which	b	where	c	that	d	there
2	a	holding	b	stabilizing	c	balancing	d	equalizing
3	a	really	b	ever	c	just	d	even
4	a	down	b	over	c	up	d	along
5	a	should	b	must	c	would	d	was
6	a	However	b	Although	c	Moreover	d	Still
7	a	damaged	b	injured	c	harmed	d	spoiled
8	a	told	b	communicated				
	c	represented	d	described				

Use of English

EXAM STRATEGY

First think of all the available options. Then decide which one fits best according to both grammar and meaning. Don't forget adverbs (e.g. *tolerantly*, *patiently*) and opposites (e.g. *intolerantly*, *impatiently*).

7 Choose the correct answers. Why is the other option wrong?

1 Remember to take hats if you're going out. You'll need some **protection / protective** against the sun.
2 I don't really like his paintings much. I find them rather **uninspiring / inspiring**.
3 She realized I wouldn't be able to move the bookcase on my own and offered to help. It was so **thoughtful / thoughtless** of her.
4 Have you seen the **attractive / attraction** new building next to the Town Hall?
5 I love those new curtains. They're such an **unappealing / appealing** shade of blue.
6 I'm sure he is capable of better work than that. His last test results were very **unimpressive / impressionable**.
7 You shouldn't speak like that to your grandmother. You should be more **respectable / respectful**.
8 Be careful with the new teacher. She has a very low **tolerance / tolerant** for bad behaviour.

8 **EXAM TASK** Complete the sentences with the correct form of the words in brackets.

1 The new boss is very .... (tolerate). She sacked someone the other day for arriving five minutes late.
2 She doesn't care about other people's feelings at all. She's so .... (think).
3 Despite wearing a lot of .... (protect) clothing, there were bruises all over his chest.
4 I think you should apologize. What you said was very .... (respect).
5 I'm not sure I like that colour at all. It's rather .... (appeal).
6 She gave an .... (inspire) talk to her students about the importance of art.
7 I can't see the .... (attract) of the theatre. I much prefer to see a film.
8 Did you see the fantastic amount of money she raised for charity? It was really most .... (impress).

Speaking

EXAM STRATEGY

Remember that the examiner may sometimes play the role of your superior, as well as the role of your friend. You should express suggestions, agreements and disagreements in more formal language if he/she is playing the role of your superior.

9 Are the phrases suggestions, agreements and disagreements? Which of them are formal and which informal? Read the exam task. Which of the phrases would you need for this particular task?

a Absolutely.
b Actually, I believe ... .
c Certainly.
d I can't do that.
e I thought it would be a good idea to ... .
f I was thinking about ... .
g Let's ... .
h Not at all. In fact, ...
i That's a bad idea.
j Yeah!

10 **EXAM TASK** Your school wants to host an event to support a local charity. As a representative of the student council, you want to explain to the head teacher how the students could be involved in organizing this fund-raising event. Include the following points:

- reason for letting the students host the event
- how to organize the fund-raising event
- who would be responsible for organizing the event
- the most suitable date for the event and why

Writing

EXAM STRATEGY

When writing an article, remember to use plenty of adjectives and adverbs to make your descriptions richer and your article more personal and convincing.

11 Form adjectives and adverbs from the words below. Look up the meaning of any words you do not know. How could you use them in the exam task below?

- obvious ■ deny ■ question ■ appear ■ vision
- evidence ■ consequence

12 **EXAM TASK** One of the popular sports clubs near your school has been sold and the new owner is planning huge changes. Write an article for the school magazine. Include the following points:

- Describe the sports club and what the planned changes are.
- Describe the last time you used the sports club.
- Give your opinion on the changes and reasons why.
- State what you think should happen next.

Exam insight 2

Reading

EXAM STRATEGY

Working out what each paragraph is about will help you to locate where to put the missing sentences. Make sure the sentence you put in the gap fits with the topic of the paragraph.

1 Read the text. Work out what the topic of each paragraph is and match the headings below to the paragraphs.

1 How the museum started
2 What will happen in the future
3 How Norcross started collecting
4 Why there were only toasters
5 Introducing a very unusual museum
6 What the museum was like

2 **EXAM TASK** Complete the text with sentences A–F.

A Unfortunately, events conspired against them, and it was not to be. Eventually, however, there was better news.
B He was running an art gallery and bar when he hit upon the novel idea of putting a toaster on each table so that customers could make their own toast.
C Whilst wandering the streets of Seattle a few years ago, I encountered my all-time favourite museum: the Toaster Museum.
D It attracted visitors from all over the world, as well as media attention from places as far afield as Canada, Japan and Britain.
E Initially, these were stored in a back room leading off the studio and not put on display.
F In an appliance museum, it would be easy to mistake a toaster for some other sort of appliance.

A ☐ What's the weirdest museum you've ever been in? One where there's an accumulation of all sorts of junk? One with a wide-ranging variety of all sorts of different objects? Or something more specialist? ¹.............
That's right – a collection dedicated entirely to the contraption in your kitchen that turns your bread into toast every morning.

B ☐ I was curious as to how such an esoteric place had been conceived and fell into conversation with Eric Norcross, the owner. There was no grand design to his museum. It happened more or less by accident.
²............. The idea took off. As a result, Norcross was always on the lookout for extra appliances. One day he came across a Toast-O-Lator, an unusual toaster where the toast travels through from one side to the other. That toaster turned him into a collector.

C ☐ Sadly, the gallery had to close. After a short hiatus, Norcross and his wife opened a new art gallery and studio, and continued to collect toasters for their own amusement. ³............. However, they drew the attention of so many people that the Norcrosses ended up giving occasional impromptu tours. Before too long, they decided there was only one thing to do: open the Toaster Museum.

D ☐ Although only open for about five years, the Toaster Museum was a great success. ⁴............. Toasters were lined up on display with cards detailing the names and dates of the manufacturer. There was also information about the history of toasters – the first electric one was produced in the early 20th century – and about how they are manufactured today. What seemed continually to fascinate visitors was the design, innovation and effort that had gone into creating what is, after all, just a common kitchen appliance.

E ☐ At first, the Norcrosses wondered whether it was ludicrous to devote a whole museum to just one appliance. In fact, visitors often asked whether they were going to diversify into kettles or coffee machines. However, Eric Norcross argued that it was simplicity that made the museum unique. ⁵............. But by displaying only toasters, it was possible to gain an overview of the development and history of the toaster; to see how change, development and evolution had unfolded over the years; and to appreciate the varied, interesting and unusual work and vision that had gone into its design and creation.

F ☐ After five years, the museum closed. The Norcrosses moved first to Portland, Oregon, then to Charlottesville, Virginia, each time with the intention of once again putting on display their collection of over 550 toasters.
⁶............. The Henry Ford Museum in Dearborn, Michigan agreed to acquire the whole collection. Although it is not yet known when the collection will be available for public viewing, all is not lost. The museum also agreed to preserve the Norcrosses' fascinating internet resource: www.toaster.org. Whenever I make toast for breakfast, I always think of the Toast Museum.

Listening

EXAM STRATEGY

First, get a general idea of what each recording is about. Make notes of any answers you think you have found. The second time you listen, get a more detailed understanding. Check the answers you have and listen for the ones you don't have.

3 🔊 **3.17** Listen and answer the questions below.

Which recording talks about
1 genetic modifications to animals?
2 using genetics to alter the condition and characteristics of an unborn child?
3 demonstrations against genetically modified (GM) foods?

4 **EXAM TASK** 🔊 **3.17** Listen again. Choose the correct answers.

Recording 1
1 What kind of recording are you listening to?
   a an expert's advice on GM foods
   b a news report about some peaceful demonstrations
   c an advertisement for a company producing food
2 Which sentence is true about the food company Monsanto?
   a It employs people in over fifty countries.
   b It labels all its GM products.
   c It believes people should be able to say what they believe.

Recording 2
3 The man believes that
   a milk makes him sick and gives him stomach problems.
   b scientists are irresponsible.
   c genetic engineering has been going on for a long time.
4 The woman thinks that
   a scientists are unaware of the consequences of their actions.
   b GM crops are OK, but not GM animals.
   c farmers practise a form of genetic engineering.

Recording 3
5 The speaker wants to
   a advise his listeners.
   b persuade his listeners.
   c describe something to his listeners.
6 The speaker thinks that
   a we should make use of genetics to improve the human race.
   b there is little connection between a person's genes and their personality.
   c a responsible society does not interfere with the genes of an unborn baby.

Use of English

EXAM STRATEGY

Try and work out what kind of word (what part of speech) is likely to fill each gap. This will make it easier to decide which word to put into the gap.

5 Read the text once to get an idea of what it is about. Then read it again and decide which part of speech (adjective, noun, verb, etc.) should go in each gap. Choose the part of speech from the list below. You may use some parts of speech more than once.
- verb (e.g. *faces, blame, spent*)
- noun (e.g. *music, food, tent*)
- adjective (e.g. *better, poor, next*)
- preposition (e.g. *of, in, to*)
- modal verb (e.g. *might, could, should*)
- adverb (e.g. *fast, quickly, carefully*)

- conjunction (e.g. *when, but, and*)
- article (e.g. *a, an, the*)

1 .... 5 ....
2 .... 6 ....
3 .... 7 ....
4 .... 8 ....

6 **EXAM TASK** Complete the text with appropriate words.

TENT NIGHTMARE AT FESTIVAL SITE

Has there been a hurricane? Is this the beginning of a new waste-disposal site? No, it's what the site of an open-air music festival ¹.................... like when all the festival-goers have left. Obviously, there are ².................... usual mountains of beer cans and piles of food packaging. However, the biggest headache that faces the organizers of this year's well-known Gilded Tree Festival in the west of England has been the 10,000 tents that festival-goers have left ³.................... .

'We ⁴.................... not really blame our customers,' said spokeswoman, Kate Wilson, for the Gilded Tree organization. 'When a three-person tent costs only as much as a couple of CDs or music downloads, you know it's not going to last that ⁵.................... . You might just as well leave it behind. We do encourage people to take their tents home with them. We also suggest that ⁶.................... they spent more money and bought a tent of better quality, it might last them a lifetime of camping holidays rather than just one festival. We did try recycling the tents ⁷.................... donating them to aid charities, but most are of such poor quality that the charities weren't interested.'

Gilded Tree is ⁸.................... ways of reducing the number of abandoned tents at next year's festival.

Use of English

EXAM STRATEGY

Think about how the words before and after each gap will help you to decide what part of speech you need. If the gap is before an adjective, you will need an adverb. If the gap is after an adjective, you will need a noun.

7 Read the sentences and answer the questions.
1 She'll take office at the .... of the year.
   Will the word in the gap be a noun or a verb?
2 He's proposing a new set of ....
   Will the noun in the gap be singular or plural?
3 We're suffering because of the .... crisis.
   Will the word in the gap be an adjective or an adverb?
4 .... will be given to people on low incomes.
   Will the word in the gap be a noun or an adjective?
5 Profits this year have been .... good.
   Will the word in the gap be an adjective or an adverb?

6 We are expecting a .... in sales following our advertising campaign.
Will the noun in the gap be singular or plural?

7 Our new boss has .... for a review of all job descriptions.
Will the verb form in the gap be a present participle or a past participle?

8 Despite the sunny weather, sales of T-shirts were ....
Will the adjective in the gap be positive or negative in meaning?

8 EXAM TASK Complete the text with the correct form of the words in brackets.

THE POPULATION TIME BOMB

A report out yesterday warned that the government is not yet ready to face the challenges of an ¹.................. (increase) aging population. Current ².................. (predict) point to a 50% increase in the number of over 65s and a doubling of over 85s over the next fifteen years.

The report recommended a radical ³.................. (transform) of health and social care in order to address this situation. It warned that many people would have ⁴.................. (adequate) savings or pensions to cope, and suggested that the government should provide far clearer ⁵.................. (inform) about amounts people could expect to receive in ⁶.................. (retire).

The report concluded that ⁷.................. (politics) leaders should take action to fully engage with the ⁸.................. (imply) of the report.

Speaking

EXAM STRATEGY

The examiner's first question after you've described the picture usually asks you to speculate about the situation it presents. You could be asked about someone's reasons, feelings, intentions or thoughts. There's no single correct answer to this, but remember that, just like all your answers, you need to justify it.

9 Look at the photo in the exam task. Below are examples of questions asking for speculation. Try to answer the questions, making sure that you justify your answers.
- Where might this woman be going? What makes you think so?
- Do you think this woman just bought her own apartment? Why / why not?
- Do you think the woman's parents are upset that she's leaving? Why / why not?

10 EXAM TASK Look at the photo and answer the questions.
1 What do you think this young woman has packed into her suitcase and backpack? What makes you think so?
2 Have you ever been on a long journey on your own?
3 If you had ten minutes to leave your home, what would you take with you? Why?
4 Tell us about a situation when you lost something valuable to you.

Writing

EXAM STRATEGY

When writing a letter, remember to write on every point in the instructions, otherwise you will lose marks.

11 Complete the sentences with the words below. What kind of letter would each of them be useful for? Which could you use for the letter in the exam task?

■ behalf ■ bring ■ concerning ■ express ■ invite ■ request ■ response

1 I am writing in .... to the advertisement in last Sunday's *Daily News* .... a vacancy in your Customer Relations department.
2 I am writing to .... permission to use the town park for a charity fund-raising concert.
3 I am writing to .... my dissatisfaction with the meal my wife and I had at your restaurant.
4 I am writing on .... of my school student council to .... you to our 'An Evening with Writers' event.
5 I am writing to .... your attention to the unacceptable state of the pavements in our area.

12 EXAM TASK You have read an article in a health and fitness magazine in which the author claims that gyms and fitness clubs take advantage of our laziness, because after all, you can keep fit by simply changing your lifestyle and attitude to food. Write a letter to this magazine. Include the following points:
■ Give your opinion on the subject and justify it.
■ Describe the health and fitness lifestyle of a friend who is a perfect example of the argument you are supporting.
■ Give details of some healthy-eating initiatives in your school.
■ State how you will (or will not) change your lifestyle as a result of this article.

Exam insight 3

Reading

EXAM STRATEGY

Read the questions carefully. If you cannot immediately find the right answer, first eliminate the options that are wrong. Then examine the remaining possibilities carefully and decide which is correct.

1 Read the texts and answer the question below for each text.

What kind of text is this?
a a review in a newspaper
b an email or letter
c an article in a newspaper
d a noticeboard announcement

2 **EXAM TASK** Read the texts again and choose the correct answers.

1 The *Encyclopaedia Britannica*
a was a constant size until the 1930s.
b will now be available in a Kindle edition.
c will no longer be published in book form.
d has always been reprinted every year.
2 The transition to digital
a was a tough decision.
b was a difficult period for the company.
c has been inevitable for some time.
d will lead to a decrease in sales.
3 The *Encyclopaedia Britannica*
a brings in the majority of the earnings to the company that owns it.
b can now be more accurate than ever.
c will soon be available as an app.
d will make its digital database available in print.

A

THE END OF AN ERA

Britannica goes online

It's happened. But it was always bound to happen. After over 240 years of continuous print versions, the *Encyclopaedia Britannica*, arguably the greatest ever English-language encyclopaedia, will only be available online. It will never again be produced in a paper edition. First published between 1768 and 1771, it originally contained just three volumes. By the fourth edition (1801–1810) that figure had increased to twenty volumes. From the mid-1930s, a process of 'continuous revision' was adopted: the encyclopaedia was reprinted each year, with articles changed and updated according to the latest information.

Then came the digital age. Top sales for the printed encyclopaedia were in 1990 when 120,000 sets of the fifteenth 32-volume edition were sold. Six years later, that figure had fallen dramatically to just 40,000. It was not, therefore, a tough decision to go online.

'The transition has not been that difficult,' says company president Jorge Cauz. 'Everyone understands we needed to change. We are the only company that I know of, so far, that has made the transition from traditional media to the digital sphere, and managed to be profitable and grow.'

In fact, the encyclopaedia itself already forms only a small part of the company (Encyclopaedia Britannica Inc.) as a whole. Subscriptions and apps bring in only 15% of earnings. Today, by far the largest part of the remaining 85% will come from other educational services and products, an area which the company has been involved in for some considerable time. 'Today our digital database is much larger than what we can fit in a print set,' wrote Cauz in a company announcement. 'And it is up-to-date because we can revise it within minutes any time we need to, and we do it many times each day.'

B

I have been asked by the Head of Resources to make a case for the purchase of an online subscription to the *Encyclopaedia Britannica*, to be accessible to all students in the college.

The main argument centres around the availability of a number of online encyclopaedias and databases which provide free, rather than subscription, access to information – Wikipedia perhaps being the most well-known of these. Indeed, it is true that Wikipedia contains a vast knowledge database and has 3.9 million articles compared to *Britannica*'s 120,000. It also receives far more 'hits' per day than *Britannica*. However, this is probably because it is free.

One has to remember that Wikipedia is an open source tool that anyone can contribute to or alter. There are many well-documented examples of Wikipedia providing inaccurate information. The important factor here is that *Britannica* has an outstanding reputation for accuracy.

Although there have been criticisms of *Britannica*'s accuracy in the past, most recently in 2010 when there was an inaccurate entry about the Irish Civil War, these are highly unusual occurrences, and *Britannica* is generally regarded as the very height of excellence. Jorge Cauz, the President of Encyclopaedia Britannica Inc., asserted last year that '*Britannica* … will always be factually correct.'

Another important factor is that *Britannica* includes, and always has included, articles by leading scholars. Past contributors have included such important figures as Sigmund Freud, Albert Einstein and Marie Curie. Where else could our students have access to such scholarship?

As well as the main encyclopaedia, *Britannica* provides a number of online editions and apps that are particularly suitable for college use: for example, a Student Encyclopaedia and an Online Academic Edition. Such well-researched and well-written resources would, I feel, be a great asset to our college and I would urge you to approve their purchase.

4 The *Encyclopaedia Britannica*
  a has always been accurate.
  b can be contributed to by anyone.
  c is larger than Wikipedia.
  d contains articles by leading academics.
5 What is the main purpose of text B?
  a To compare two things.
  b To persuade someone to do something.
  c To order someone to do something.
  d Describe something in detail.
6 The writer is most probably writing to
  a the Principal of the college.
  b the Head of Resources.
  c the students at the college.
  d a friend.

Listening

EXAM STRATEGY

Read the question carefully before you listen. Remember: the words you hear will probably not be the same as in the question. There are many different ways of saying the same thing in English. Be careful – if the words you hear are the same as in the question, they might well not be the answer.

3 Match phrases 1–8 to phrases a–h with similar meanings.

1 I like to browse.
2 It's so easy to carry around.
3 It looks really good.
4 I like to support them.
5 I think it's wrong to do it.
6 It often causes problems.
7 I like to buy over the internet.
8 I had a terrible conscience about it.

a It's not nearly so convenient.
b It's beautiful.
c It's so portable.
d I like to see what's available.
e I felt really bad about it.
f I feel guilty about doing it.
g I like to help them to keep going.
h I prefer to purchase online.

4 **EXAM TASK** 3.18 Listen to five speakers taking about their attitudes to e-books and 'real' books. Match options A–F to speakers 1–5. There is one option that you do not need.

This speaker
A feels guilty about buying e-books.
B likes to chat about what is on people's bookshelves.
C will always buy some books just to own them and enjoy them.
D feels that there will always be a demand for some kinds of books.
E likes to sit in cafés and read.
F no longer buys real books.

Speaker 1		Speaker 4	
Speaker 2		Speaker 5	
Speaker 3			

Use of English

EXAM STRATEGY

Look at the words and think about how you would use them. This will help you to decide where to put them.

5 Complete the sentences with the correct form of the words in exercise 6. There are two words that you do not need.

1 New words .... come into the language from the world of technology.
2 I .... that they were speaking Finnish, even though I don't understand the language.
3 Working as a dictionary editor is a bit like being a ....: I'm always trying to track down new words and their meanings.
4 A 'cat', meaning someone who knows a lot about jazz music, first .... the dictionary in the 1920s.
5 'Bitcoin', a digital currency that does not need a bank, made its first .... in the dictionary in 2013.
6 As a writer, she was .... by Joseph Conrad, a great author who wrote in English even though it was not his native language.
7 He's .... Tolstoy's *War and Peace* and turning it into a TV drama.
8 Although it was a .... expense, we bought a twenty-volume copy of the *Oxford English Dictionary*.

6 **EXAM TASK** Complete the text with the correct form of the words below. There are two words that you do not need.

■ adapt ■ frequent ■ detect ■ recognize ■ inspire
■ appear ■ include ■ enter ■ consider

1,000 NEW WORDS IN THE DICTIONARY

When does a new word reach adulthood? Probably when it receives the ¹.............. it deserves by being put in the dictionary. Every year, approximately 1.8 billion new words are ²............... Most of them ³.............. almost as quickly as they come on the scene. Some hang around for longer - a few years, maybe. And around 1,000 a year gain ⁴.............. to *Oxford Dictionaries Online*.
Oxford Dictionaries keep a track of new words and their usage, noting the source and ⁵.............. of use. Then, when the evidence is sufficient, a new word is ⁶.............. for addition to their dictionaries of current English.
Among the new words ⁷.............. this year are: 'selfie' (a photo you take of yourself), 'phablet' (a smartphone with a large screen, somewhere between a phone and a tablet computer) and 'silly money' (a ridiculously large amount of money).

Use of English

EXAM STRATEGY

Decide what part of speech is needed to fill each gap (noun, verb, adjective or adverb). Then work out the correct form of the word in brackets. Check the meaning of the sentence, too. Remember that opposites are always possible.

7 Read the sentences in exercise 8. Decide which part of speech is needed to fill each gap: noun, verb, adjective or adverb. Decide if any of the words need to be negative.

1 ....
2 ....
3 ....
4 ....
5 ....
6 ....
7 ....
8 ....

8 **EXAM TASK** Complete the sentences with the correct form of the words in brackets.

1 He had a wonderful .... (child), growing up on a farm in the south of England.
2 .... (admit), she can be quite rude, but she is by far the best person for the job.
3 We recently discovered some long-lost cousins. We didn't even know of their .... (exist) until a few months ago!
4 He was delighted. You should have seen the .... (express) on his face.
5 They've lived in the village all their lives. They really do need to .... (broad) their outlook on life.
6 We've been studying the story of .... (evolve) – how animals gradually developed.
7 It was supposed to be a thriller, but it was so .... (excite) I walked out before the end.
8 There's no way I can arrive by 7 a.m. I'm afraid it's a complete .... (possible).

Speaking

EXAM STRATEGY

Try to develop your answers by including different arguments with examples. Use linking expressions to make your language more natural.

9 Match the expressions below to categories A–D. Then add two more expressions to each category.

- for instance ■ apart from that ■ now that ■ besides
- yet ■ since ■ nevertheless ■ still ■ such as
- in particular ■ seeing that ■ what's more ■ even so

A Adding more points on the same topic
B Moving to contrasting points
C Giving examples
D Talking about reasons

10 **EXAM TASK** You wish to sign up for a language course and you see these two adverts. Compare and contrast them. Include the following points:

- Which advert seems more convincing and why?
- Explain why you are rejecting the other advert.
- State the ways in which you can learn languages.
- Do you think it is important to speak many languages in today's 'global village'?

Writing

EXAM STRATEGY

When writing an article, try to write an introduction that will interest the reader and that avoids clichés and sweeping generalizations. Things to include are: asking rhetorical questions; citing shocking statistics; describing a situation in detail or quoting a famous person.

11 Which of the following is a good opening for the exam task below? Match openings A–C to the categories above and then write your own openings for the remaining categories.

a The average American teenager spends over three hours a day watching TV and will watch even more as he or she grows older.
b Mum, Dad and their two children are sitting at dinner. But they're not sitting around the table; instead they're sitting in a semi-circle so that they can all watch their favourite TV programme while eating. That, unfortunately, seems to be a very typical picture in many homes in the 21st century.
c Nowadays, everyone has at least one TV at home and wastes way too much time watching it.

12 **EXAM TASK** There is a discussion in your school magazine about the educational role of TV. Write an article to give your opinion on the topic. Include the following points:

- Give your opinion of news programmes on TV.
- Recommend an educational TV programme that supports your argument.
- Describe an educational programme that you watched recently.
- Say what other things television is useful for.

Exam insight 4

Reading

EXAM STRATEGY

Look at the words before and after each gap. Look for links between these words, and words in the sentences that have been taken out. These links will help you to put the sentences in the right places.

1 Read the text in exercise 2 quickly to get an idea of what it is about. Then read it more carefully and answer the questions. Use the bold words in sentences A–F in exercise 2 to help you.

Paragraph 1
'The result looks exactly like …' – **The result of what?**

Paragraph 2
'In fact, demand …' – **Demand for what?**

Paragraph 3
' … carbon dioxide emissions … methane emissions …' – **What kind of issues are these?**

Paragraph 4
'Humans have a tendency to enjoy meat.' – **How might this affect the issue being discussed?**

Paragraph 5
'Nor was there …' – **In what way is the word 'Nor' important? What does it tell you?**

Paragraph 6
'There are many steps …' – **What steps are these?**
'… to address that issue.' – **What issue?**

2 **EXAM TASK** Complete the text with sentences A–F.

A **And, increasingly**, inhabitants of developing countries, India and China in particular, are consuming more and more meat.
B Dr Post's research, therefore, and **these** new technological developments, are of vital importance.
C There was no fat in his burger, which explained the dryness and the rather bland taste.
D The only **natural** ingredients used were egg and breadcrumbs to help hold everything together, and beetroot juice and saffron to give colour.
E Adding fat and blood cells is already on the agenda. **At the moment**, they can only work with small pieces of meat.
F Can we really afford to increase the natural production of meat whilst **ignoring environmental concerns**?

Listening

EXAM STRATEGY

Try and identify the purpose of each text. What is the speaker trying to do and why? This will help you to understand what the speaker is saying.

A BURGER? CERTAINLY – THAT'LL BE €250,000

It looks like a burger. It tastes more or less like a burger. But it costs €250,000. What is it? It's the world's first artificial burger, created by Dr Mark Post and his team at Maastricht University. Three months ago, the process started with the extraction of stem cells from two different types of cow. These cells were grown in a laboratory and eventually turned into muscle fibre. The fibres were then straightened out and eventually pressed together to produce a burger. ¹_____ The result looks exactly like the real thing.

This project has far-reaching implications for the food industry and for food supply. The population of the world is expected to rise to 9.5 billion by 2070. ²_____ In fact, demand is predicted to double by the middle of the century. Where is it all going to come from? Is it possible to increase sufficiently the supply of naturally grown meat?

Already, 30% of the Earth's ice-free land is devoted to animals, either for grazing or for growing animal feed. Farm animals alone account for 5% of carbon dioxide emissions, but also an enormous 40% of methane emissions, a much more powerful and destructive greenhouse gas. ³_____ Post reckons that his laboratory-grown meat reduces energy use by 70% and cuts the need for land and water by 90%.

Of course, the best way to reduce the consumption of meat would be to encourage people to eat less, even to become vegetarian. However, that is an unlikely prospect. Richard Wrangham, a Professor at Harvard University, argues that eating meat is very much a part of our evolution. Learning how to cook and eat meat was one of the reasons that our brains were able to grow as big as they did. Humans have a tendency to enjoy meat. ⁴_____ 'People are going to continue wanting meat,' says Prof Wrangham, 'and a system of meat production that reduces environmental and ethical costs will be a great benefit.'

Most importantly of all, though, how does this new meat taste? The first artificial burger was cooked and tasted by a nutrition scientist and a food writer. Their verdict was 'close to meat' and 'not that juicy'. However, Dr Post was not unhappy. ⁵_____ Nor was there any blood in it. Dr Post and his team are working on introducing these elements into their next prototype.

What, then, does the future really hold for Dr Post and his team? There are many steps to take before anything like large-scale manufacture can be started. ⁶_____ They will need to develop new technologies to address that issue. It will be essential that the new product looks and tastes exactly like the real thing. Finally, any new food product would need to be tested and approved by the Food Standards Agency. All this will take time, money and effort. Yet the end product may make a substantial contribution to conserving the Earth's resources.

3 🔊 **3.19** Listen to the recordings. In which one is someone
   a trying to persuade the listener to do something?
   b giving information to the listener?
   c describing a situation?

4 **EXAM TASK** 🔊 **3.19** Listen again and choose the correct answers.

Recording 1
1 The people are talking about
   a different ways of blending food.
   b different interpretations of what 'fusion food' is.
   c the differences between European and Asian cuisine.
2 Wolfgang Puck is famous for
   a fusing Chinese and Malay cuisine.
   b fusing European and Asian cuisine.
   c being the founder of the 'fusion food' movement.

Recording 2
3 Where is the speaker reporting from?
   a An airport hotel.
   b A very busy upmarket restaurant.
   c Some open-air food stalls and restaurants.
4 The people who work there
   a are actually richer than they look.
   b are extremely well dressed.
   c work in offices during the day.

Recording 3
5 The speaker's aim is to
   a praise the location of the restaurant.
   b advertise Asian cuisine.
   c invite the listeners to a new eating place.
6 The food in the new restaurant is a fusion of
   a Malay Chinese and Indian cuisines.
   b Malaysian and Singaporean cuisines.
   c many Asian cuisines.

> **EXAM STRATEGY**
>
> For each question, check that the answers you have not chosen are wrong. Decide why they are wrong.

Use of English

> **EXAM STRATEGY**
>
> Remember how words often go together in particular patterns (e.g. *dangerous criminal*, *violent hatred*) or sometimes groups of words (e.g. *in the middle of*, *to express doubts about*, *heart and mind*). Think about these patterns when finding a word to fill the gap.

5 Match words 1–5 to words a–e.
   1 heart   a benefits
   2 blood   b fat
   3 saturated   c disease
   4 fat   d pressure
   5 health   e content

6 Complete the sentences with an appropriate preposition.
1 She's much fitter than she was, compared .... this time last year.
2 He was very unpopular for a time, but he's back .... favour now.
3 You should eat more fruit and vegetables. They are very good .... you.
4 I came .... the conclusion that she was wrong.
5 Unfortunately, he went rather deaf .... later life.

7 **EXAM TASK** Read the text. Choose the correct answers.

> Is there really a diet that will help you live longer? Increasingly, doctors and researchers are thinking ¹............... there is. For example, the inhabitants of the San Blas islands have an astonishingly low ²............... of heart disease: only nine in 100,000 people, compared to eighty-three in 100,000 among the Panamanians who live on the mainland. But why? There is an increasing body of evidence to suggest that diet plays a major role. What kind of diet?
>
> Most of us know about avoiding saturated fats, eating a lot of fruit and vegetables, and eating fish that is ³............... in omega-3 fats. However, there are some food and drink items, once thought of as unhealthy, that ⁴............... recently been reassessed as being good for your health.
>
> Nuts, for instance, were not on the list of healthy foods because of their fat ⁵................ However, most of the fat they contain is unsaturated and protects against heart disease, so they are now back in favour. In the San Blas islands, researchers have come to the conclusion that heart disease is so rare ⁶............... the islanders eat large quantities of dark chocolate. One of the ingredients of chocolate actually lowers blood pressure. Also on this list is coffee. A number of ⁷............... suggest that coffee has measurable health benefits and may even reduce the risk of dementia in later life.
>
> At last! I can now finish my day ⁸............... usual with a coffee and a bar of nutty chocolate. And I no longer have to feel guilty!

1 a how   b that   c why   d what
2 a rate   b grade   c kind   d portion
3 a strong   b great   c high   d elevated
4 a are   b were   c had   d have
5 a ingredient b items   c content d structure
6 a because   b although   c since   d when
7 a exams   b studies   c tests   d research
8 a like   b so   c the   d as

Use of English

8 What words can you generate from the following?

increase: *increasing, increased, increasingly*
expand: ....
produce: ....
drama: ....
develop: ....
export: ....
environment: ....
weak: ....

9 **EXAM TASK** Complete the text with the correct form of the words in brackets.

FISH FARMING – THE FUTURE

The ever-rising worldwide demand for animal products is set to have a major impact on the way we look after and harvest fish. The UN Food and Agriculture Organization estimates that the oceans have been overfished to such an extent that the wild fish left will not be enough to meet the needs of a growing and ¹..................... (increase) rich world population. As a result, food companies have taken the situation into their own hands and there has been a major ²..................... (expand) in the fish farming industry. This has been especially true in Asia, which now accounts for over 90% of global ³..................... (produce). Interviewed recently about her views on the subject, Diana Atwell of the World Fish Organization said: 'The most ⁴..................... (drama) rise is likely to be in China and India, and the rest of Asia, with their growing middle classes.'

For this ⁵..................... (develop) in the industry to be successful, however, strict rules and regulations need to be in place to head off potential disaster. By the middle of the last decade, Chile was the world's second largest ⁶..................... (export) of salmon and trout, with a business worth over £1 billion a year. But some scientists who visited and studied the Chilean operation, along with a large number of ⁷..................... (environment) campaigners, were quick to point out that the regulations were not of a high enough standard, and, in fact, contained many obvious ⁸..................... (weak). What followed was an outbreak of disease which wiped out huge numbers of fish. 'The industry will continue to grow,' says Diana Atwell, 'but there is an urgent need for controls and inspections to guarantee hygiene and quality.'

Speaking

10 Correct the mistakes in the sentences.
1 I would to choose the first show.
2 This dish seems as the most appealing to me.
3 The first slogan sounds more convincingly.
4 I'd rather to not go to an open-air restaurant.
5 I'd prefer being part of the first team.

11 **EXAM TASK** Look at the pictures. Read the statement and give your opinion about it. Respond to any counter-arguments appropriately.

Schools should do more to help young people choose their future profession.

Informed choice is the key to your future.

Writing

EXAM STRATEGY

Remember that if you are writing a for and against essay, you should present both arguments. If you are only required to give your opinion, you should just present one point of view.

12 Which of a–d below would be suitable for a for and against essay and which for an opinion essay?
a Lives of rich people can be negative as well as positive.
b Healthy diet and nutrition should be part of the school curriculum.
c It is not advisable for parents to give their children absolutely everything.
d There are many advantages to GM food; however, there are also some drawbacks.

13 **EXAM TASK** Most people are in favour of school canteens only offering healthy food. Write an essay giving your opinion on the subject. Include the following points:

- Describe what sort of food your school canteen offers.
- Describe what food students can buy elsewhere during the school day.
- Describe the last time you ate in the school canteen and what you ate.
- Suggest a possible solution to the problem of offering healthy food and also making the school canteen popular with students.

Exam insight 5

Reading

1 Below are two texts about engineering and engineers.
   1 Which text might you find in
      a a dictionary of biography?
      b a newspaper?
   2 Which text
      a reports on a new initiative by a company?
      b gives facts about someone's life?
   3 Answer the questions.
      a What was Dyson's first original invention?
      b What is his most famous invention?
      c Which of his inventions has not been successful?
      d What does the Sevcon company make?
      e What problem does the company have?

2 **EXAM TASK** Read the texts and choose the correct answers.

A

Sir James Dyson (b. 2 May 1947)

Dyson was born in Cromer, Norfolk, UK and attended Gresham's School, Holt from 1956 to 1965. He spent a year at the Byam Shaw School of Art, followed by four years at the Royal College of Art, where he studied furniture and interior design. His career as an inventor began at the Royal College of Art and, shortly after leaving, he created his first original invention: the Ballbarrow – a garden wheelbarrow that had a ball at the front instead of a wheel.

In the late 1970s, Dyson developed what would become his trademark invention: the bagless vacuum cleaner. With the UK market in disposable vacuum cleaner bags standing at £100 million, he found that he was unable to interest any of the major vacuum cleaner manufacturers in his product. He therefore started production in Japan, where he won the International Design Fair prize in 1991. He opened a research centre and factory in Malmesbury in Wiltshire in 1993. And the Dyson Dual Cyclone vacuum cleaner quickly became the fastest-selling UK vacuum cleaner of all time, and one of the most popular brands in the country.

More recent inventions by Dyson include a washing machine, called the ContraRotator, which was not a success; the Air Blade, a fast hand drier; and the Air Multiplier, a fan without blades, both of which have proved very popular.

However, Dyson's success has not been without its difficulties, from the rejection of his ideas and inventions to the copying of his products. Every year his company spends millions of pounds dealing with the theft of the company's intellectual property. One of the earliest cases was when Dyson took Hoover UK to court for copying his Dyson Dual Cyclone, and he won around £3 million. He has also been strongly criticized for moving some of his production from England to Malaysia, a move he insists was essential to allow further investment in research and development.

1 Which of these statements about James Dyson is true?
   a He is an engineer by training.
   b He started inventing things after he left art college.
   c He spent five years studying art.
   d He invented the first wheelbarrow.
2 Major vacuum cleaner companies were not interested in Dyson's invention because
   a it was made in Japan.
   b they made too much money selling disposable bags.
   c it hadn't yet won a design award.
   d Dyson had his own factory.
3 Dyson had problems because
   a people stole millions of pound from his factories.
   b he was not able to move production to Malaysia.
   c he found it difficult to reproduce his ideas.
   d Hoover UK made a vacuum cleaner that was too similar to his.

B

Engineering company Sevcon is by no means a household name in the UK, yet it is a major global player in the design and manufacture of control systems for electronic vehicles. The company has been in business since 1961 and employs around 100 people in the north-east of England.

Despite its huge reputation in the industry and the obvious attraction of working for a world leader in innovation and design, the recruitment of engineers has been proving problematic for Sevcon – so much so that the company has set up its own sponsorship scheme for university students.

Sevcon is investing £200,000 in eight students, taking them through engineering degree courses at Newcastle and Northumbria universities over the next four years. Sevcon covers the students' tuition fees for the course; the students work for Sevcon during their holidays. Provided that the students pass all their exams, they are guaranteed a job at Sevcon at the end of their course, which they are obliged to take up for a period of twelve months. After that, they are free to stay or to leave.

'We hope that once they have been up here, worked and studied here, loved us for who we are and what we do, they will want to stay,' says chief executive, Matt Boyle. 'It's a good investment for us. The potential opportunities for our business are tantalizing, and we need skilled staff to help us achieve that.'

With a desperate shortage of good engineering students coming out of British universities, Matt Boyle is hoping that Sevcon has gone some way to solving its staffing crisis.

4 What would be the best headline for the second article?
   a Problems for engineering students in the UK
   b Universities enrol too few engineering students
   c UK company finances engineering students through university
   d UK company leads the world in electronic innovation

5 Sevcon wants to
  a become better known in the UK.
  b attract more engineers to work for it.
  c set up its own university course.
  d recruit 100 engineers over four years.
6 Which of the following sentences is a fact, not an opinion?
  a British universities are producing too few engineers.
  b The sponsorship scheme will solve Sevcon's recruitment problem.
  c Sevcon has a good working environment.
  d Sevcon is set to grow enormously in the future.

Listening

EXAM STRATEGY

Read the questions before you listen. When you read the questions, think about what kind of language (words, phrases and sentences) might be used and which might help you to find the right answer.

3 **3.20** Read the questions for the recordings. Then look at the words and phrases below. Mark each item 1, 2 or 3 according to which recording you think you will hear it in. Listen and check.

■ Better education helps … ■ … the political microscope … ■ … make them and their families sick ■ … the earliest surviving written word … ■ … an international charity helping to … ■ … the developing world …
■ … one of the foremost experts in linguistics … ■ … donate …
■ The taxation system is not helping people …
■ … criminal justice system … ■ … paperwork and bureaucracy … ■ … subjective …

4 **EXAM TASK** **3.20** Listen and choose the correct answers.

Recording 1
1 What is the purpose of this recording?
  a To give listeners an item of news.
  b To ask listeners for money.
  c To explain some health problems.
2 What does Aquarius ultimately hope to achieve?
  a To provide better food for the population.
  b To provide better education to children.
  c To give people the chance to escape poverty.

Recording 2
3 Who chose the most important 100 words in English?
  a The *Daily Mail*.
  b A language expert.
  c A team of linguists.
4 Where was the word 'roe' found?
  a On the bone of a small deer.
  b On a sheep's bone.
  c On a wall.

Recording 3
5 What is the main intention of the speaker?
  a To get fairer taxes.
  b To improve the police.
  c To get elected.
6 The speaker thinks that
  a People who work hard are not rewarded enough.
  b Good health and education systems make society fairer.
  c The present government is addressing the right issues.

Use of English

5 Match the verbs to the meanings.

a
drop in	go to sleep
drop off	leave
drop back	fall behind
drop out	visit

b
take up	look like
take after	start
take on	leave
take off	employ

6 Cross out the most unlikely option in each box where there is a choice.

commercial	radio
	break
	success
	win

a reversal of	policy
	fortunes
	vehicles
	roles

7 **EXAM TASK** Complete the text with appropriate words.

Steve Jobs 1955–2011

Steve Jobs was born in California in 1955, to a Syrian father and a Swiss-American mother. Adopted at ¹……………… by Paul and Clara Jobs, he went to school in Cupertino and then enrolled in Reed College, Portland, Oregon. However, he stayed only a semester before dropping ²………………. Eventually, Jobs settled on a job at Atari Inc., but that too was short-lived, as he soon took ³……………… to spend seven months travelling in India.

On his return, Jobs returned to Atari, but, by 1975, had left to found Apple Computers with neighbourhood friend Steve Wozniak. Wozniak single-handedly invented the first Apple Computer, which sold for $666.66. By 1980, the Apple computer was on its third version, the company was listed on the stock market, and Jobs and Wozniak were ⁴……………… millionaires.

In 1985, Jobs resigned. He moved on to found a new company: NeXTStep. The company was not a commercial ⁵.......................... However, it was a NeXTStep computer that Tim Berners-Lee used to invent the World Wide Web. During this time, Jobs also started graphics company Pixar and became involved with the Disney Corporation.

In 1996, Apple acquired NeXTStep and Jobs ⁶.......................... to the Apple boardroom. This heralded a remarkable reversal of ⁷.......................... for the company: from near bankruptcy in 1996 to profitability in 1998. By 2011, Apple was the world's most valuable public company.

In 2004, Jobs was diagnosed with cancer. ⁸.......................... his condition initially responded to treatment, he died on 5 October 2011. He will be remembered as a great entrepreneur and inventor, and as a charismatic pioneer of the personal computer revolution.

Use of English

8 Which part of speech should go into each gap? Why?

1 All .... must leave the building until the police declare it safe.
2 She's very .... She just won't take 'no' for an answer.
3 I wouldn't accuse him of ...., but who else suddenly has lots of money?
4 I've never worked with him. I only know him ....
5 This class caters for people of all ...., from beginner to advanced.
6 I'll try to get it for you by Friday if at all .... possible.
7 I .... wanted a first edition of that book.
8 She was .... in her attempt to reach the final of the competition, winning her semi-final easily.

9 **EXAM TASK** Complete the sentences with the correct form of the words in brackets.

1 We've moved from the city centre into a quiet .... (reside) area.
2 I'm so depressed. It's been raining .... (persist) all day.
3 He told me .... (honest) that he had no idea who had taken my book.
4 It's not that he's .... (social). I think he's just rather shy.
5 I know he can't see well, but his .... (able) doesn't stop him from living a full life.
6 The conditions inside a 19th century prison were absolutely .... (human).
7 He designed his own computer to his own .... (specify).
8 She was very upset that her application didn't .... (success).

Speaking

EXAM STRATEGY

When justifying your choice/rejection of the photos, try to avoid using the same arguments for two pictures.

10 Which of these justifications use the same argument for both pictures?

a This school seems boring, while the other one looks interesting.
b School A looks traditional, and I think traditional methods of learning work best because they've been tested for years. On the other hand, school B looks like it's all about fun, and I'm afraid I would focus only on that and wouldn't work very hard.
c This teacher looks very strict and serious, and I don't like that. I like the other teacher because he looks like a lenient teacher, and I think his lessons would be fun.

11 **EXAM TASK** Look at the three photos. You have to choose one of them to include in a poster on the theme of 'the dark side of technology'. Answer the following questions:

- Which photo will you choose and why? Why are you rejecting the other two photos?
- Do you play computer games? How often?
- Should computer games that are too violent be banned completely?

Writing

12 **EXAM TASK** Some people say that politicians cannot be successful unless they have an online presence. Write an essay presenting arguments for and against. Include the following points:

- Describe how politicians can promote themselves online.
- Explain the benefits and disadvantages of this.
- Describe other ways in which politicians can make themselves heard.
- Describe how you think politicians could engage more with young people.

Grammar reference and practice 1

1.1 Tenses revision

Present simple and present continuous

We use the present simple:
- to talk about routines or habits (often with adverbs of time, e.g. *always*, *sometimes*, *never*).
  Does your school always celebrate 'We Day'?
  Yes, it does. / No, it doesn't.
- to talk about facts and general truths.
  We meet many different challenges in life, but we don't always overcome them.
- with verbs that describe states: *believe*, *hate*, *have*, *know*, *like*, *need*, *prefer*, *see*, *seem*, *think*, *understand*, *want*.
  I think that global poverty is the most important issue in the world today.

We use the present continuous:
- to describe an action that is happening now, or around now (often with time expressions, e.g. *right now*, *at the moment*).
  Today we're collecting money for an important charity.
- to describe a temporary, changing or developing situation.
  Is your local community becoming more co-operative?
  Yes, it is. / No, it isn't.
- to describe irritating habits (often with *always*).
  He's always checking his texts on his mobile phone.

State verbs

We never use continuous tenses with state verbs, e.g. *believe*, *know*, *understand*, *like*, etc.
We believe his promises.
NOT ~~We're believing his promises.~~
He hasn't understood the argument.
NOT ~~He hasn't been understanding the argument.~~

Past simple and past continuous

We use the past simple:
- to talk about a completed action that happened in the past.
  Did you travel to the USA last year?
  Yes, I did. / No, I didn't.
- to describe two or more actions that happened one after the other.
  He climbed over the wall and jumped in through the window.
- to talk about two connected actions that happened at around the same time.
  When we saw the fire, we called the emergency services.

We use the past continuous:
- to describe a scene in the past or an action that was happening at a particular time.
  She was waving at us, but we weren't looking at her.
- to talk about a longer action that happens at the same time as a shorter action, or a longer action that is interrupted by a shorter action.
  Were you listening to the radio when you heard the news? Yes, I was. / No, I wasn't.
  I remembered her name while she was talking.

Present perfect and present perfect continuous

We use the present perfect:
- to talk about actions that happened at some unspecified point in the past.
  She's experienced many extraordinary things in her life.
- to talk about experiences with *never*, *already*, *just* and *yet*.
  They've already raised £5,000 for charity, but they haven't achieved their target yet.
- to talk about actions that began in the past, but continue up to the present moment, often with *for* and *since*.
  How long have you been part of this organization?
  I've been a member for fifteen years.

We use the present perfect continuous:
- to talk about actions that began in the past, but continue up to the present, often with *for* and *since*.
  He's been campaigning for a change in policy for six years.
- to talk about an action that has happened repeatedly in the past and that is still happening now.
  We haven't been sitting idly at home, we've been working to improve the situation.
- to talk about a very recent action which has either just finished or which has just been interrupted.
  You look very tired. Have you been working hard?
  Yes, I have. / No, I haven't.

Past perfect

We use the past perfect to talk about something that happened before something else in the past.
He couldn't read and write because he had never been to school.

1 Match 1–6 to a–f to make sentences.

1 I've been following his blog since
2 I usually spend the summer at the beach, but this year
3 I wasn't studying yesterday because
4 I did very well in the test because
5 I remembered the phone number
6 I left home when I was sixteen and

a I was helping my friend to fix his car.
b I moved to England to find work.
c I heard about it from friend.
d I had studied hard for several weeks.
e I'm doing some voluntary work for an overseas charity.
f while I was dialing it.

Grammar reference and practice 1

2 Choose the correct words.

1 Where **do you usually go / are you usually going** on holiday?
2 They **didn't hear / haven't heard** from him since last July.
3 He **drove / was driving** to work when he **saw / was seeing** the accident.
4 I **had never experienced / never experienced** such a reaction before then.
5 It's **developing / develops** into a very challenging project.
6 Where **did you first learn / have you first learned** about this initiative?
7 Sorry I'm late. **Did you wait / Have you been waiting** long?
8 They **left / were leaving** their jobs in the city and **had started / started** up their own travel company.

3 Complete the text with the correct form of the verbs in brackets. Sometimes more than one answer is possible.

My life ¹.......................... (change) dramatically in 2010, when I ².......................... (lose) my job as an accountant. My father ³.......................... (die) the year before, and he ⁴.......................... (leave) me some money. I ⁵.......................... (look) at some travel magazines and I ⁶.......................... (think) about spending the money on an exotic holiday, when I ⁷.......................... (hear) a programme on the radio about orphanages in India. 'I ⁸.......................... (want) to make a difference,' I thought to myself. 'Why ⁹.......................... (I / dream) about holidays when I can help other people?' Since then, I ¹⁰.......................... (travel) several times to India and I ¹¹.......................... (help) to rebuild an orphanage in Calcutta. It ¹².......................... (be) an amazing experience.

1.2 ■ Past perfect and past perfect continuous

We use the past perfect to describe completed events that happened before another event in the past (often with time expressions such as *by the time*, *when*, *before*, *after* and *until*).
She had already learned how read and write by the time she started school.

We use the past perfect continuous:
- to describe ongoing activities leading up to a more recent past event.
  They had been walking for hours when they saw the house in the distance.
- to give background information about an event.
  She was concerned because he hadn't been sleeping well recently.
- to emphasize the duration of an activity.
  We'd been dancing for hours and we were tired.

1 Choose the correct sentence endings.

1 By the time he reached the prison gates,
  a a large crowd had already gathered to greet him.
  b a large crowd had already been gathering to greet him.
2 When the visitors arrived at the island,
  a they had travelled for many days.
  b they had been travelling for many days.
3 His head ached and his eyes were sore because
  a he had studied since five o'clock in the morning.
  b he had been studying since five o'clock in the morning.
4 Until I read Mandela's autobiography,
  a I hadn't realized that he had spent twenty-seven years in prison.
  b I hadn't been realizing that he had spent twenty-seven years in prison.
5 We heard about the riot
  a after we had left the building.
  b after we had been leaving the building.
6 They were angry because
  a they had waited for many hours.
  b they had been waiting for many hours.

2 Complete the sentences. Use the past perfect or past perfect continuous form of the verbs below.

■ not finish ■ work ■ look for ■ swim ■ climb
■ not expect ■ shop

1 She .... for thirty minutes before she realized that she couldn't see the shore.
2 He .... the speech before the crowd began to cheer.
3 By the time we reached the top of the mountain, we .... over 300 metres.
4 She .... so many people to come until she arrived and the room was full.
5 He was extremely tired because he .... hard all day.
6 How long .... (you) the book before you found it?
7 We .... for hours by the time we found the gift we wanted to buy.

Grammar reference and practice 2

2.1 Future tenses

Present simple

We use the present simple to talk about future events that are based on a schedule or timetable.
School finishes at half past three in the afternoon.

Present continuous

We use the present continuous to talk about arrangements for a future time.
We're meeting our friends at the Opera House tonight.

will + infinitive

We use *will* and *won't* to talk about:
- promises and hopes for the future, often with verbs like *hope*, *expect* or *promise* + *that* (you can omit *that*).
  I promise (that) I'll finish my geography project.
- predictions, often after *I think* or *I don't think*, or future facts that we are certain about.
  We don't think (that) the weather will be very good tomorrow.
  Our children's lives will be very different from ours.
- future facts or future predictions that we are less certain about, with *probably*.
  They probably won't come to the lecture this afternoon.
- things we decide to do at the moment of speaking (instant decisions, offers, promises).
  Look at this mess! I'll tidy up.

going to + infinitive

We use *be* + *going to* to talk about:
- intentions and plans.
  I'm going to think more carefully about where my food comes from.
- predictions about the future based on evidence, for example something we can see in the present.
  Look at that car! It's going to crash!

may / might

We use *may* or *might* when we are less certain about the future. There is very little difference in meaning between the two words.
We may / might go to the beach. It depends on the weather.

1 Choose the correct words.
1. Tomorrow we're **going to / will** decorate our house: we've already bought the paint and the brushes.
2. A Where's your homework, Anna?
   B I promise I'm **finishing / 'll finish** it tonight, Mr James.
3. I hope we **might not / won't** destroy our marine environment.
4. Your train **leaves / is leaving** at half past five.
5. She**'s going to / might** visit Uluru when she goes to Australia. She hasn't decided yet.
6. Ellen Jones **comes / is coming** to dinner later.

2 Write questions and answers using the correct form of *be going to*, the present simple, *will* or *may / might*.
1. A What / you / do / at the weekend?

   B I don't know yet. I / go swimming or I / visit / my cousins in London.

2. A What time / the film / start?

   B The doors / open / at 5.30 p.m. / but / the film / not start / until 5.50 p.m.

3. I think / you / enjoy / this book.

4. She / not / return / to college / after the holiday. She / work / at her mother's company.

5. I think / we / much more concerned / global warming in the future.

6. By 2050 / everyone on the planet / probably / live / for over 100 years.

2.2 Future continuous, future perfect and future perfect continuous

Future continuous

We use the future continuous with a future time expression to talk about an action that will be in progress at a certain time in the future.
This time tomorrow, we'll be moving to our new house!
We also use the future continuous to talk about a future action that is fixed or decided. A time expression is not always necessary.
Will Pete be playing at the concert?

Future perfect

We use the future perfect to talk about a completed action or event in the future. We often use *by* or *before* + a time expression to say when the action will be finished.
Everything will have changed by the time you get back.
They won't have finished the work before the weekend.
A time expression is not always necessary.
There's no doubt she will have entertained her audience, but will she have changed their minds?

Future perfect continuous

We use the future perfect continuous to talk about an action that will continue up to a particular time in the future.
How long will you have been studying when you graduate?
We often use the future perfect continuous with a time expression with *for* to focus on the duration of an activity.
I will have been working for ten weeks on this project by the time I finally complete it.

Grammar reference and practice 2 111

Grammar reference and practice 2

1 Complete the sentences with the correct future forms below.

- will have been travelling ■ will be travelling
- will have travelled

1 She .... to six countries in six months by February.
2 I .... across Australia next month.
3 We .... for more than four weeks by the time we finally arrive in Darwin.

- won't have studied ■ will have been studying
- won't be studying

4 By the time I take my final exam, I .... at this college for four years.
5 They .... all the tenses in English by the end of this year.
6 She .... ecology next year. She really doesn't enjoy the subject.

2 Complete the sentences with the correct form of the verbs in brackets. Use the future continuous, future perfect or future perfect continuous.

1 By this time next year I .... (visit) every major city in the UK.
2 Over the next month they .... (appear) at all the major music festivals in the UK.
3 You read so fast! You .... (read) the whole book before dinner!
4 He'll be furious when we finally arrive – he .... (wait) for us for three hours!
5 This time next month, we .... (sit) on a beach and .... (relax) in the sunshine.
6 When we finish this trip we .... (wear) the same clothes for six months.

2.3 ■ Future time clauses

Time clauses link an event in the time clause with another event in the main clause.

- Future time clauses begin with time words like *until* (up to a point in time), *as soon as* (at the moment when / immediately after), *by the time* (one event will be completed before another), *while* (during a period of time), *unless* (if not), *before*, *after* and *when*.
  I'll look after your things until you come home.
  By the time you read this, I will be in Paris!
  Don't touch the animals unless you want to get hurt.
- When the time clause comes at the beginning of a sentence, we separate it from the main clause with a comma.
  When we've arrived at our destination, we'll unpack our suitcases and explore the town.
- We often use the present simple or future tenses in the main clause. There is little difference in meaning. We **never** use *will / won't* after the future time clauses.
  As soon as you arrive, we'll have some food.
  NOT ~~As soon as you will arrive, ...~~

1 Complete sentence b so that it has a similar meaning to sentence a.

1 a I'll buy the tickets and then I'll call you.
  b As soon as ....
2 a If he doesn't read the guidebook, he won't understand what he's looking at.
  b Unless ....
3 a When you arrive at the hotel, it will already be dark.
  b By the time ....
4 a We will be happy when we know what the result is.
  b Until ....
5 a She will be studying for the exam and at the same time he will be rebuilding his house.
  b While ....
6 a When I leave the house, I'll lock the doors.
  b Before ....

2.4 ■ Modifying adverbs with gradable and non-gradable adjectives

Gradable adjectives describe qualities that you can measure, e.g. *knowledgeable, tedious, interesting*. We can say a person is more or less *knowledgeable*. With gradable adjectives we use grading adverbs, e.g. *a little bit*, *particularly*, *very*.
Our tour guide was very knowledgeable.
Non-gradable adjectives describe qualities that are absolute or extreme, e.g. *ideal, awesome, overwhelming*. They cannot be used as comparative adjectives. We cannot say that something is more or less *ideal*: either it is ideal or it is not. With non-gradable adjectives we use non-grading adverbs, e.g. *utterly, absolutely*.
Your suggestion is absolutely ideal.
The adverbs *quite, really, pretty* and *fairly* can be used with both types of adjectives. With gradable adjectives, they emphasize the nature, whereas with non-gradable adjectives they describe the degree. *Quite* means 'fairly' when used with gradable adjectives, and it means 'to the greatest degree' when used with non-gradable adjectives.
I found the film quite tedious.
The experience has been quite overwhelming.

1 Choose the correct words.

1 My new exercise routine is **not particularly** / **totally** exhausting.
2 The whole meal was fantastic, and the dessert was **particularly** / **fairly** delicious.
3 There was something **a little bit** / **utterly** extraordinary about her performance.
4 It's a shame the concert was **absolutely** / **really** disappointing.
5 The new shopping centre is **absolutely** / **very** enormous.
6 Since her first TV role she has become **quite** / **utterly** well-known.

Grammar reference and practice 3

3.1 Articles

a / an

We use *a / an*:
- with non-specific things.
  I want to read a magazine.
- the first time we mention something.
  I can see a tall house in the distance.
- with any member of a group or jobs.
  He's a football player. She's a teacher.
- to express *each* or *per*.
  My father eats three eggs a day.

We use *a* before words that begin with a consonant. We use *an* before words that begin with a vowel or a silent 'h'.
She's an honest friend, but she isn't an outgoing person.

the

We use *the*:
- with specific things.
  I want to read the magazine on the table.
- with things that have already been mentioned.
  I can see a tall house in the distance. The house is red.
- when there is only one of something.
  The Prime Minister made an important announcement.
- with superlative adjectives.
  She's the fastest runner in our school.
- with a general statement about all the things referred to by that noun.
  Scientists believe that the woolly mammoth became extinct because of climate change.
- with adjectives like *wealthy*, *unemployed*, *disabled*, to talk about groups of people who share a characteristic.
  This new law is intended to protect the elderly.
- with countries that include words like *kingdom*, *states* or *republic*.
  the USA, the UK, the Republic of Ireland
- with countries and islands that have plural nouns.
  the Maldives, the Orkneys
- with rivers, seas, oceans, canals, forests, deserts, gulfs, peninsulas and geographical areas.
  the Nile, the Alps, the Lake District, the Black Forest
- with names of hotels, famous buildings and organizations.
  the United Nations, the Hilton Hotel
- with families.
  We're going to visit the Wilsons tonight.

no article

We use no article:
- with things in general or before general plural nouns.
  He's got blue eyes.
- with abstract nouns.
  Some people believe that love conquers everything.
- with uncountable nouns.
  I like fish but I hate fruit.
- with most countries, towns, streets, lakes, mountains, continents and islands.
  France, Paris, Church Road, Lake Titicaca.
- with languages and nationalities.
  He's Chinese but he speaks English perfectly.

1 Complete the sentences with *a(n)*, *the* or – (no article).

1. Last year I went to .... the UK where I visited .... London and went to .... British Museum.
2. I was filled with .... sadness when I heard about .... tragic death of .... Queen.
3. My sister is .... student in .... Madrid.
4. She's got .... enormous bedroom with .... purple curtains, ... designer furniture and .... pink ceiling.
5. He's not .... best singer in the world, but he writes .... amazing songs.
6. She's .... Brazilian, so she speaks .... Portuguese.
7. I need .... holiday. A trip down .... Nile would be amazing!
8. That's .... boy I told you about yesterday. His father is .... actor.

3.2 Determiners

We use the following determiners to talk about quantity before countable and uncountable nouns.

- We use *any* in negative sentences. We can modify *any* with *hardly*, meaning 'almost no'.
  There were hardly any boats at sea.
- We use *some* in affirmative sentences and offers.
  Some students in the class agreed with her.
- We use *a lot of* to mean a large number or amount.
  There were a lot of people working on the art show.
- We use *none of* to mean 'not any'. We can modify *none of* with *almost*, meaning 'not quite'. We don't generally use *of* when there is no other determiner (e.g. article or possessive). Instead we use *no*.
  (Almost) none of the students finished their homework.
  We've got no plans this weekend.
- *All (of)* can modify nouns and pronouns. It is used to talk about a whole amount. We can modify *all* with *almost*, meaning 'not quite'. Before a noun with no determiner, we don't usually use *of*.
  All fish is horrible! NOT ~~All of fish is horrible!~~

We use the following determiners with countable nouns:
- We use *few* meaning 'not enough' or 'a small number of' and *a few* to mean 'a small number of'.
  Few people clean up their rubbish.
  A few people turned up to help clean the beach.
- We often use *many* in negatives and questions. We can add *too* or *far too* in front of *many* and *few* to modify them. *Far* means a greater amount. We use *many of* in front of determiners and pronouns.
  There were (far too) many people on the beach.
  How many of you went to the beach?

Grammar reference and practice 3

- We use *several* to talk about more than two but not many.
  There were several plastic bottles floating in the sea.
- We use the following determiners with uncountable nouns.
- We use *much* with negatives and questions. We can modify *much* with *far too* meaning a great amount. We don't generally use *of* when there is no other determiner (e.g. article or possessive).
  She spent (far too) much money on those flip-flops.
- We use *little* to mean 'not enough' or 'a small amount' and *a little* to mean 'a small amount'.
  Fish need little feeding.
  There's a little milk left in the fridge.

1 Choose the correct words.

1. We've got **much / little** money, but we've got **a lot of / much** friends.
2. She's sad because **too much / several** of her relatives forgot her birthday.
3. We can't make bread because we've got **hardly any / lots of** flour.
4. There are **almost no / almost none of** cars here.
5. **Almost no / Almost none of** the pens work.
6. Can I have **a little / a few** help, please? I've got **a few / a little** questions about this work.

3.3 ■ Verb patterns

When two verbs appear together in a sentence, the first one can be followed by the infinitive (with or without *to*) or the *-ing* form of the verb.

- Verbs with *-ing* (*avoid, consider, discuss, enjoy, finish, imagine, recommend, suggest*)
  Have you finished reading the book?
- Infinitive with *to* (*agree, hope, plan, afford, need, prefer, intend, refuse*)
  She agreed to talk to us, but refused to help.
- Object + infinitive with *to* (*ask, expect, get, help, inspire, want*)
  She inspired me to write my first novel.
- Object + infinitive without *to* (*let* and *make*)
  They must let him see the results.
  She made him finish his work.

Some verbs change their meaning depending on whether they are followed by infinitive with *to* or verb + *-ing*.

- *remember / forget + -ing*: remember / forget something
  I remember meeting Fred at a party and I'll never forget hearing him sing!
- *remember / forget + to*: something you should do or want to do
  Please remember to lock the door when you go out!
- *regret + -ing*: be sorry for doing something
  I regret not telling her about the party.
- *regret + to*: give some bad news
  I regret to tell you that you weren't successful.
- *try + -ing*: do something as an experiment
  I tried cooking with butter instead of oil, but I didn't like the taste.
- *try + to*: attempt to do something which is difficult
  She tried to climb the mountain, but she didn't reach the top.

- *like + -ing*: enjoy
  I like swimming but I hate surfing.
- *like + to*: do something as a habit
  I like to swim every morning before work.
- *stop + -ing*: no longer do something
  I stopped talking to Henry.
  (I don't talk to Henry any more.)
- *stop + to*: stop in order to do something different
  I stopped to talk to Henry.
  (I stopped my other activities in order to talk to Henry.)
- *go on + -ing*: continue to do something
  Shall we go on looking at these pictures or not?
- *go on + to*: do something after completing something else
  We talked about books and then went on to discuss politics.

1 Complete the sentences with the correct form of the verbs in brackets.

1. Please don't stop .... (sing).
2. I think I'll try .... (wear) my new jeans.
3. They refused .... (listen) to us, even though we tried .... (persuade) them.
4. I don't remember .... (switch) the oven off this morning. Maybe I should go home and check!
5. We like .... (walk) home in the afternoon because the bus is usually very full.
6. She ate four biscuits and then went on .... (have) a huge piece of cake.

3.4 ■ Ordering events in a story

To describe one action that happens before another action we can use *having* + past participle and *after* + *-ing*. The first clause is separated by a comma.
Having run to the station, she caught the train.
After spending all afternoon by the pool, he went to the beach.
To describe an action that happens at the same time as another action we can use a present participle or *as* + past simple. The first clause is separated by a comma.
Seeing them across the street, he called out.
As she walked past the shops, she saw exactly the dress she was looking for.

1 Match 1–5 to a–e to make sentences.

1. Listening to the radio,
2. After looking in the shed,
3. Having completed university,
4. As I boarded the plane,
5. Wanting some food,

a. I saw someone acting suspiciously.
b. I fell asleep.
c. they found the cat hiding there.
d. he went to the fridge.
e. she started looking for a job.

Grammar reference and practice 4

4.1 ▪ Talking about habitual behaviour

used to

We use *used to*:
- to talk about repeated past actions or habits.
  We used to spend the weekends at our aunt's house.
- to describe states in the past.
  Did you use to be scared of spiders when you were a child? Yes, I did, but I'm not scared of them now.
  We didn't use to live in the city, we used to live in a small village in the country.

Note the difference between:
- *used to* (repeated past actions, habits or states in the past that no longer happen now)
- *get used to* (become accustomed to; previously strange, but normal now)
- *be used to* (be accustomed to now; part of everyday life)

1 Rewrite the sentences that are incorrect.

1 I am used to love watching hospital dramas on TV, but now I'm not interested in them.

2 I know your job is difficult at the moment, but you will get used to it.

3 She doesn't get used to having such a big breakfast, she usually just has a piece of toast.

4 Did you use to go to my school?

5 I can't be used to the cold weather in this country!

6 We are used to cold water because we go swimming in the sea every morning.

would

We use *would*:
- to talk about repeated past actions or habits.
  We would spend the weekends at our aunt's house.

We **cannot** use *would* to talk about past states:
She used to be happy. NOT *She would be happy.*
They used to be able to play the piano. NOT *They would be able to play the piano.*
I used to have a pet frog. NOT *I would have a pet frog.*

Past simple

We use the past simple:
- to talk about repeated past actions and to say how long a situation went on for.
  For ten years we spent the weekends at our aunt's house.
- to describe states in the past.
  Were you scared of spiders when you were a child? Yes, I was, but I'm not scared of them now.
  We didn't live in the city, we lived in a small village in the country.

We have to use the past simple:
- to describe things in the past that happened only once.
  She moved to Cardiff in 2007.
  NOT *She would move to Cardiff in 2007.*
  NOT *She used to move to Cardiff in 2007.*

2 Complete the sentences with *would* or *used to*. If both are possible, use *would*.

1 When we lived in Brighton, my father .... (go) swimming in the sea every morning.

2 I .... (have) a small green bicycle when I was younger.

3 .... (you / believe) in ghosts when you were a child?

4 While they were on holiday, they .... (not / get) up before ten o'clock in the morning.

5 She .... (not / understand) her maths teacher at her last school.

6 Every year, in the summer, we .... (travel) three hundred kilometers to visit our grandmother in Birmingham.

7 She .... (like) sugar in her coffee, but now she hates it.

8 We .... (always / walk) home through the park when we finished school.

Present simple

We use the present simple:
- to talk about habits and repeated behaviour in the present.
  We spend the weekends at our aunt's house.

will

We use *will*:
- to express irritation or criticism.
  He will keep on losing the TV remote control.
- to describe typical behaviour.
  We will sometimes eat out in the evening.

Present continuous

We use the present continuous:
- to talk about repeated actions and events if they are around the time of speaking.
  Katie is seeing a lot of James at the moment.
- to describe habits that that are annoying. We often use *always*, *forever*, or *constantly* for emphasis.
  Your brother is always borrowing my phone!
  Why are you constantly complaining about the weather?

3 Choose the correct sentence endings.

1 My computer was stolen at the weekend
  a so I'm using the computer in the library this week.
  b so I use the computer in the library this week.

2 My friends
  a would talk when I want to watch TV. It's so irritating.
  b will talk when I want to watch TV. It's so irritating.

3 I've got a new fitness routine.
  a I'm always going for a swim after work.
  b I always go for a swim after work.

Grammar reference and practice 4

4 I'm not happy with my new phone,
  a the battery's always running out.
  b the battery always runs out.
5 She's never late for work;
  a she always leaves the house at 7 a.m.
  b she will leave the house at 7 a.m.
6 I'm not surprised you are upset but
  a you are talking to him angrily.
  b you will talk to him angrily.

4.2 Future in the past

When we're talking about the past, we sometimes want to refer to things which were in the future at that time.

would

We use *would*:
- to talk about general future possibilities, predictions, or expectations, but not definite plans. We use *would* especially when the future event was in the very distant future or lasted a long time.
  The discovery of antibiotics in 1929 would revolutionize medical care in the 20th century.
  Some of my friends believed the world would end in the year 2000.

was / were going to

We use *was / were going to*:
- to talk about plans or intentions.
  She was going to finish her homework, but then she decided to go out instead.
- to make a prediction.
  Some of my friends believed the world was going to end in the year 2000.

was / were to

We use *was / were to*:
- to talk about events that took place. We can also use *would* to convey the same meaning.
  He was to become a world-famous physicist by the time he was twenty-five.
  He would become a world-famous physicist by the time he was twenty-five.

was / were about to

We use *was / were about to*:
- to talk about an event that was in the very near future or events that took place immediately after another event.
  The war was over and the victory celebrations were about to begin.
- with a *when* time clause to describe an interrupted event.
  The doctors were about to perform the operation when they realized that the patient was still awake.

1 **Match 1–6 to a–f to make sentences.**
1 She was going to meet him at two o'clock
2 She was about to leave the house
3 She had always felt that
4 Her decision to leave her job
5 She thought her day had been pretty bad
6 She was going to town to meet the man

a when the phone rang.
b but then he phoned to say he would be late.
c but things were about to get much worse.
d would affect the rest of her life.
e who would eventually become her husband.
f her life would change when she left university.

2 **Rewrite the sentences using the words in brackets.**
1 We had planned to visit our grandmother over the weekend, but then we changed our minds. (going)
2 They intended to leave the house when they realized the windows were still open. (about)
3 We didn't know at the time that he would become so famous. (was)
4 In less than two months, we were going to leave school and begin the rest of our lives. (would)
5 We had packed our suitcases and we were going to begin our journey very soon. (about)
6 I believed that our situation would get far worse. (going)

3 **Complete the text with the verbs in brackets and *would, was / were going to, was / were to* or *was / were about to*. Sometimes more than one answer is possible.**

At 9.00 a.m. on 12 April 1961, Yury Gagarin [1]............... (become) the first cosmonaut to travel into space. His spacecraft, Vostok 1, launched at 9.07 a.m.; its mission [2]............... (orbit) the Earth once at a maximum altitude of 187 miles.
Gagarin studied at a trade school near Moscow and [3]............... (work) as a moulder in a factory. Instead he took a course in flying and went into the Soviet Air Force. He graduated in 1957 and only four years later [4]............... (enter) space.
Gagarin completed his mission, orbiting the Earth in 1 hour 29 minutes. The success of Vostok 1 [5]............... (make) him famous and [6]............... (advance) the fierce competition between the Soviet Union and the USA to send a man to the moon.
After his first flight, Gagarin [7]............... (never go) into space again, but he helped to train other cosmonauts. No one predicted that he [8]............... (die) in an accident on a routine flight just seven years after his historic mission.

Grammar reference and practice 5

5.1 Advice, obligation and prohibition

Advice

We use *should(n't)* + infinitive to give advice.
Should I look up new words in a dictionary? You should have a dictionary but you shouldn't use it every time you can't understand a word.

Ought to + infinitive and *should* + infinitive are very similar, but *should* is much more frequently used than *ought to*. The question form of *ought* is rarely used.
You ought to listen more to the teacher.

We use *had better (not)* + infinitive to give advice or a warning. Even though *had* is the past simple form of *have*, we use *had better* to give advice about the present or future. The question form of *had better* is very rarely used.
You'd better talk to her about the problem tomorrow.
You'd better not worry about it.

Obligation

We use *must* + infinitive to express necessity or strong obligation. The feeling of obligation is 'internal': it usually comes from the speaker him/herself.
I must write to thank my grandmother for the money she sent me.

We use *have to* + infinitive to express necessity or strong obligation. The feeling of obligation usually comes from an external source.
All students have to be at school by 8.00 a.m.

We use *need to* + infinitive to express mild obligation, usually from an external source. There is often a sense that fulfilling the obligation will benefit the speaker.
I need to finish my homework by Saturday morning because I want to go out in the afternoon.

We use *don't have to / needn't / don't need to* + infinitive to express lack of obligation.
You have to dress smartly for the wedding but you don't have to / needn't / don't need to wear a hat.

Prohibition

We use *mustn't* + infinitive to express strong prohibition.
You mustn't copy my essay! That's cheating!

1 Complete the sentences with the verbs below.

- needn't work ■ shouldn't work ■ mustn't work
- must work ■ have to work ■ should work

1 I .... harder this term. I don't want to fail my exams again.
2 We .... on this project tonight. We don't have to hand it in until Friday.
3 You .... so hard. You're always getting headaches.
4 You .... in the library. It's much quieter than your bedroom and you'll get more done.
5 Students .... on the library computers. These are for the teachers' use only.
6 We all .... on this new project for the next six months.

2 Rewrite the sentences using the words in brackets.

1 It's necessary for us to pay for this language course by Wednesday. (have to)
2 I advise you to listen to an English radio station for fifteen minutes every day. (should)
3 Students are not permitted to use their mobile phones in the classroom. (mustn't)
4 It's not necessary for you to live in France in order to learn French. (don't need to)
5 I don't think it's a good idea for them to go out tonight. (shouldn't)
6 We feel obliged to phone our cousins this evening. (must)

5.2 Past modals

Regret

We use *should have / shouldn't have / ought to have* + past participle to express regret or disapproval about something in the past and to say what the right thing to do was. The question form and negative past forms of *ought* are rarely used.
He shouldn't have been so rude to her. He should have apologized for his behaviour.
(He was rude. He didn't apologize.)
They ought to have revised before the exam.
(They didn't revise.)

Necessity

We use *needed to / had to* + infinitive to say that something was necessary in the past.
We needed to speak to the administrator before we could join the class. Then we had to sign some documents.

Lack of necessity

We use *didn't have to* + infinitive when something was not necessary and it **didn't** happen.
They didn't have to take an exam at the end of the course.
(They didn't take an exam.)
We use *needn't have* + past participle when something was not necessary and it **did** happen.
We needn't have run to the station. The train was delayed, so we had plenty of time.
(We ran to the station but it wasn't necessary.)
We use *didn't need to* when something was not necessary. It can mean that it **did** happen or that it **didn't** happen.
We didn't need to bring a book to read on the train. We spent the whole journey chatting.
(Maybe we brought a book and maybe we didn't, but a book wasn't necessary.)

Grammar reference and practice 5

1 Choose the correct words.
1 They **didn't have to hide / shouldn't have hidden** her bag. She was very upset about it.
2 We **needn't have driven / didn't have to drive** to the cinema. The bus service is excellent. Now we can't find a parking space!
3 You **should have brought / didn't need to bring** an umbrella. You're soaking wet!
4 I **needn't have made / didn't have to make** any food for the party, so I didn't.
5 They **had to leave / should have left** their car in the car park and walk from there to the theatre.
6 He **ought to have woken / didn't have to wake** up earlier. Now he's going to be late.

5.3 ■ Talking about ability

Ability in the present
We use *can / can't* + infinitive to talk about ability in the present.
Bella can act but she can't sing.
We can also use *be able to / not be able to* + infinitive. This form is far less common but we **must** use *be able to* after verbs that take the infinitive or *-ing*:
I like being able to speak Japanese. NOT ~~I like can speak Japanese.~~
I want to be able to skateboard. NOT ~~I want can skateboard.~~

Ability in the past
We use *could / couldn't* + infinitive to talk about general ability in the past.
My brother could run faster than anyone else in his class.
We also use *could / couldn't* with verbs of perception: *see, hear, feel, taste, smell, understand, know,* etc.
We could see the stage from our seats but we couldn't hear the actors' voices very well.
We use *was / were able to* + infinitive, *succeeded in* + *-ing* or *managed to* + infinitive to talk about ability on a specific occasion in the past.
They were able to build a new theatre on the grounds of the old one.
They succeeded in driving across the desert.
We managed to reach our destination.

Ability in the future
We use *will be able to* to talk about ability in the future.
She will be able to give us a lift to college after she passes her driving test.
We use *can / can't* to talk about specific arrangements in the future.
I can meet you at the library tomorrow, but I can't stay for long because I've got a tennis lesson.

1 Choose the correct sentence in each pair.
1 a We could feel the cold wind in our faces.
  b We succeeded in feeling the cold wind in our faces.
2 a I hate can't understand my cousins when they speak German.
  b I hate not being able to understand my cousins when they speak German.
3 a They managed in persuading him to change his mind.
  b They managed to persuade him to change his mind.
4 a We could leave the country before the beginning of the winter next year.
  b We were able to leave the country before the beginning of the winter next year.
5 a Will you be able to compete in next month's race?
  b Will you can compete in next month's race?
6 a She stopped being able to ride a bike after the car accident.
  b She stopped could ride a bike after the car accident.

2 Rewrite the sentences using the words in brackets.
1 It was difficult, but I was able to finish my work before breakfast. (managed to)
2 No one was speaking to her and she didn't understand why. (couldn't)
3 We don't have enough money now, but next year we're going to buy a new computer. (able to)
4 It's great because I can see the mountains from my bedroom window. (able to)
5 It wasn't possible for us to go on holiday last year. (not able to)
6 I tried to find a holiday job and I was successful. (succeeded in)

Grammar reference and practice 6

6.1 Speculation about the past, present and future

Speculation about the past

We use *must have* + past participle to show that we are certain that something happened in the past.
He's carrying a newspaper. He must have bought it at the newsagent's.
We use *can't have* + past participle to show that we are certain something didn't happen in the past. It is not possible to use *mustn't have* to speculate about the past.
She can't have been playing football last night. I saw her at Lisa's party. NOT ~~She mustn't have been playing football last night.~~
We use *may have / could have / might have* + past participle to express possibility about the past.
I don't know why Marie is looking so sad. She may have heard some bad news.
I can't find my jacket. I could have left it at school.
She might have spoken to the teacher about her problems, but I think it's unlikely.

Speculation about the present and future

We use *have to / must* + infinitive to express certainty about the present or future. We use *have to* and *must* to show that we are certain about something happening now. *Must* is more commonly used than *have to*.
She must be Tessa's sister. She looks just like her.
They have to be lying. Their story doesn't make sense.
We use *can't* + infinitive to show that we are certain something isn't true. It is not possible to use *mustn't* instead of *can't*.
She can't be eating strawberries – she hates them!
NOT ~~She mustn't be eating strawberries.~~
We use *may / could / might* + infinitive to express possibility about the present or future.
They may call us tomorrow with more news. I don't know.
She could find out her exam results next weekend.
We might go out tonight. We haven't decided yet.

Expressions of probability and possibility

Certainty
- *be bound to* + infinitive
  They're bound to contact you very soon.
- *It's safe to say that / I'm almost sure that / It's not possible that* + main clause
  It's safe to say that we will see his picture on the news tonight.
  I'm almost sure that they've left the country.
  It's not possible that there's no more information available about this.

Possibility
It looks like / He/She looks as if / It seems likely that / most probably + main clause
It looks like he has moved out of this house.
She looks as if she's heard some bad news.
It seems likely that we will be staying here for a while.

1 Choose the correct words.
1 They **must / can't** have heard some bad news. They look very shocked.
2 He **must / could** be Jessie's friend. I'm not sure.
3 **It's not possible / It seems likely** that the story is a hoax. I've seen clear evidence that it's true.
4 She **can't / might** be our new teacher. She's only nineteen years old!
5 You **have to / can't** be telling the truth. I don't believe a word of what you're saying.
6 They **must / might** have sold the story to the newspaper, but I don't think it's very likely.

2 Read the questions and then make speculations. Use *can't have, might have* or *must have* and the correct form of the verbs in brackets.
Where is David?
1 He .... (go out). I just walked past his house and no one was there.
2 He .... (go) to Marie's house. They had a huge argument last week and now they're not talking to each other.
3 He .... (decide) to catch a bus into town. I'm not sure.
Why is the window broken?
4 My brother .... (kick) a ball through it. He was playing football in the garden this morning. But he's usually very careful.
5 The dog .... (do) it. Look! There's some glass in his paw.
Why are your friends laughing?
6 Jane .... (tell) them a funny joke. Her jokes always make people laugh.
Is this note from Paul?
7 No. Paul .... (write) that note. It's definitely not his handwriting.
8 I'm not sure. Marie .... (see) who wrote it – why don't you ask her?

3 Rewrite the sentences using the words in brackets.
1 It's possible that my brother has bought a new phone.
  My brother .... a new phone. (could)
2 I'm certain that the girl on the sofa is wearing my jacket.
  The girl on the sofa .... my jacket. (must)
3 It's not possible that my friends have seen this film.
  My friends .... this film. (can't)
4 We will probably visit our grandparents at the weekend.
  I'm .... at the weekend. (almost sure)
5 He will definitely be listening to this radio programme.
  He .... to this radio programme. (bound)
6 I think the government will soon change its economic policy.
  It .... its economic policy. (seems likely)

Grammar reference and practice 6   119

Grammar reference and practice 6

7 I think it's likely that the film will be a success.
The film .... a success. (might)

8 I'm convinced that your brother has forgotten my birthday.
Your brother .... my birthday. (must)

6.2 ■ Emphasis and inversion

There are many different ways of making a sentence more emphatic. After *What / All they did was* … we use infinitive with or without *to*.

| They fooled the public. | → | What they did was (to) fool the public. |

| They fooled the public. | → | All they did was (to) fool the public. |

After *What happened was (that)* … we need a subject and a verb. We can put *that* before the subject.

| They fooled the public. | → | What happened was (that) they fooled the public. |

To show emphasis we use *It was* + noun or noun clause + relative pronoun (*who / that*) + relative clause.

| The bright lights in the sky stopped him from seeing the girl in the road. | → | It was the bright lights in the sky that stopped him from seeing the girl in the road. |

We can also make a sentence more emphatic by putting a negative or limiting adverb (or adverbial phrase) at the front. These include: *hardly, seldom, not only, never, never before, no way, rarely, no sooner … than*. After the adverb or phrase, the word order is inverted: auxilary + subject. If there is no auxilary verb, add *do, does* or *did*.

People had seldom been so confused.	→	Seldom had people been so confused.
They not only go to the cinema, but they go to the theatre.	→	Not only do they go to the cinema, but they go to the theatre.
We had never experienced this before.	→	Never before had we experienced this.

1 Put the words in order to make emphatic sentences.

1 going to watch / am / I / no way / this programme / .

2 the presentation / was / what happened / to / no one came / that / .

3 but / he direct / it / the film, / not only / he funded / did / .

4 I / so / felt / seldom / embarrassed / had / .

5 surprised / that / the reaction / of / us / it was / the audience / .

6 they / a film / was / to / did / produce / what / .

7 got / that / what happened / was / the director's daughter / the main part / .

2 Complete sentence b so that it has a similar meaning to sentence a.

1 a She had never seen such shocking footage before.
b Never before ....

2 a The excellent cinematography made the documentary really moving.
b It was ....

3 a We had not only wasted our money, but we had also wasted our time.
b Not only ....

4 a The story spread via the internet and was trending within hours.
b What happened ....

5 a He used crowd funding to pay for his film.
b What he did was ....

6 a They changed the music and rewrote some of the script.
b All they did ....

7 a The prime minister revealed that there had been some disagreements within the party.
b It was ....

8 a There has rarely been such an extraordinary reaction.
b Rarely ....

9 a We had never heard such an emotional speech before.
b Never before ....

Grammar reference and practice 7

7.1 Conditionals

Second conditional

We use the second conditional to talk about an imaginary or unlikely situation and its imagined result. It can describe present and future situations.

If we had more time, we would visit Japan.
We would visit Japan if we had more time.
It is possible to use other modals in the result clause.
If they could see the evidence, they might believe us.
We can also use *unless* in second conditional sentences.
She wouldn't move house unless she won a lot of money.
We can use *were* instead of *was*, especially in formal style.
If I were you, I would spend more time with my family.

Third conditional

We use the third conditional to talk about unreal situations in the past. The condition is imaginary, because we cannot change what happened. Consequently, the result is also impossible. *Unless* is never used in third conditional sentences.

If you had studied, you would have passed the exam.
You would have passed the exam if you had studied.
It is possible to use other modals in the result clause.
If you'd mentioned it earlier, I might have been able to do something about it.
If we hadn't taken the wrong road, we could have got there sooner.

1 Match 1–8 with a–h to make sentences.
1 If I had caught the earlier train,
2 If I had a million dollars,
3 If I lived on a desert island,
4 If I became President of the world,
5 If I could speak French,
6 If I had spoken to him,
7 If I hadn't read the newspaper article,
8 If I had known about this problem yesterday,

a I might have been able to help.
b I would understand this film.
c I wouldn't have believed it.
d I would buy a house with a swimming pool.
e I would spend more money on the environment.
f I would get bored very quickly.
g I would have arrived in time.
h he wouldn't have been so upset.

7.2 Mixed conditionals

When the time reference in the 'If' clause is different from the time reference in the main clause, we use a 'mixed conditional' sentence. This is a mix of second and third conditionals in the same sentence. Mixed conditionals describe an unreal situation: either a past condition with a present result, or a present condition with a past result.

3rd conditional (past) | 2nd conditional (present)
If I hadn't switched off my alarm clock, | I wouldn't be late now.
(I switched my alarm clock off in the past and I am late now.)
2nd conditional (present) | 3rd conditional (past)
If she believed in ghosts, | that story would have terrified her.
(She doesn't believe in ghosts and the story did not terrify her.)

2 Read the sentences and then choose the best description of the situation.
1 If James was more friendly, he would have enjoyed the party more.
  a James isn't friendly and he didn't enjoy the party.
  b James isn't friendly, so he won't enjoy the party.
2 If you had paid attention, you wouldn't be so confused.
  a I didn't pay attention and I was confused.
  b I didn't pay attention, so I'm confused now.
3 If we hadn't eaten that cake, we would be hungry.
  a We ate the cake so we're not hungry now.
  b We didn't eat the cake because we weren't hungry.
4 If they didn't know the hotel manager, they wouldn't have got such a good room.
  a They know the hotel manager, so they got a good room.
  b They don't know the hotel manager, so they didn't get a good room.
5 If I had a mobile phone, I would have called you.
  a I don't have a mobile phone, so I can't call you.
  b I don't have a mobile phone, so I didn't call you.
6 If they had stayed at home, they wouldn't be in trouble.
  a They are staying at home and now they are in trouble.
  b They didn't stay at home and now they are in trouble.

Grammar reference and practice 7

3 Complete sentence b so that it has a similar meaning to sentence a. Use mixed conditional sentences.

1. a I spent all my money yesterday and I haven't got any today.
   b If I hadn't ...., I .... some today.
2. a She doesn't have a car, so she didn't drive to the beach last weekend.
   b If she ...., ... to the beach last weekend.
3. a We love camping in Cornwall, so we went camping in Cornwall last July.
   b If we didn't ...., ... in Cornwall last July.
4. a They failed their exams last term, so now they have to take them again.
   b If they ...., ... them again now.
5. a I didn't meet my brother at the station and now he is angry with me.
   b If I ...., ... angry with me now.
6. a They don't understand Japanese, so they bought a Japanese phrase book for their holiday.
   b If they ...., ... a Japanese phrase book for their holiday.

7.3 ■ Unreal situations

We can use different expressions to make suppositions about the present or the past.

Unreal situations in the present

We use *Imagine / Suppose / Supposing* + past simple / present simple to describe a possible situation in the present / future. We can use either the past simple or the present simple to convey the same meaning.
Imagine / Suppose I bought a coat. I'd be much warmer.
Imagine / Suppose I buy a coat. I'd be much warmer.
(I haven't got a coat, but I might buy one.)
We use *I'd rather / sooner* + infinitive to describe a preference in the present.
I could take the train today, but I'd rather / sooner take the bus.
(I want to take the bus but I haven't decided yet.)
We use *I'd rather / sooner* + past simple to describe a preference in the present.
We live in France, but I'd rather / sooner we lived in Spain.
(We live in France, but I want to live in Spain)
We use *It's as if / though* + past simple / present simple to describe a supposition about the present. We can use either the past simple or the present simple to convey the same meaning.
It's as if / though she doesn't want to talk to anyone.
It's as if / though she didn't want to talk to anyone.
(I suppose that she doesn't want to talk to anyone).

Unreal situations in the past

We use *Imagine / Suppose / Supposing* + past perfect to describe an unreal situation in the past.
Imagine / Suppose / Supposing I'd bought a coat last weekend. I'd be much warmer now.
(I didn't buy a coat last weekend. Now I am cold.)
We use *I'd rather / sooner* + *have* + past participle to describe a preference in the past for something that didn't happen.
I took the train, but I'd rather have taken the bus.
(I took the train, but I wanted to take the bus.)
We use *I'd rather / sooner* + past perfect to describe a preference in the past for something that didn't happen. It has the same meaning as *I'd rather / sooner* + *have* + past participle.
We lived in France, but I'd rather / sooner we had lived in Spain.
(We lived in France, but I wanted to live in Spain)
We use *It was as if / though* + past perfect to describe a supposition about the past that you believe is very unlikely / impossible.
It was as if he had forgotten how to swim.
(It seemed, in the past, that he had forgotten how to swim – but you think that's very unlikely.)

1 Rewrite the sentences using the words in brackets.

1. I studied geography at college, but I wanted to study economics. (rather)
2. It seemed that Ted had decided to start a new life. (as if)
3. If I had taken my dog to the vet yesterday, he wouldn't be so ill now. (suppose)
4. Tom might go to college next year, but really he wants to get a job. (sooner)
5. You bought opera tickets, but I wanted you to buy theatre tickets. (rather)
6. I haven't read this magazine, but if I did, I'd probably enjoy it. (imagine)
7. We're going to Florida this year, but I wanted to go on safari in Tanzania. (rather)

Grammar reference and practice 8

8.1 The passive

The passive is formed with the verb *be* + past participle of the main verb. The tense of a passive construction is determined by the tense of the verb *be*. For example:
The goods are taken (by a lorry) to the supermarket.
(present simple)
The animals were being fed when the storm began.
(past continuous)
We use the passive:
- when we are more interested in the action than in the person / thing who performs the action.
  The food industry has been transformed over the last fifty years.
- when we don't know who / what performs the action, or when it is clear from the context who / what performs the action.
  A decision to ban pesticides has been taken.

When we want to say who / what performs an action in a passive sentence, we use the preposition *by*.
We were advised by an agricultural expert to update our farming methods.

1 Rewrite the passive sentences in the active.
1. Too much meat is being eaten.
   People ....
2. Fruit and vegetables are often cultivated in gardens.
   People often ....
3. A change in the law had already been made by the government.
   The government ....
4. A large cake was taken from the kitchen during the night.
   During the night someone ....
5. A table at this restaurant could have been booked last night.
   We ....
6. A new fish and chip shop has been opened.
   They ....
7. The regulations about food hygiene will be updated next month.
   They ....
8. Nothing was being done about the problem.
   People ....

2 Rewrite the active sentences in the passive without saying who / what performs the action.
1. Someone had moved the boxes of fruit to the back of the lorry.
2. People were inventing new dishes.
3. They have reorganized the aisles in the supermarket.
4. Someone will investigate this problem in more detail.
5. You should have put this milk in the fridge.
6. They grow cocoa beans in Ghana.
7. People are questioning the government's policies.
8. Someone released the animals from the laboratory.

8.2 More passive structures

We use *being* + past participle after the following verbs: *like, dislike, hate, enjoy, prevent, avoid, stop, finish, imagine, remember, suggest, miss, practice, object*.
I enjoyed being guided around the chocolate factory.
We use *to be* + past participle after the following verbs: *expect, want, prefer, persuade, order, deserve, begin, hope*.
We expect our food to be prepared in advance.
We use *being* + past participle after the following prepositions: *about, with, without, in, at, of, for*.
I'm interested in being selected for this year's competition.

1 Complete the sentences with the correct form of the verbs in brackets.
1. He doesn't like .... (tell) what to do.
2. We're looking forward to .... (show) around your new office.
3. I'm not scared of .... (criticize).
4. They should avoid .... (drive) by my brother. He's a dreadful driver!
5. I want this food .... (reheat). It's cold.
6. We hope .... (move) to a better hotel room this afternoon.
7. We'd prefer .... (take) by you to the exhibition tomorrow.
8. They're complaining about .... (charge) extra for their breakfast.

8.3 The passive: verbs with two objects

Active sentences with two objects

Some active sentences have two objects: a direct object and an indirect object. There are two possible ways of expressing these sentences.
My sister sent me two books. OR My sister sent two books to me.
The direct object is *two books*. The indirect object is *me*.
We put *to* or *for* before the indirect object when the indirect object comes after the direct object.

Grammar reference and practice 8

Passive sentences with two objects

There are also two ways of expressing the passive form of these sentences.

I was sent two books by my sister. OR *Two books were sent to me by my sister.*

We put *to* or *for* before the indirect object, when the indirect object comes after the passive verb.

to or for

Verbs with *to* that can take two objects include: *send, give, write, lend, offer, post, read, show, sell, introduce, teach*
Verbs with *for* that can take two objects include: *buy, bring, make, find, keep, cook, get, save, build*

1 Put the words in order to make passive sentences.

1 given / diary / she / a / was / .

2 sent / to / flowers / were / my / some / sister / .

3 been / some / the / for / computers / have / new / bought / school / .

4 equipment / the / to / be / lent / students / will / .

5 a / was / I / meal / delicious / cooked / .

6 built / office / they / new / were / a / .

2 Rewrite the sentences in exercise 1 in a different way using the passive.

1
2
3
4
5
6

3 Rewrite the active sentences. Use two different passive sentences.

1 He bought Ingrid a book on Italian cooking.

2 We showed the audience our new invention.

3 They lent me a dictionary.

4 Someone cooked her an amazing meal.

5 They saved you a piece of cake.

6 Someone has offered Rachel a new job.

7 They're bringing him a replacement oven.

8 Someone has sold us a broken phone.

8.4 ■ The passive with reporting verbs

Passive sentences can be used to make a text more impersonal, using reporting verbs such as *believe, claim, consider, know, report, say, think*. Some verbs can be used with different constructions.

With *believe, claim, report* and *say* we use *It* + passive (past or present) + *that*.

It is believed that around half a million people joined the protests.

With *know* and *consider* we use subject + passive (past or present) + *to do something*.

In some cultures, coins are considered to bring you good luck.

With *think* and *know* we use subject + passive (past or present) + *to have done something*.

The guitarist was known to have performed the piece over a thousand times.

With *believe* and *say* we use subject + passive (past or present) + *to be doing something*.

Police are said to be investigating his criminal connections.

1 Complete the sentences with the reporting verb in the present simple.

1 They .... (say / work) a cure for lung cancer.

2 The fire .... (think / start) in the warehouse.

3 It .... (claim) that he completed the painting in under a day.

4 The fossil .... (know / be) over 100 million years old.

5 The drug .... (consider / be) completely safe.

6 The suspect .... (know / commit) three robberies since last week.

Grammar reference and practice 9

9.1 ■ Reported speech

Tense changes

We use reported speech when we want to tell someone about something that another person said. The following tenses change:

Direct speech	Reported speech
Present simple 'I need a new computer.'	Past simple He said that he needed a new computer.
Present continuous 'We're working on a new invention.'	Past continuous She said that they were working on a new invention.
Present perfect 'She's lost her mobile phone.'	Past perfect He said that she had lost her mobile phone.
Past simple 'I didn't understand the instructions.'	Past perfect He said that he hadn't understood the instructions.
Past perfect 'I'd already seen the film,' said Mari.	Past perfect Mari said that she'd already seen the film.
Modals	
can 'I can't get into my Facebook account.'	could He said that he couldn't get into his Facebook account.
will 'We'll buy a 3D TV next year.'	would They said that they would buy a 3D TV the following year.
must 'We must install the new software.'	had to She said that we had to install the new software.

Pronouns, possessive adjectives, determiners, time references and place references often change, too.

Direct speech	Reported speech
'Our email isn't working today,' they said.	They said that their email wasn't working that day.
'I forgot my password yesterday,' she said.	She said that she had forgotten her password the day before.
'We left our laptops here last week,' he said.	He said that they had left their laptops there the week before.
'I don't like this website,' she said.	She said that she didn't like that website.

The following tenses do not change:

Direct speech	Reported speech
Past perfect 'He had already tested the new plane.'	Past perfect She said that he had already tested the new plane.
Modals	
would 'Would you like to use my computer?'	would She asked me if I would like to use her computer.
should 'I think you should leave.'	should He said he thought I should leave.
could 'He could go home.'	could She said he could go home.
had better 'She'd better improve her work.'	had better He said she'd better improve her work.

We don't change the tense, time or place words when the reporting verb is in the present, present perfect, or future.

I was here yesterday.	She says that she was here yesterday.
We didn't expect to win.	They've said that they didn't expect to win.
We're too busy to come tomorrow.	They'll say that they're too busy to come tomorrow.

1 Rewrite the reported sentences in direct speech.

1 She said that she had bought an amazing new MP3 player.
2 He said that he was testing a new video game.
3 They say that they didn't use a calculator to solve these maths problems.
4 Sarah told me that she would reply to my email the following day.
5 I think he'll say that he didn't leave the house yesterday.
6 She told him that he had to finish the work soon.

Yes / No questions

To report a *yes / no* question, we use the structure *ask* (+ object) + *if / whether* + affirmative word order.
Did you fix your Wi-Fi? → He asked (me) if / whether I had fixed my Wi-Fi.

Wh- questions

To report a *wh-* question, we use the structure *ask* (+ object) + *wh-* + affirmative word order.
Where is your camera? → He asked (me) where my camera was.

Grammar reference and practice 9

1 Put the words in order to make reported questions.
1. her / he / the headphones / when / had / asked / bought / she / .
2. Tom / work / she / if / would / meet / he / her / after / asked / .
3. angry with / Rick / was / asked / whether / I / him / me / .
4. switched off / they / he / hadn't / asked / why / the computer / them / .
5. doing / what / there / asked / we / us / she / were / .
6. if / him / asked / he / plane / they / repair / their / could / .

2 Complete sentence b so that it has a similar meaning to sentence a.
1. a 'Did you watch the TV programme about inventors last night?'
   b He asked me ....
2. a 'Why aren't you answering my calls?'
   b She asked John ....
3. a 'Are you happy with your new tablet?'
   b Sophie asked her mother ....
4. a 'Can you help me with my homework?'
   b He asked me ....
5. a 'Where have you decided to go on holiday?'
   b They asked him ....
6. a 'What will you do after this project?'
   b He asked her ....

9.2 ■ Verb patterns in reported speech

We can use several different structures to report people's speech:

- verb + *that* + reported statement
  admit, agree, announce, apologize, boast, claim, confess, deny, explain, insist, promise, say
  We admitted that we had copied the plans.
  She promised that she would call him the following day.
- verb + object + *that* + reported statement
  remind, tell, warn
  They reminded us that they had already changed the instructions.
  He warned me that I would find the course very challenging.
- verb + infinitive with *to*
  agree, demand, offer, promise, refuse
  I agreed to leave at once.
  She refused to speak to us.

- verb + object + infinitive with *to*
  advise, ask, beg, encourage, forbid, invite, order, persuade, remind, tell, warn
  He persuaded us to buy the more expensive model.
  She told them not to wait for her.
- verb + gerund
  admit, deny, recommend, suggest
  We admitted cheating in our final exams.
  They suggested moving to a different part of the country.
- verb + preposition + gerund
  apologize for, boast of / about, confess to, insist on
  I apologized for forgetting his birthday.
  He insisted on speaking to the manager.
- verb + object + preposition + gerund
  accuse (someone) of, congratulate (someone) on, criticize (someone) for, warn (someone) against
  They criticized us for leaving early.
  She accused me of stealing her ideas.

1 Choose the correct words.
1. She boasted about **getting** / **to get** top marks in the exam.
2. He told me **restart** / **to restart** the computer.
3. She suggested **to call** / **calling** the help desk.
4. We denied **ignoring** / **us to ignore** the instructions.
5. They congratulated **that we won** / **us on winning** the science prize.
6. She reminded them **to finding out** / **that they would find out** the results the following morning.

2 Complete sentence b so that it has a similar meaning to sentence a.
1. a 'I'm sorry that I lost your mobile phone.'
   b He apologized ....
2. a 'You should get a new camera.'
   b She recommended ....
3. a 'You are not allowed to use this science lab at lunch time.'
   b The teacher forbade ....
4. a 'Well done! You've passed your driving test.'
   b She congratulated ....
5. a 'Yes, it's true. I ate your sandwich.'
   b I confessed ....
6. a 'I will buy you a new bag tomorrow.'
   b He promised ....
7. a 'Would you like to go to this science show with me?'
   b He invited ....
8. a 'I'm not going to drive you to college today.'
   b She refused ....

Grammar reference and practice 10

10.1 ■ Defining and non-defining relative clauses

We use relative clauses to connect two ideas. A relative clause comes immediately after a noun.

Defining relative clauses

Defining relative clauses give information that identifies the noun they are used with. If we took out the relative clause, the sentence would not make sense. Relative clauses are introduced by relative pronouns: *that*, *who*, *which*, *whom*, *whose*.
The speech that / which the politician made was very powerful.
I met a man whose aunt had worked for John F Kennedy.
We can also use adverbs: *where*, *why*, *when*.
I've never been to a place where you can't buy coffee.
Could you explain why you are opposed to this suggestion?
When combining two sentences, we do not repeat the subject or object of the relative pronoun.
This TV programme is about the civil rights activist whom we were discussing yesterday.
NOT This TV programme is about the civil rights activist whom we were discussing him yesterday.
The relative pronoun *who(m)*, *which* or *that* can be omitted when it refers to the object of the relative clause (but not when it is the subject).
She'd read the book which / that had moved so many people.
BUT She was studying the book (which / that) she had borrowed from the library.

1 Cross out the relative pronoun if possible.
1 He refused to talk to the woman who had criticized his policies.
2 The disagreement was over a message that she had left on his phone.
3 I'm not convinced by the evidence that he presented.
4 No one in our family understood the programme which was on TV last night.
5 She's the same girl whom you invited to the lecture.
6 They elected the man who had promised to campaign for tax reductions.

Sentence-relative clauses

A sentence-relative clause gives extra information about the sentence as a whole, not just the noun before it. The clause is introduced by *which*.
The experiment was a success, which proved her theory.

Non-defining relative clauses

A non-defining relative clause gives extra information about the subject. The sentence makes sense without it.
The relative clause, introduced by *which*, is between commas. The commas have a similar function to brackets.
This newspaper, which is strongly opposed to the new government, is a very popular paper.

We can use *which*, *when*, *where*, *who* and *whose* in non-defining relative clauses. We do not repeat the subject or object when we combine two sentences.
This book, which has a red cover, is very boring.
NOT This book, which has a red cover, it is very boring.
We can't use *that* in non-defining relative clauses.
NOT This book, that has a red cover, is very boring.
A non-defining relative clause does not have to come between two other clauses. It can be followed by a full stop if it comes at the end of a sentence.
Last year she broke off all communication with her family, who were devastated by her actions.

1 Rewrite the sentences. Use defining or non-defining clauses.
1 The house is now a community centre. I grew up there.
   The house .... is now a community centre.
2 The speech lasted two hours. It was very powerful.
   The speech .... was very powerful.
3 My brother has got a new job. His wife is a professional singer.
   My brother .... has got a new job.
4 The man is waiting at the bank. We saw him yesterday.
   The man .... is waiting at the bank.
5 I will never forget the day. We heard that John F Kennedy had been shot.
   I will never forget .... had been shot.
6 The children were all very tired. They were arguing with each other.
   The children .... were arguing with each other.

10.2 ■ Participle clauses

We can also use a clause introduced by a participle to connect ideas. The participle can be an *-ing* form (present participle) or an *-ed* form (past participle).
A present participle replaces an active verb in the present or the past.
Do you know the girl who is talking to my brother?
Do you know the girl talking to my brother?
He followed the car which was speeding along the road.
He followed the car speeding along the road.
The participle can only replace a relative pronoun when it refers to the subject of the relative clause, not the object. The participle can replace *that*, *which* and *who*, but not *when*, *where* or *whose*.
The train which I was travelling in was late.
NOT The train I travelling in was late.

Grammar reference and practice 10

A past participle replaces a passive verb, which can be in the present or past.
The lecture, <u>which was given</u> by a visiting professor, was excellent.
The lecture, <u>given</u> by a visiting professor, was excellent.
The coffee, <u>which is produced</u> in Ghana, is delicious.
The coffee, <u>produced</u> in Ghana, is delicious.
If the relative clause includes a negative verb, we simply put 'not' in front of the participle, whether an active or a passive participle.

That boy who isn't listening to the music but is talking loudly on his phone is actually my brother!	→	That boy not listening to the music but talking loudly on the phone is actually my brother!
The coffee, which isn't produced in Kenya, but in Ghana, is delicious.	→	The coffee, not produced in Kenya, but in Ghana, is delicious.

1 Rewrite the sentences using participle clauses.

1 The man is walking into your garden. He is a friend of my father's.

2 The book was first published in 1969. It is still relevant today.

3 I don't understand the grammar point. It was taught in today's lesson.

4 At the end of the street there is a sign. It points to the library.

5 This is a very old house. It is believed by many to be haunted.

6 He was driving the car. It was travelling at 30 km per hour.

10.3 ▪ Relative clauses: other structures

Relative clauses after pronouns and determiners

We can use relative clauses after the following words:
all, any(thing), every(thing), few, little, many, much, no(thing), none, some(thing), someone, that, those
A few words were <u>all</u> that he would say on the subject.
There were <u>many</u> who complained, but <u>none</u> who were prepared to take action.
I've heard <u>something</u> which will interest you.
Many people saw the programme last night, but <u>those</u> who missed it can watch the repeat tomorrow.

Compound relative pronouns

We can introduce relative clauses with *whenever* (at any time), *whatever* (anything that), *whoever* (anyone who), *wherever* (at any place), *whichever* (any … which) (where these is a choice between things), *however* (in any way).

You can arrive at any time. We will be waiting for you.	→	Whenever you arrive, we will be waiting for you.
It doesn't matter which place she goes to, she always gets lost.	→	She always gets lost, wherever she goes.
Anyone who visits the school after 9 a.m. must park in the road.	→	Whoever visits the school after 9 a.m. must park in the road.

Relative clauses with prepositions

With *who, whom* or *which* the preposition can go at the start or the end of the relative clause.
The box <u>in which</u> I keep my old diaries has got a heavy lock. (formal)
The box <u>which</u> I keep my old diaries <u>in</u> has got a heavy lock. (informal)
The preposition **cannot** go before the relative pronoun *that*.
The box that I keep my old diaries in has got a heavy lock.
NOT ~~The box in that I keep my old diaries has got a heavy lock.~~
When we use phrasal verbs ending in a preposition in relative clauses, we must keep the preposition with the verb.
The five-year-old (whom) I look after on Saturday mornings is very naughty.
NOT ~~The five-year-old after whom I look on Saturday mornings is very naughty.~~

1 Rewrite the sentences using the words in brackets.

1 I saw the small boy hiding under a car. The car was very powerful. (under)
   The car .... was very powerful.

2 It doesn't matter which course you choose. You will enjoy it. (whichever)
   .... you will enjoy it.

3 Yesterday I met someone. She has read your book. (who)
   Yesterday .... has read your book.

4 They ran away from the dog. The dog was very frightening. (which)
   The .... was very frightening.

5 Some people have visited the exhibition. They have found it very interesting. (those)
   .... have found it very interesting.

6 It doesn't matter how angry you were. You shouldn't have shouted at him. (however)
   .... you shouldn't have shouted at him.

Wordlist
This list contains the key words from the Student's Book

Unit 1

attentive (adj) /əˈtentɪv/ listening or watching carefully and with interest
benefit (n) /ˈbenɪfɪt/ an advantage that sth gives you; a helpful and useful effect that sth has
blow (n) /bləʊ/ a negative setback
commitment (n) /kəˈmɪtmənt/ a promise to do sth or to behave in a particular way
compassion (n) /kəmˈpæʃn/ a strong feeling of sympathy for people who are suffering and a desire to help them
compassionate (adj) /kəmˈpæʃənət/ feeling or showing sympathy for people who are suffering
conquer (v) /ˈkɒŋkə(r)/ to become very popular or successful in a place
conundrum (n) /kəˈnʌndrəm/ a confusing problem or question that is very difficult to solve
courage (n) /ˈkʌrɪdʒ/ the ability to do sth dangerous, or to face pain or opposition, without showing fear
courageous (adj) /kəˈreɪdʒəs/ showing courage
dedicated (adj) /ˈdedɪkeɪtɪd/ working hard at sth because it is very important to you
dedication (n) /ˌdedɪˈkeɪʃn/ the hard work and effort that sb puts into an activity or purpose because they think it is important
determined (adj) /dɪˈtɜːmɪnd/ making a firm decision to do it and you will not let anyone prevent you
determination (n) /dɪˌtɜːmɪˈneɪʃn/ the quality that makes you continue trying to do sth even when this is difficult
dignified (adj) /ˈdɪɡnɪfaɪd/ calm and serious and deserving respect
dignity (n) /ˈdɪɡnəti/ a calm and serious manner that deserves respect
gape (v) /ɡeɪp/ to stare at sb/sth with your mouth open because you are shocked or surprised
gawp (v) /ɡɔːp/ to stare at sb/sth in a rude or stupid way
gaze (v) /ɡeɪz/ to look steadily at sb/sth for a long time, either because you are very interested or surprised, or because you are thinking of sth else
get over it (phr v) /ɡet ˈəʊvə(r) ɪt/ to deal with or gain control of sth
glance (v) /ɡlɑːns/ to look quickly at sth/sb
glare (v) /ɡleə(r)/ to look at sb/sth in an angry way
glimpse (n) /ɡlɪmps/ a look at sb/sth for a very short time, when you do not see the person or thing completely
gradual (adj) /ˈɡrædʒuəl/ happening slowly over a long period; not sudden
(a) great deal (n) /ɡreɪt diːl/ a large quantity
ground-breaking (adj) /ˈɡraʊndbreɪkɪŋ/ making new discoveries; using new methods
haggard (adj) /ˈhæɡəd/ looking very tired because of illness, worry or lack of sleep
hindrance (n) /ˈhɪndrəns/ a person or thing that makes it more difficult for sb to do sth or for sth to happen
humble (adj) /ˈhʌmbl/ showing you do not think that you are as important as other people
humility (n) /hjuːˈmɪləti/ the quality of not thinking that you are better than other people
incremental (adj) /ˌɪŋkrəˈmentl/ Increase or adding on, especially in a regular series
ingenuity (n) /ˌɪndʒəˈnjuːəti/ the ability to invent things or solve problems in clever new ways
innovative (adj) /ˈɪnəveɪtɪv/ introducing or using new ideas, ways of doing sth, etc.
inspiration (n) /ˌɪnspəˈreɪʃn/ the process that takes place when sb sees or hears sth that causes them to have exciting new ideas or makes them want to create sth
inspirational (adj) /ˌɪnspəˈreɪʃənl/ providing inspiration
interim (adj) /ˈɪntərɪm/ intended to last for only a short time until sb/sth more permanent is found
obstacle (n) /ˈɒbstəkl/ a situation, an event, etc. that makes it difficult for you to do or achieve sth
optimism (n) /ˈɒptɪmɪzəm/ a feeling that good things will happen and that sth will be successful
overcome (v) /ˌəʊvəˈkʌm/ to succeed in dealing with or controlling a problem that has been preventing you from achieving sth
patience (n) /ˈpeɪʃns/ the ability to stay calm and accept a delay or sth annoying without complaining
peek (v) /piːk/ to look at sth quickly and secretly because you should not be looking at it
penalize (v) /ˈpiːnəlaɪz/ to put sb at a disadvantage by treating them unfairly
perfectionism (n) /pəˈfekʃənɪzəm/ a person who likes to do things perfectly and is not satisfied with anything less
perseverance (n) /ˌpɜːsɪˈvɪərəns/ the quality of continuing to try to achieve a particular aim despite difficulties
persistence (n) /pəˈsɪstəns/ the fact of continuing to try to do sth despite difficulties, especially when other people are against you and think that you are being annoying or unreasonable
persistent (adj) /pəˈsɪstənt/ determined to do sth despite difficulties, especially when other people are against you and think that you are being annoying or unreasonable
resourceful (adj) /rɪˈsɔːsfl/ good at finding ways of doing things and solving problems, etc.
resourcefulness (n) /rɪˈzɔːsfʊlnɪs/ the ability to be resourceful
revolutionary (adj) /ˌrevəˈluːʃənəri/ involving a great or complete change
self-assurance (n) /ˌself əˈʃʊərəns/ belief in your own abilities or strengths
self-control (n) /ˌself kənˈtrəʊl/ the ability to remain calm and not show your emotions even though you are feeling angry, excited, etc.
self-defence (n) /ˌself dɪˈfens/ sth you say or do in order to protect yourself when you are being attacked, criticized, etc.
self-interest (n) /ˌselfˈɪntrəst/ one's personal interest or advantage, especially when pursued without regard for others
self-obsession (n) /ˌselfəbˈseʃən/ the state of being interested in yourself, your happiness, motivations and interests to the exclusion of other things
self-preservation (n) /ˌself prezəˈveɪʃn/ the fact of protecting yourself in a dangerous or difficult situation
self-sacrifice (n) /ˌselfˈsækrɪfaɪs/ the act of not allowing yourself to have or do sth in order to help other people
selflessness (adv) /ˈselfləsnəs/ thinking more about the needs, happiness, etc. of other people than about your own
singlemindedness (n) /ˌsɪŋɡlˈmaɪndəd/ only thinking about one particular aim or goal because you are determined to achieve sth
squint (v) /skwɪnt/ to look at sth with your eyes partly shut in order to keep out bright light or to see better
striking (adj) /ˈstraɪkɪŋ/ interesting and unusual enough to attract attention
tolerance (n) /ˈtɒlərəns/ the willingness to accept or tolerate sb/sth, especially opinions or behaviour that you may not agree with, or people who are not like you
willing (adj) /ˈwɪlɪŋ/ not objecting to doing sth; having no reason for not doing sth
willingness (n) /ˈwɪlɪŋnəs/ the quality or state of being prepared to do sth; readiness

Unit 2

abandoned (adj) /əˈbændənd/ left and no longer wanted, used or needed
absolutely (adv) /ˈæbsəluːtli/ used to emphasize that sth is completely true
accessible (adj) /əkˈsesəbl/ that can be reached, entered, used, seen, etc.
advisable (adj) /ədˈvaɪzəbl/ sensible and a good idea in order to achieve sth
amicable (adj) /ˈæmɪkəbl/ done or achieved in a polite or friendly way and without arguing
asteroid (n) /ˈæstərɔɪd/ any one of the many small planets that go around the sun
attractive (adj) /əˈtræktɪv/ pleasant to look at
audible (adj) /ˈɔːdəbl/ that can be heard clearly
awesome (adj) /ˈɔːsəm/ very impressive or very difficult and perhaps rather frightening
bay (n) /beɪ/ a part of the sea, or of a large lake, partly surrounded by a wide curve of the land
benefit (of) (n) /ˈbenɪfɪt/ an advantage that sth gives you; a helpful and useful effect that sth has
boarded-up (adj) /ˈbɔːdɪd ʌp/ when a window, door, etc. is covered with wooden boards
bus shelter (n) /ˈbʌs ʃeltə(r)/ a structure with a roof where people can stand while they are waiting for a bus
care (for) (n) /keə(r)/ the process of caring for sb/sth and providing what they need for their health or protection
collectible (adj) /kəˈlektəbl/ worth collecting because it is beautiful or may become valuable
considerable (adj) /kənˈsɪdərəbl/ great in amount, size, importance, etc.
constellation (n) /ˌkɒnstəˈleɪʃn/ a group of stars that forms a shape in the sky and has a name
crumbling (adj) /ˈkrʌmblɪŋ/ break or fall apart into small fragments, especially as part of a process of deterioration
cycle path (n) /ˈsaɪkl pɑːθ/ a part of a road that only bicycles are allowed to use
decline (v) /dɪˈklaɪn/ a continuous decrease in the number, value, quality, etc. of sth
demand (for) (n) /dɪˈmɑːnd/ a very firm request for sth
derelict (adj) /ˈderəlɪkt/ not used or cared for and in bad condition
destroy (v) /dɪˈstrɔɪ/ to damage sth so badly that it no longer exists, works, etc.
disappointing (adj) /ˌdɪsəˈpɔɪntɪŋ/ not as good, successful, etc. as you had hoped
diverse (adj) /daɪˈvɜːs/ very different from each other and of various kinds
edible (adj) /ˈedəbl/ fit or suitable to be eaten
efficient (adj) /ɪˈfɪʃnt/ doing sth well and thoroughly with no waste of time, money, or energy
eligible (adj) /ˈelɪdʒəbl/ a person who is eligible for sth or to do sth, is able to have or do it because they have the right qualifications, are the right age, etc.
endanger (v) /ɪnˈdeɪndʒə(r)/ to put sb/sth in a situation in which they could be harmed or damaged
enormous (adj) /ɪˈnɔːməs/ extremely large
estuary (n) /ˈestʃuəri/ the wide part of a river where it flows into the sea
extraordinary (adj) /ɪkˈstrɔːdnri/ unexpected, surprising or strange
extremely (adv) /ɪkˈstriːmli/ to a very high degree
fairly (adv) /ˈfeəli/ to some extent but not very
fashionable (adj) /ˈfæʃnəbl/ following a style that is popular at a particular time
flexible (adj) /ˈfleksəbl/ able to change to suit new conditions or situations
flourishing (adj) /ˈflʌrɪʃɪŋ/ developing rapidly and successfully
galaxy (n) /ˈɡæləksi/ any of the large systems of stars, etc. in outer space
glacier (n) /ˈɡlæsiə(r)/ a large mass of ice, formed by snow on mountains, that moves very slowly down a valley
grasp (of) (n) /ɡrɑːsp/ an understanding of sth
grassland (n) /ˈɡrɑːslænd/ a large area of open land with wild grass
handful (of) (n) /ˈhændfʊl/ the amount of sth that can be held in one hand
harsh (adj) /hɑːʃ/ cruel, severe and unkind
high-rise building (n) /haɪ raɪz ˈbɪldɪŋ/ very tall and having a lot of floors
horrible (adj) /ˈhɒrəbl/ very bad or unpleasant; used to describe sth that you do not like
ice floe (n) /ˈaɪs fləʊ/ a large area of ice, floating in the sea
ideal (adj) /aɪˈdiːəl/ perfect; most suitable
inaccessible (adj) /ˌɪnækˈsesəbl/ difficult or impossible to reach or to get
incomprehensible (adj) /ɪnˌkɒmprɪˈhensəbl/ impossible to understand

Wordlist

incredible (adj) /ɪnˈkredəbl/ impossible or very difficult to believe
industrial estate (n) /ɪnˌdʌstriəl ɪˈsteɪt/ an area especially for factories, on the edge of a town
inevitably (adv) /ɪnˈevɪtəbli/ as is certain to happen
inhabited (adj) /ɪnˈhæbɪtɪd/ with people or animals living there
irresistible (adj) /ˌɪrɪˈzɪstəbl/ so strong that it cannot be stopped or resisted
kid-friendly (adj) /kɪd ˈfrendli/ suitable for children
knowledge (of) (n) /ˈnɒlɪdʒ/ the information, understanding and skills that you gain through education or experience
knowledgeable (adj) /ˈnɒlɪdʒəbl/ knowing a lot
last-minute (adj) /lɑːst ˈmɪnɪt/ done, decided or organized just before sth happens or before it is too late
legible (adj) /ˈledʒəbl/ clear enough to read
(a) little bit (adv) /ˈlɪtl bɪt/ somewhat
magnificent (adj) /mægˈnɪfɪsnt/ extremely attractive and impressive; deserving praise
meteorite (n) /ˈmiːtiəraɪt/ a piece of rock from outer space that hits the Earth's surface
moon (n) /muːn/ the round object that moves around the earth once every 27½ days and shines at night by light reflected from the sun
mountain range (n) /ˈmaʊntən reɪndʒ/ a series of mountain ridges alike in form, direction, and origin
navigable (adj) /ˈnævɪgəbl/ wide and deep enough for ships and boats to sail on
neglected (adj) /nɪˈglektɪd/ not receiving enough care or attention
not particularly (adv) /nɒt pəˈtɪkjələli/ not very
overwhelming (adj) /ˌəʊvəˈwelmɪŋ/ very great or very strong
parking meter (n) /ˈpɑːkɪŋ miːtə(r)/ a machine beside the road that you put money into when you park your car next to it
pedestrian crossing (n) /pəˌdestriən ˈkrɒsɪŋ/ a part of a road where vehicles must stop to allow people to cross
peninsula (n) /pəˈnɪnsjələ/ an area of land that is almost surrounded by water but is joined to a larger piece of land
plain (n) /pleɪn/ a large flat area of land; the Great Plains
planet (n) /ˈplænɪt/ a large round object in space that moves around a star (such as the Sun) and receives light from it
pointless (adj) /ˈpɔɪntləs/ having no purpose
pond (n) /pɒnd/ a small area of still water, especially one that is artificial
pretty (adv) /ˈprɪti/ to some extent
profound (adj) /prəˈfaʊnd/ felt or experienced very strongly
prosperous (adj) /ˈprɒspərəs/ rich and successful
quite (adv) /kwaɪt/ to some degree
recognizable (adj) /ˈrekəgnaɪzəbl/ easy to know or identify
refurbished (adj) /ˌriːˈfɜːbɪʃt/ a room, building, etc. that has been decorated in order to make it more attractive, more useful, etc.
relevance (of) (n) /ˈreləvəns/ closely connected with the subject you are discussing or the situation you are thinking about
remote (adj) /rɪˈməʊt/ far away from places where other people live
renovate (v) /ˈrenəveɪt/ to repair and paint an old building, a piece of furniture, etc. so that it is in good condition again
respect (for) (n) /rɪˈspekt/ a feeling of admiration for sb/sth because of their good qualities or achievements
responsibility (for) (n) /rɪˌspɒnsəˈbɪləti/ a duty to deal with or take care of sb/sth
road sign (n) /rəʊd saɪn/ a sign near a road giving information or instructions to drivers
robust (adj) /rəʊˈbʌst/ strong and healthy
sense (of) (n) /sens/ a feeling about sth important

sensible (adj) /ˈsensəbl/ able to make good judgements based on reason and experience rather than emotion
shabby (adj) /ˈʃæbi/ in poor condition because of long use or lack of care
solar system (n) /ˈsəʊlə sɪstəm/ the sun and all the planets that move around it
speed bump (n) /spiːd bʌmp/ a raised area across a road that is put there to make traffic go slower
spellbinding (adj) /ˈspelbaɪndɪŋ/ holding your attention completely
star (n) /stɑː(r)/ a large ball of burning gas in space that we see as a point of light in the sky at night
stifling (adj) /ˈstaɪflɪŋ/ to feel unable to breathe, or to make sb unable to breathe, because it is too hot and/or there is no fresh air
stream (n) /striːm/ a small, narrow river
subsistence (lifestyle) (n) /səbˈsɪstəns/ the state of having just enough money or food to stay alive
sun (n) /sʌn/ the star that shines in the sky during the day and gives the earth heat and light
swamp (n) /swɒmp/ an area of ground that is very wet or covered with water and in which plants, trees, etc. are growing
tedious (adj) /ˈtiːdiəs/ lasting or taking too long and not interesting
thriving (adj) /ˈθraɪvɪŋ/ to become, and continue to be, successful, strong, healthy, etc.
totally (adv) /ˈtəʊtəli/ wholly and completely
tundra (n) /ˈtʌndrə/ the large flat Arctic regions of northern Europe, Asia and N America where no trees grow and where the soil below the surface of the ground is always frozen
unacceptable (adj) /ˌʌnəkˈseptəbl/ that you cannot accept, allow or approve of
unappealing (adj) /ˌʌnəˈpiːlɪŋ/ not attractive or pleasant
universe (n) /ˈjuːnɪvɜːs/ the whole of space and everything in it, including the earth, the planets and the stars
utterly (adv) /ˈʌtəli/ used to emphasize how complete sth is
valuable (adj) /ˈvæljuəb/ very useful or important
very (adv) /ˈveri/ used before adjectives, adverbs and determiners to mean 'in a high degree' or 'extremely'
vibrant (adj) /ˈvaɪbrənt/ full of life and energy
visible (adj) /ˈvɪzəbl/ that can be seen
wasteful (adj) /ˈweɪstfl/ using more of sth than is necessary; not saving or keeping sth that could be used
well-known (adj) /ˈwel ˈnəʊn/ known about by a lot of people
worthwhile (adj) /ˌwɜːθˈwaɪl/ worth spending time, money or effort on

Unit 3

abstract (adj) /ˈæbstrækt/ based on general ideas and not on any particular real person, thing or situation
accumulate (v) /əˈkjuːmjəleɪt/ to gradually get more and more of sth over a period of time
aluminium (n) /ˌæljəˈmɪniəm/ of, pertaining to, or containing aluminium
amass (v) /əˈmæs/ to collect sth, especially in large quantities
antique (adj) /ænˈtiːk/ old and often valuable
belongings (n) /bɪˈlɒŋɪŋz/ the things that you own which can be moved, for example not land or buildings
bin (v) /bɪn/ to throw away
breathtaking (adj) /ˈbreθteɪkɪŋ/ very exciting or impressive (usually in a pleasant way)
broad (adj) /brɔːd/ wide
broad-minded (adj) /ˌbrɔːd ˈmaɪndɪd/ willing to listen to other people's opinions and accept behaviour that is different from your own
bronze (adj) /brɒnz/ to be a gold brown colour
chest of drawers (BrE) **dresser** (NAmE) (n) /ˌtʃest əv ˈdrɔːz/ /ˈdresə/ a piece of furniture with drawers for keeping clothes in
clear out (phr v) /klɪə(r) aʊt/ to make something empty and clean by removing things or throwing things away

clutter (n) /ˈklʌtə(r)/ having too many things, so that it is untidy
coin (n) /kɔɪn/ a small flat piece of metal used as money
colourful (adj) /ˈkʌləfl/ full of bright colours or having a lot of different colours
contemporary (adj) /kənˈtemprəri/ belonging to the same time
controversial (adj) /ˌkɒntrəˈvɜːʃl/ causing a lot of angry public discussion and disagreement
cooker (BrE) **stove** (NAmE) (n) /ˈkʊkə(r)/ /stəʊv/ a large piece of equipment for cooking food, containing an oven and gas or electric rings on top
copper (adj) /ˈkɒpə(r)/ reddish-brown in colour
crushed (adj) /krʌʃt/ pulverized, rendered into small, disconnected fragments
curtains (BrE) **drapes** (NAmE) (n) /ˈkɜːtnz/ /dreɪps/ pieces of cloth that are hung to cover a window
dated (adj) /ˈdeɪtɪd/ old-fashioned; belonging to a time in the past
decaying (adj) /dɪˈkeɪɪŋ/ implies the deterioration from sound condition
delicate (adj) /ˈdelɪkət/ easily damaged or broken
drop out of (phr v) /drɒp aʊt əv/ to no longer take part in or be part of sth
dustbin (BrE) **trash can** (NAmE) (n) /ˈdʌstbɪn/ /ˈtræʃkæn/ a large container with a lid, used for putting rubbish/garbage in, usually kept outside the house
fast-paced (adj) /fɑːst peɪst/ including a lot of things happening quickly
flat (BrE) **apartment** (NAmE) (n) /flæt/ /əˈpɑːtmənt/ a set of rooms for living in, usually on one floor of a building
garden (BrE) **yard** (NAmE) (n) /ˈgɑːdn/ /jɑːd/ a piece of land next to or around your house where you can grow flowers, fruit, vegetables, etc.
German (adj) /ˈdʒɜːmən/ of or pertaining to Germany, its inhabitants, or their language
get rid of (v) /get rɪd əv/ to make yourself free of sb/sth that is annoying you or that you do not want; to throw sth away
handmade (adj) /ˌhæn(d)ˈmeɪd/ made by hand, not by machine, and typically therefore of superior quality
heap of (n) /hiːp əv/ a lot of sth
heartbreaking (adj) /ˈhɑːtbreɪkɪŋ/ a strong feeling of sadness
helmet (n) /ˈhelmɪt/ a type of hard hat that protects the head, worn, for example, by a police officer, a soldier or a person playing some sports
help out (phr v) /help aʊt/ to help sb, especially in a difficult situation
highly respected (adj) /ˈhaɪli rɪˈspektɪd/ admired by many people for their achievements or good qualities
hoard (v) /hɔːd/ to accumulate for preservation, future use, etc., in a hidden or carefully guarded place
huge (adj) /hjuːdʒ/ extremely large in size or amount
Indian (adj) /ˈɪndiən/ a type of cuisine, often eaten as a take away
jewels (n) /ˈdʒuːəlz/ pieces of jewellery or decorative objects that contain precious stones
junk (n) /dʒʌŋk/ things that are considered useless or of little value
lift (BrE) **elevator** (NAmE) (n) /lɪft/ /ˈelɪveɪtə/ a moving platform or cage for carrying passengers or freight from one level to another, as in a building
loads of (n) /ˈləʊdz əv/ a large number or amount of sb/sth; plenty
mask (n) /mɑːsk/ a covering for part or all of the face, worn to hide or protect it
mind-blowing (adj) /ˈmaɪnd bləʊɪŋ/ very exciting, impressive or surprising
mountains of (n) /ˈmaʊntənz əv/ a very large amount or number of sth
much-anticipated (adj) /mʌtʃ ænˈtɪsɪpeɪtɪd/ to feel or realize beforehand
mummy (n) /ˈmʌmi/ a body of a human or an animal that has been mummified

never-ending (adj) /ˌnevər ˈendɪŋ/ seeming to last for ever

object (n) /ˈɒbdʒɪkt/ a thing that can be seen and touched, but is not alive

opt out (phr v) /ˈɒpt aʊt/ the act of choosing not to be involved in an agreement

paper (adj) /ˈpeɪpə(r)/ made of paper or paperlike material

pick out (phr v) /pɪk aʊt/ to choose sb/sth carefully from a group of people or things

piles of (n) /paɪlz əv/ a quantity of things heaped together

plastic (adj) /ˈplæstɪk/ made of plastic

possession (n) /pəˈzeʃn/ sth that you have or own

pottery (n) /ˈpɒtəri/ pots, dishes, etc. made with clay that is baked in an oven

product (n) /ˈprɒdʌkt/ a thing that is grown or produced, usually for sale

reach out (to) (phr v) /riːtʃ aʊt/ to be seen or heard by sb

rectangular (adj) /rekˈtæŋɡjələ(r)/ a flat shape with four straight sides, two of which are longer than the other two, and four angles of 90°

ripped (adj) /rɪpt/ torn, either partly or into separate pieces

rubbish (n) /ˈrʌbɪʃ/ things that you throw away because you no longer want or need them

run out (of) (phr v) /rʌn aʊt/ to use up or finish a supply of sth

rusty (adj) /ˈrʌsti/ covered with rust

sculpture (n) /ˈskʌlptʃə(r)/ a work of art that is a solid figure or object made by carving or shaping wood, stone, clay, metal, etc.

self-defeating (adj) /ˌself dɪˈfiːtɪŋ/ causing more problems and difficulties instead of solving them; not achieving what you wanted to achieve but having an opposite effect

silk (adj) /sɪlk/ to be made from a type of fine smooth cloth made from silk thread

smooth (adj) /smuːð/ completely flat and even, without any lumps, holes or rough areas

sort out (phr v) /sɔːt aʊt/ to organize the contents of sth; to tidy sth

spill out (phr v) /spɪl aʊt/ to fill a container and go over the edge

spread out (phr v) /spred aʊt/ to stretch your body or arrange your things over a large area

stacks of (n) /stæks ɒv/ a large number or amount of sth; a lot of sth

statue (n) /ˈstætʃuː/ a figure of a person or an animal in stone, metal, etc, usually the same size as in real life or larger

striking (adj) /ˈstraɪkɪŋ/ interesting and unusual enough to attract attention

stuff (n) /stʌf/ used to refer to a substance, material, group of objects, etc. when you do not know the name

stunning (adj) /ˈstʌnɪŋ/ extremely attractive or impressive

tablet (n) /ˈtæblət/ a flat piece of stone that has writing on it

take out (phr v) /ˈteɪk aʊt/ to move sth from one place to another

tangled (adj) /ˈtæŋɡld/ twisted together in an untidy way

tap (BrE) faucet (NAmE) (n) /tæp/ /ˈfɔːsɪt/ a device that controls the flow of water from a pipe

thing (n) /θɪŋ/ an object whose name you do not use because you do not need to or want to, or because you do not know it

thought provoking (adj) /ˈθɔːt prəvəʊkɪŋ/ making people think seriously about a particular subject or issue

throw out (phr v) /θrəʊ aʊt/ to get rid of sth that you no longer want

tiny (adj) /taɪni/ very small in size or amount

tool (n) /tuːl/ an instrument such as a hammer, screwdriver, saw, etc. that you hold in your hand and use for making things, repairing things, etc.

torch (BrE) flashlight (NAmE) (n) /tɔːtʃ/ /ˈflæʃlaɪt/ a small electric lamp that uses batteries and that you can hold in your hand

transparent (adj) /trænsˈpærənt/ allowing you to see through it

triangular (adj) /traɪˈæŋɡjələ(r)/ shaped like a triangle

troubling (adj) /ˈtrʌblɪŋ/ causing stress or anxiety

vase (n) /vɑːz/ a container made of glass, etc, used for holding cut flowers or as a decorative object

wardrobe (BrE) closet (NAmE) (n) /ˈwɔːdrəʊb/ /ˈklɒzɪt/ a large cupboard for hanging clothes in which is either a piece of furniture or built into the wall

weapon (n) /ˈwepən/ an object such as a knife, gun, bomb, etc. that is used for fighting or attacking sb

wear out (phr v) /weə(r) aʊt/ to become, or make sth become, thin or unusuable, usually because it has been used too much

well documented (adj) /wiːl ˈdɒkjumentɪd/ having a lot of written evidence to prove, support or explain it

well earned (adj) /ˌwel ˈɜːnd/ much deserved

well known (adj) /ˌwel ˈnəʊn/ known about by a lot of people

wide ranging (adj) /ˌwaɪd ˈreɪndʒɪŋ/ including or dealing with a large number of different subjects or areas

winding (adj) /ˈwaɪndɪŋ/ having a curving and twisting shape

witty (adj) /ˈwɪti/ able to say or write clever, amusing things

wooden (adj) /ˈwʊdn/ made of wood

Unit 4

addiction (n) /əˈdɪkʃn/ the condition of being addicted to sth

aggression (n) /əˈɡreʃn/ feelings of anger and hatred that may result in threatening or violent behaviour

artery (n) /ˈɑːtəri/ any of the tubes that carry blood from the heart to other parts of the body

baldness (n) /ˈbɔːldnəs/ having little or no hair on the head

be in two minds (idiom) /bi ɪn tuː maɪndz/ to be unable to decide what you think about sb/sth, or whether to do sth or not

bone (n) /bəʊn/ any of the hard parts that form the skeleton of the body of a human or an animal

brain (n) /breɪn/ the organ inside the head that controls movement, thought, memory and feeling

break sb's heart (idiom) /breɪk ˈsʌmbədiːz hɑːt/ to make sb feel very unhappy

burden (n) /ˈbɜːdn/ a duty, responsibility, etc. that causes worry, difficulty or hard work

cause (n) /kɔːz/ the person or thing that makes sth happen

change your mind (idiom) /tʃeɪndʒ jɔː(r) maɪnd/ to change a decision or an opinion

come to your senses (idiom) /kʌm tə jɔː(r) sensɪz/ cause someone to (or start to) think and behave reasonably after a period of folly or irrationality

cross your mind (idiom) /krɒs jɔː(r) maɪnd/ to come into your mind

deafness (n) /ˈdefnəs/ the state of being unable to hear anything or unable to hear very well

depression (n) /dɪˈpreʃn/ a medical condition in which a person feels very sad and anxious and often has physical symptoms such as being unable to sleep, etc.

dig your heels in (idiom) /dɪɡ jɔː(r) hiːlz ɪn/ to refuse to do sth or to change your mind about sth

disability (n) /ˌdɪsəˈbɪləti/ a physical or mental condition that means you cannot use a part of your body completely or easily, or that you cannot learn easily

dismally (adv) /ˈdɪzməli/ causing or showing sadness

engineer (n) /ˌendʒɪˈnɪə(r)/ a person whose job involves designing and building engines, machines, roads, bridges, etc.

flowing (adj) /ˈfləʊɪŋ/ (especially of long hair or clothing) hanging or draping loosely and gracefully

give sb a piece of your mind (idiom) /ɡɪv ˈsʌmbədi ə piːs ɒv jɔː(r) maɪnd/ to tell sb that you disapprove of their behaviour or are angry with them

go out of your mind (idiom) /ɡəʊ aʊt ɒv jɔː(r) maɪnd/ to be unable to think or behave in a normal way

hard to swallow (idiom) /hɑːd tə ˈswɒləʊ/ difficult to accept or not easy to believe

heart (n) /hɑːt/ the organ in the chest that sends blood around the body, usually on the left in humans

imperfection (n) /ˌɪmpəˈfekʃn/ a fault or weakness in sb/sth

keep in mind (idiom) /kiːp ɪn maɪnd/ to remember sb/sth

lifeless (adj) /ˈlaɪfləs/ dead or appearing to be dead

liver (n) /ˈlɪvə(r)/ a large organ in the body that cleans the blood and produces bile

lung (n) /lʌŋ/ either of the two organs in the chest that you use for breathing

make up your mind (idiom) /meɪk ʌp jɔː(r) maɪnd/ to decide sth

mind (n) /maɪnd/ the part of a person that makes them able to be aware of things, to think and to feel

(there is) more to sb than meets the eye (idiom) /ðeə(r) ɪz mɔː(r) tə ˈsʌmbədi ðæn miːts ðə aɪ/ a person or thing is more complicated or interesting than you might think at first

obesity (n) /əʊˈbiːsəti/ the condition of being very fat, in a way that is not healthy

pearly (adj) /ˈpɜːli/ of or like a pearl

rib (n) /rɪb/ any of the curved bones that are connected to the spine and surround the chest

screen (n) /skriːn/ the flat surface at the front of a television, computer, or other electronic device, on which you see pictures or information

shift (v) /ʃɪft/ to move, or move sth, from one position or place to another

short-sighted (adj) /ˌʃɔːt ˈsaɪtɪd/ able to see things clearly only if they are very close to you

shrivelled (adj) /ˈʃrɪvld/ to become or make sth dry and wrinkled as a result of heat, cold or being old

skin (n) /skɪn/ the layer of tissue that covers the body

skull (n) /skʌl/ the bone structure that forms the head and surrounds and protects the brain

slip your mind (idiom) /slɪp jɔː(r) maɪnd/ to forget sth or forget to sth

(have) sth on your mind (idiom) /həv ˈsʌmθɪŋ ɒn jɔː(r) maɪnd/ if sb/sth is on your mind, you are thinking and worrying about them/it a lot

spine (n) /spaɪn/ the row of small bones that are connected together down the middle of the back

stomach (n) /ˈstʌmək/ the organ inside the body where food goes when you swallow it

take your mind off sth (idiom) /teɪk jɔː(r) maɪnd ɒf ˈsʌmθɪŋ/ to make you forget about sth unpleasant for a short time

vein (n) /veɪn/ any of the tubes that carry blood from all parts of the body towards the heart

warts and all (idiom) /wɔːts ænd ɔːl/ including all the bad or unpleasant features of sb/sth

watery (adj) /ˈwɔːtəri/ of or like water

(a) weight off your shoulders (idiom) /weɪt ɒf jɔː(r) ˈʃəʊldəz/ to relieve yourself of a burden, normally sth that has been troubling/worrying you

Unit 5

abuse (n) /əˈbjuːs/ rude and offensive remarks

add on (phr v) /ˈæd ɒn/ make an addition to

as far as I know (idiom) /əz fɑː(r) əz aɪ nəʊ/ used to say that you think you know, remember, understand, etc. sth but you cannot be completely sure, especially because you do not know all the facts

as soon as possible (idiom) /əz suːn əz ˈpɒsəbl/ as quickly, much, soon, etc. as you can

at some point (idiom) /æt səm pɔɪnt/ a non-specific time in the future

Definitions adapted from *Oxford Advanced Learner's Dictionary* 8th edition

Wordlist

back cover (n) /bæk ˈkʌvə/ the back part of the cover of a book or magazine
bibliography (n) /ˌbɪbliˈɒɡrəfi/ a list of books, etc. that have been used by sb writing an article, etc.
by the way (idiom) /baɪ ðə weɪ/ used to introduce a comment or question that is not directly related to what you have been talking about
bye for now (idiom) /baɪ fɔː(r) naʊ/ used to express good wishes when parting or at the end of a conversation
carry on (phr v) /ˈkæri ɒn/ to continue without stopping
cheer on (phr v) /tʃɪə(r) ɒn/ to give shouts of encouragement to sb in a race, competition, etc.
chilling (adj) /ˈtʃɪlɪŋ/ frightening, usually because it is connected with sth violent or cruel
cling on (phr v) /klɪŋ ɒn/ to be unwilling to get rid of sth, or stop doing sth
come on (phr v) /ˈkʌm ɒn/ used in orders to tell sb to hurry or to try harder
complex (adj) /ˈkɒmpleks/ made of many different things or parts that are connected
contents page (n) /kənˈtents peɪdʒ/ a list of the different sections that are contained in a book
dust jacket (n) /ˈdʌst dʒækɪt/ a paper cover on a book that protects it but that can be removed
empower (v) /ɪmˈpaʊə(r)/ to give sb the power or authority to do sth
enable (v) /ɪˈneɪbl/ to make it possible for sb to do sth
enclose (v) /ɪnˈkləʊz/ to build a wall, fence, etc. around sth
encourage (v) /ɪnˈkʌrɪdʒ/ to give sb support, courage or hope
enlarge (v) /ɪnˈlɑːdʒ/ to make sth bigger
ensure (v) /ɪnˈʃʊə(r)/ to make sure that sth happens or is definite
entitle (v) /ɪnˈtaɪtl/ to give sb the right to have or to do sth
entrust (v) /ɪnˈtrʌst/ to make sb responsible for doing sth or taking care of sb
expressive (adj) /ɪkˈspresɪv/ showing or able to show your thoughts and feelings
for what it's worth (idiom) /fɔː(r) wɒt ɪts wɜːθ/ used to emphasize that what you are saying is only your own opinion or suggestion and may not be very helpful
for your information (idiom) /fɔː(r) jɔː(r) ˌɪnfəˈmeɪʃn/ used to tell sb that they are wrong about sth
from my point of view (idiom) /frɒm maɪ pɔɪnt ɒv vjuː/ your personal judgment or opinion about sth
front cover (n) /frʌnt ˈkʌvə(r)/ a book cover is any protective covering used to bind together the pages of a book
glossary (n) /ˈɡlɒsəri/ a list of technical or special words, especially those in a particular text, explaining their meanings
go on (phr v) /ɡəʊn/ to continue
gripping (adj) /ˈɡrɪpɪŋ/ exciting or interesting in a way that keeps your attention
hardback (n) /ˈhɑːdbæk/ a book that has a stiff cover
index (n) /ˈɪndeks/ a list of names or topics that are referred to in a book, etc, usually arranged at the end of a book in alphabetical order or listed in a separate file or book
insightful (adj) /ˈɪnsaɪtfʊl/ showing a clear understanding of a person or situation
intricate (adj) /ˈɪntrɪkət/ having a lot of different parts and small details that fit together
keep on (phr v) /kiːp ɒn/ to speak to sb often and in an annoying way about sb/sth
laugh out loud (jargon) /lɑːf aʊt laʊd/ extremely funny
live on (phr v) /lɪv ɒn/ to have enough money for the basic things you need to live
meaningful (adj) /ˈmiːnɪŋfl/ intended to communicate or express sth to sb, without any words being spoken
move on (phr v) /muːv ɒn/ to start doing or discussing sth new
moving (adj) /ˈmuːvɪŋ/ causing you to have deep feelings of sadness or sympathy
on the point of (phr v) /ɒn ðə pɔɪnt ɒv/ at the moment immediately before a specified condition, action, etc, is expected to begin
in my humble opinion (idiom) /ɪn maɪ ˈhʌmbl əˈpɪnjən/ a phrase introducing the speaker's opinion
paperback (n) /ˈpeɪpəbæk/ a book that has a thick paper cover
perceptive (adj) /pəˈseptɪv/ having or showing the ability to see or understand things quickly, especially things that are not obvious
pinnacle (n) /ˈpɪnəkl/ the most important or successful part of sth
point out (phr v) /pɔɪnt aʊt/ to mention sth in order to give sb information about it or make them notice it
preface (n) /ˈprefəs/ an introduction
protagonist (n) /prəˈtæɡənɪst/ the main character in a play, film or book
quirky (adj) /ˈkwɜːki/ an aspect of sb's personality or behaviour that is a little strange
riveting (adj) /ˈrɪvɪtɪŋ/ so interesting or exciting that it holds your attention completely
ruthless (adj) /ˈruːθləs/ determined to get what you want and not caring if you hurt other people
slip on (phr v) /ˈslɪp ɒn/ to put clothes on or to take them off quickly and easily
spine (n) /spaɪn/ the narrow part of the cover of a book that the pages are joined to
switch on (phr v) /swɪtʃ ɒn/ to turn a light, machine, etc. off/on by pressing a button or switch
take your point (idiom) /teɪk jɔː(r) pɔɪnt/ accept the validity of someone's idea or argument
thanks in advance (phr) /θæŋks ɪn ədˈvɑːns/ used to show that you are grateful to sb for sth they have done
the point is (idiom) /ðə pɔɪnt ɪz/ stating in your opinion the meaning about what is actually happening
throw on (phr v) /θrəʊ ɒn/ to put on a piece of clothing quickly and carelessly
title page (n) /ˈtaɪtl peɪdʒ/ a page at the front of a book that has the title and the author's name on it
too much information /tuː mʌtʃ ˌɪnfəˈmeɪʃn/ an expression indicating that someone has revealed information that is too personal and made the listener or reader uncomfortable
touching (adj) /ˈtʌtʃɪŋ/ causing feelings of pity or sympathy; making you feel emotional
transcend (v) /trænˈsend/ to be or go beyond the usual limits of sth
turn on (phr v) /ˈtɜːn ɒn/ to start sth by pressing a switch or a button
up to a point (idiom) /ʌp tə ə pɔɪnt/ to some degree but not completely
urge on (phr v) /ɜːdʒ ɒn/ to encourage sb to do sth or support them so that they do it better
villain (n) /ˈvɪlən/ the main bad character in a story, play, etc.
you only live once (interjection) /juː ˈəʊnli lɪv wʌns/ motto to convey that one should take risks and live life to the fullest because you probably won't get another chance to do it

Unit 6

accountability (n) /əˌkaʊntəˈbɪləti/ responsible for your decisions or actions and expected to explain them when you are asked
(set the) agenda (n) /əˈdʒendə/ a list of items to be discussed at a meeting
archival footage (n) /ˈɑːkaɪvl ˈfʊtɪdʒ/ film or video footage from the past that can be used in other films
(to be) armed (with) (adj) /ɑːmd/ furnished with weapons
audio engineer (n) /ˈɔːdiəʊ ˌendʒɪˈnɪə(r)/ a person whose job it is to alter and balance the levels of different sounds as they are recorded
axe (v) /æks/ to get rid of a service, system or sb's job
back (v) /bæk/ to give help or support
ban (v) /bæn/ to decide or say officially that sth is not allowed
bid (v) /bɪd/ to offer to provide a service for a particular price, in competition with other companies
boom (n) /buːm/ a sudden increase in trade and economic activity
(expose) corruption (n) /kəˈrʌpʃn/ dishonest or illegal behaviour, especially of people in authority
costume designer (n) /ˈkɒstjuːm dɪˈzaɪnə/ a person who designs costumes for plays and films
cover-up (n) /ˈkʌvər ʌp/ action that is taken to hide a mistake or illegal activity from the public
(lack) credibility (n) /ˌkredəˈbɪləti/ the quality that sb/sth has that makes people believe or trust them
crowd funding (n) /ˈkraʊdfʌndɪŋ/ the practice of funding a project or venture by raising many small amounts of money from a large number of people, typically via the internet
curb (v) /kɜːb/ to control or limit sth, especially sth bad
delve (into) (v) /delv/ to search for sth inside a bag, container, etc.
devastated (adj) /ˈdevəsteɪtɪd/ extremely upset and shocked
docu-ganda (n) film that uses documentary style to spread propaganda
explore (v) /ɪkˈsplɔː(r)/ to travel to or around an area or a country in order to learn about it
fly-on-the-wall (style) (adj) /flaɪ ɒn ðə wɔːl/ doing sth or watching/filming sb without them noticing
gem (n) /dʒem/ a precious stone that has been cut and polished and is used in jewellery
go viral (phr v) /ɡəʊ ˈvaɪrəl/ an image, video, or link that spreads rapidly through a population by being frequently shared with a number of individuals online
(make) headlines (n) /ˈhedlaɪn/ the most important items of news, at the beginning of a news programme or at the start of a newspaper article
in one's element (idiom) /ˈelɪmənt/ doing what you are good at and enjoy
in step with (idiom) /ɪn step wɪð/ having ideas that are the same as other people's
in the limelight (idiom) /ɪn ðə ˈlaɪmlaɪt/ the centre of public attention
in the offing (idiom) /ɪn ðə ˈɒfɪŋ/ likely to appear or happen soon
lighting (n) /ˈlaɪtɪŋ/ the arrangement or type of light in a place
location (n) /ləʊˈkeɪʃn/ a place where sth happens or exists
out of character (idiom) /aʊt ɒv ˈkærəktə(r)/ not typical of a person's character
out of favour (idiom) /aʊt ɒv ˈfeɪvə(r)/ disapproval or support for sb/sth
out on a limb (idiom) /aʊt ɒn ə lɪm/ not supported by other people
out of one's depth (idiom) /aʊt ɒv jɔː(r) depθ/ to be in a situation that you cannot control
plea (n) /pliː/ an urgent emotional request
prop (n) /prɒp/ a small object used by actors during a performance
quit (v) /kwɪt/ to stop doing sth or to leave your job, school, etc.
riddle (n) /ˈrɪdl/ a question that is difficult to understand, and that has a surprising answer, that you ask sb as a game
rigged (v) /rɪɡd/ to arrange or influence sth in a dishonest way in order to get the result that you want
(spread a) rumour (n) /ˈruːmə(r)/ a piece of information, or a story, that people talk about, but that may not be true
(fall for a) scam (n) /skæm/ a clever and dishonest plan for making money
(musical) score (n) /skɔː(r)/ the music written for a film/movie or play
scramble (up) (v) /ˈskræmbl/ to move quickly, especially with difficulty, using your hands to help you

screenplay (n) /ˈskriːnpleɪ/ the words that are written for a film/movie (= the script), together with instructions for how it is to be acted and filmed
scriptwriter (n) /ˈskrɪptraɪtə(r)/ a person who writes the words for films/movies, television and radio plays
scrutinize (v) /ˈskruːtənaɪz/ to look at or examine sb/sth carefully
shot on location (idiom) /ʃɒt ɒn ləʊˈkeɪʃn/ practice of filming in an actual setting rather than on a sound stage
(trace) sources (n) /sɔːs/ a person, book or document that provides information, especially for study, a piece of written work or news
staged (scenes) (adj) /steɪdʒd/ deliberately arranged for effect
storyboard artist (n) /ˈstɔːrɪbɔːd ɑːtɪst/ a profession specialized in creating storyboards for advertising agencies and film productions
storyline (n) /ˈstɔːrɪlaɪn/ the basic story in a novel, play, film/movie, etc.
stuntman (n) /ˈstʌntmæn/ a person who does dangerous things in place of an actor
sweep (v) /swiːp/ to remove quickly with force
terrified (adj) /ˈterɪfaɪd/ very frightened
voice-over (n) /ˈvɔɪs əʊvə(r)/ information or comments in a film/movie, television programme, etc. that are given by a person who is not seen on the screen
vow (n) /vaʊ/ a formal and serious promise to do sth
vulnerable (adj) /ˈvʌlnərəbl/ weak and easily hurt physically or emotionally

Unit 7

adolescent (n) /ˌædəˈlesnt/ a young person who is developing from a child into an adult
ahead of time (adj) /əˈhed ɒv taɪm/ earlier than was expected
all the time (adv) /ɔːl ðə taɪm/ very often
(feel) at ease (idiom) /æt iːz/ to make sb feel relaxed and confident, not nervous or embarrassed
at one time (idiom) /æt wʌn taɪm/ in or during a known but unspecified past period
at the best of times (idiom) /æt ðə best ɒv taɪmz/ even when the circumstances are very good
at the same time (idiom) /æt ðə seɪm taɪm/ at one time, together
be yourself (idiom) /bi jɔːˈself/ to act naturally
before my time (idiom) /bɪˈfɔː(r) maɪ taɪm/ happening before you were born or can remember or before you lived, worked, etc. somewhere
behind the times (idiom) /bɪˈhaɪnd ðə taɪmz/ old-fashioned in your ideas, methods, etc.
breathe life into (idiom) /briːð laɪf ˈɪntə/ to improve sth by introducing new ideas and making people more interested in it
brush off (phr v) /ˈbrʌʃ ɒf/ a rejection or dismissal of sth by treating it as unimportant
call off (phr v) /ˈkɔːl ɒf/ to cancel sth
childish (adj) /ˈtʃaɪldɪʃ/ behaving in a stupid or silly way
cross off (phr v) /krɒs ɒf/ to draw a line through a person's name or an item on a list because they/it is no longer required or involved
cut off (phr v) /ˈkʌt ɒf/ to isolate or be separate
dependent (adj) /dɪˈpendənt/ needing sb/sth in order to survive or be successful
dynamic (adj) /daɪˈnæmɪk/ having a lot of energy and a strong personality
ease off (phr v) /iːz ɒf/ to become or make sth become less strong, unpleasant, etc.
elderly (adj) /ˈeldəli/ used as a polite word for 'old'
every walk of life (idiom) /ˈevri wɔːk ɒv laɪf/ every status and occupation
experienced (adj) /ɪkˈspɪəriənst/ having knowledge or skill in a particular job or activity
fend off (phr v) /fend ɒf/ to protect yourself from sth, especially by avoiding them

fight off (phr v) /faɪt ɒf/ to resist sb/sth by fighting against them/it
foolish (adj) /ˈfuːlɪʃ/ not showing good sense or judgement
for the time being (idiom) /fɔː(r) ðə taɪm ˈbiːɪŋ/ for a short period of time but not permanently
from time to time (idiom) /frɒm taɪm tə taɪm/ occasionally but not regularly
get away with (phr v) /get əˈweɪ wɪð/ to do sth wrong and not be punished for it
get up to (phr v) /get ʌp tə/ to be busy with sth, especially sth surprising or unpleasant
get your own way (idiom) /get jɔː(r) əʊn weɪ/ to get or do what you want, especially when sb has tried to stop you
give in to (phr v) /gɪv ɪn tə/ to agree to do sth you don't want
go on about (phr v) /gəʊ ɒn əˈbaʊt/ to talk about sb/sth for a long time, especially in a boring or complaining way
in next to no time (idiom) /ɪn nekst tə nəʊ taɪm/ so soon or so quickly that it is surprising
in the course of time (idiom) /ɪn ðə kɔːs ɒv taɪm/ when enough time has passed
in the nick of time (idiom) /ɪn ðə nɪk ɒv taɪm/ at the very last moment
independent (adj) /ˌɪndɪˈpendənt/ confident and free to do things without needing help from other people
inexperienced (adj) /ˌɪnɪkˈspɪəriənst/ having little knowledge or experience of sth
infantile (adj) /ˈɪnfəntaɪl/ typical of a small child, childish
juvenile (adj) /ˈdʒuːvənaɪl/ silly and more typical of a child than an adult
laugh off (phr v) /lɑːf ɒf/ to try to make people think that sth is not serious or important, especially by making a joke about it
live a charmed life (idiom) /tʃɑːmd laɪf/ to always be lucky and safe from danger
long in the tooth (idiom) /lɒŋ ɪn ðə tuːθ/ old or ageing
make off (phr v) /meɪk ɒf/ to steal sth and hurry away with it
(a) matter of life and death (idiom) /ˈmætə(r) ɒv laɪf ænd deθ/ used to describe a situation that is very important or serious
mature (adj) /məˈtʃʊə(r)/ behaving in a sensible way, like an adult
(the) milestones in life (idiom) /ˈmaɪlstəʊnz ɪn laɪf/ a very important stage or event
(a) new lease of life (idiom) /njuː liːs ɒv laɪf/ the chance to live or last longer, or with a better quality of life
(be) out of touch with (idiom) /aʊt ɒv tʌtʃ wɪð/ to not know or understand what is happening in a particular subject or area
(be) over the hill (idiom) /ˈəʊvə(r) ðə hɪl/ old and therefore no longer useful or attractive
(in the) prime of life (idiom) /praɪm ɒv laɪf/ the time of maturity when power and vigor are greatest
put off (phr v) /pʊt ɒf/ to change sth to a later time or date
self-reliant (adj) /ˌself rɪˈlaɪənt/ able to do or decide things by yourself, rather than depending on other people for help
(be) set in your ways (idiom) /set ɪn jɔː(r) -weɪz/ to have habits or opinions that you have had for a long time and that you do not want to change
set off (phr v) /set ɒf/ to begin a journey
shelf life (n) /ˈʃelf laɪf/ the length of time that food, etc. can be kept before it is too old to be sold
shrug off (phr v) /ʃrʌg ɒf/ to treat sth as if it is not important
stand on your own two feet (idiom) /stænd ɒn jɔː(r) əʊn tuː fiːt/ to be independent and able to take care of yourself
supportive (adj) /səˈpɔːtɪv/ giving help, encouragement or sympathy to sb
vulnerable (adj) /ˈvʌlnərəbl/ weak and easily hurt physically or emotionally
warn off (phr v) /wɔːn ɒf/ to tell sb to leave or stay away from a place or person, especially in a threatening way

wear off (phr v) /weə(r) ɒf/ to gradually disappear or stop
wise (adj) /waɪz/ able to make sensible decisions and give good advice because of the experience and knowledge that you have
youthful (adj) /ˈjuːθfl/ typical of young people

Unit 8

agonizing (adj) /ˈægənaɪzɪŋ/ causing great pain, anxiety or difficulty
(protect) animal (n) /ˈænɪml/ a creature that is not a bird, a fish, a reptile, an insect or a human
attack (on) (n) /əˈtæk/ strong criticism of sb/sth in speech or in writing
awe-inspiring (adj) /ˈɔː ɪnspaɪərɪŋ/ making you feel respect and admiration
bake (v) /beɪk/ to cook food in an oven without extra fat or liquid
banquet (n) /ˈbæŋkwɪt/ a formal meal for a large number of people, usually for a special occasion
barbecue (n) /ˈbɑːbɪkjuː/ an outdoor meal or party when food is cooked in this way
based (on) (n) /beɪst/ if one thing is based on another, it uses it or is developed from it
better off (without) (idiom) /ˈbetə(r) ɒf/ used to say that sb is/would be happier or more satisfied if they were in a particular position or did a particular thing
boil (v) /bɔɪl/ to cook or wash sth in boiling water
carbon emissions (n) /ˈkɑːbən ɪˈmɪʃnz/ carbon gas that is sent out into the atmosphere
Chinese (adj) /tʃaɪˈniːz/ from or connected with China
classic (adj) /ˈklæsɪk/ with all the features you would expect to find, typical
cold-blooded (adj) /ˌkəʊld ˈblʌdɪd/ showing no feelings or pity for other people
concerned (about) (adj) /kənˈsɜːnd/ worried and feeling concern about sth
countless (adj) /ˈkaʊntləs/ too many to be counted or mentioned
critical (adj) /ˈkrɪtɪkl/ extremely important because a future situation will be affected by it
depend (on) (v) /dɪˈpend/ to rely on sb/sth and be able to trust them
(traditional) dish (n) /dɪʃ/ food prepared in a particular way as part of a meal
distressing (adj) /dɪˈstresɪŋ/ making you feel extremely upset, especially because of sb's suffering
(maintain an) ecosystem (n) /ˈiːkəʊsɪstəm/ all the plants and living creatures in a particular area considered in relation to their physical environment
emergency (n) /iˈmɜːdʒənsi/ a sudden serious and dangerous event or situation which needs immediate action to deal with it
empathy (for) (n) /ˈempəθi/ the ability to understand another person's feelings, experience, etc.
face the music (idiom) /feɪs ðə ˈmjuːzɪk/ to accept and deal with criticism or punishment for sth you have done
face up to (the facts) (idiom) /feɪs ʌp tə/ to accept and deal with sth that is difficult or unpleasant
(standard) fare (n) /feə(r)/ food that is offered as a meal
(prevent) fires (n) /ˈfaɪəz/ flames that are out of control and destroy buildings, trees, etc.
fraction (of) (n) /ˈfrækʃn/ a small part or amount of sth
fry (v) /fraɪ/ to cook sth in hot fat or oil
grill (v) /grɪl/ to cook food under or over a very strong heat
(destroy a) habitat (n) /ˈhæbɪtæt/ the place where a particular type of animal or plant is normally found
(cause an) imbalance (n) /ɪmˈbæləns/ a situation in which two or more things are not the same size or are not treated the same, in a way that is unfair or causes problems
(have an) impact (n) /ˈɪmpækt/ the powerful effect that sth has on sb/sth

Definitions adapted from *Oxford Advanced Learner's Dictionary* 8th edition

Wordlist

in the face of (idiom) /ɪn ðə feɪs ɒv/ despite problems, difficulties, etc.
individual (adj) /ˌɪndɪˈvɪdʒuəl/ connected with one person/thing
ingredient (in) (n) /ɪnˈɡriːdiənt/ one of the things from which sth is made, especially one of the foods that are used together to make a particular dish
let's face it (phr v) /lets feɪs ɪt/ used to convey that one must be realistic about an unwelcome fact or situation
light (adj) /laɪt/ small in quantity, easy to digest
monstrous (adj) /ˈmɒnstrəs/ considered to be shocking and unacceptable because it is morally wrong or unfair
(conserve) nature (n) /ˈneɪtʃə(r)/ all the plants, animals and things that exist in the universe that are not made by people
on the face of it (idiom) /ɒn ðə feɪs ɒv ɪt/ used to say that sth seems to be good, true, etc. but that this opinion may need to be changed when you know more about it
(popular) order (n) /ˈɔːdə(r)/ a request for food or drinks in a restaurant, bar, etc.
outlaw (v) /ˈaʊtlɔː/ to make sth illegal
poach (v) /pəʊtʃ/ to cook food gently in a small amount of liquid
(double) portion (n) /ˈpɔːʃn/ an amount of food that is large enough for one person
(ban harmful) practices (n) /ˈpræktɪsɪz/ a way of doing sth that is the usual or expected way in a particular organization or situation
put on a brave face (idiom) /pʊt ɒn ə breɪv feɪs/ to pretend that you feel confident and happy when you do not
(wartime) ration (n) /ˈræʃn/ a fixed amount of food, fuel, etc. that you are officially allowed to have when there is not enough for everyone to have as much as they want
(overexploit) resources (n) /rɪˈsɔːs/ a supply of sth that a country, an organization or a person has and can use
result (in) (phr v) /rɪˈzʌlt/ to make sth happen
rise (in) (n) /raɪz/ an increase in an amount, a number or a level
roast (v) /rəʊst/ to cook food, especially meat, without liquid in an oven or over a fire
scramble (v) /ˈskræmbl/ to cook an egg by mixing the white and yellow parts together and heating them, sometimes with milk and butter
side (n) /saɪd/ a dish that is served with, but is subordinate to, a main course
six-course (adj) /sɪks kɔːs/ a formal meal that has six courses
slaughter (n) /ˈslɔːtə(r)/ the killing of animals for their meat
(lunchtime) snack (n) /snæk/ a small meal or amount of food, usually eaten in a hurry
(threaten a) species (n) /ˈspiːʃiːz/ a group into which animals, plants, etc. that are able to breed with each other and produce healthy young are divided
steam (v) /stiːm/ to place food over boiling water so that it cooks in the steam
stew (v) /stjuː/ to cook sth slowly, or allow sth to cook slowly, in liquid in a closed dish
stir-fry (v) /ˈstɜː fraɪ/ to cook thin strips of vegetables or meat quickly by stirring them in very hot oil
(fast-food) takeaway (n) /ˈteɪkəweɪ/ a meal that you buy at a restaurant that you eat somewhere else
thanks to (idiom) /θæŋks tə/ used to say that sth has happened because of sb/sth
threatened with (v) /ˈθretnd wɪð/ to say that you will cause trouble, hurt sb, etc. if you do not get what you want
toast (v) /təʊst/ to make sth, especially bread, turn brown by heating it in a toaster or close to heat
toxic waste (n) /ˈtɒksɪk weɪst/ poisonous waste materials
(talk) until we're blue in the face (idiom) to try to do sth as hard and as long as you possibly can but without success
wiped out (phr v) /waɪpt aʊt/ to destroy or remove sb/sth completely

Unit 9

assess (v) /əˈses/ to make a judgement about the nature or quality of sb/sth
backup (n) /ˈbækʌp/ a copy of a file, etc. that can be used if the original is lost or damaged
bug (n) /bʌɡ/ a fault in a machine, especially in a computer system or program
bulky (adj) /ˈbʌlki/ large and difficult to move or carry
close (adv) /kləʊs/ near in space or time
closely (adv) /ˈkləʊsli/ in a close relation or position in time or space
convenient (adj) /kənˈviːniənt/ useful, easy or quick to do
cookie (n) /ˈkʊki/ a computer file with information in it that is sent to the central server each time a particular person uses a network or the internet
cord (n) /kɔːd/ a piece of wire that is covered with plastic, used for carrying electricity to a piece of equipment
cumbersome (adj) /ˈkʌmbəsəm/ large and heavy; difficult to carry
cutting-edge (n) /ˌkʌtɪŋ ˈedʒ/ the newest, most advanced stage in the development of sth
data (n) /ˈdeɪtə/ information that is stored by a computer
dedicated (adj) /ˈdedɪkeɪtɪd/ working hard at sth because it is very important to you
demonstrate (v) /ˈdemənstreɪt/ to show sth clearly by giving proof or evidence
earbud(s) (n) /ˈɪəbʌd/ a very small headphone that is worn inside the ear
early adopter (n) /ˈɜːli əˈdɒptə(r)/ a person who starts using a product or technology as soon as it becomes available
elegant (adj) /ˈelɪɡənt/ attractive and showing a good sense of style
emerging technologies (n) /ɪˈmɜːdʒɪŋ tekˈnɒlədʒiz/ new technologies that are currently developing or will be developed over the next five to ten years, and which will substantially alter the business and social environment
examine (v) /ɪɡˈzæmɪn/ to consider or study an idea, a subject, etc. very carefully
exorbitant (adj) /ɪɡˈzɔːbɪtənt/ much too high
(launch with) fanfare (n) /ˈfænfeə(r)/ a large amount of activity and discussion on television, in newspapers, etc. to celebrate sb/sth
firewall (n) /ˈfaɪəwɔːl/ a part of a computer system that prevents people from getting at information without permission, but still allows them to receive information that is sent to them
fragile (adj) /ˈfrædʒaɪl/ easily broken or damaged
groan-inducing (adj) /ɡrəʊn ɪnˈdjuːsɪŋ/ an act that causes someone to groan
hallmark(s) (n) /ˈhɔːlmɑːk/ a feature or quality that is typical of sb/sth
handset (n) /ˈhændset/ the part of a telephone that you hold close to your mouth and ear to speak into and listen
handy (adj) /ˈhændi/ easy to use or to do
hard (adv) /hɑːd/ with great effort
hardly (adv) /ˈhɑːdli/ almost none
hard-wearing (adj) /ˌhɑːd ˈweərɪŋ/ that lasts a long time and remains in good condition
(to) have legs (idiom) /həv leɡz/ to continue to be of interest
headset(s) (n) /ˈhedset/ a pair of headphones, especially one with a microphone attached to it
high (adv) /haɪ/ at or to a position or level that is a long way up from the ground or from the bottom
highly (adv) /ˈhaɪli/ with admiration or praise
innovative (adj) /ˈɪnəveɪtɪv/ introducing or using new ideas, ways of doing sth, etc.
just (adv) /dʒʌst/ only
justly (adv) /ˈdʒʌstli/ according to what is morally right or fair
keypad (n) /ˈkiːpæd/ a small set of buttons with numbers on used to operate a telephone, television, etc.

late (adv) /leɪt/ arriving, happening or done after the expected, arranged or usual time
lately (adv) /ˈleɪtli/ recently
lightweight (adj) /ˈlaɪtweɪt/ made of thinner material and less heavy than usual
murmur (reassurances) (v) /ˈmɜːmə(r)/ to say sth in a soft quiet voice that is difficult to hear or understand
obsolete (adj) /ˈɒbsəliːt/ no longer used because sth new has been invented
plain (adj) /pleɪn/ simple or basic in character
pricey (adj) /ˈpraɪsi/ overpriced, too expensive
prove (v) /pruːv/ to use facts, evidence, etc. to show that sth is true
reasonable (adj) /ˈriːznəbl/ fair, practical and sensible
sink (v) /sɪŋk/ to go down below the surface or towards the bottom of a liquid or soft substance
sleek (adj) /sliːk/ having an elegant smooth shape
spam (n) /spæm/ advertising material sent by email to people who have not asked for it
spyware (n) /ˈspaɪweə(r)/ software that enables a user to obtain covert information about another's computer activities by transmitting data covertly from their hard drive
(tech) start-ups (n) /ˈstɑːt ʌps/ connected with starting a new business or project
suggest (v) /səˈdʒest/ to put forward an idea or a plan for other people to think about
Trojan (n) /ˈtrəʊdʒən/ a Trojan horse, or Trojan, is a hacking program that is a non-self-replicating type of malware
under age (idiom) /ˈʌndəreɪdʒ/ not legally old enough to do a particular thing
under attack (adj) /ˈʌndə(r) əˈtæk/ subjected to enemy attack or censure
under control (idiom) /ˈʌndə(r) kənˈtrəʊl/ to be being dealt with successfully
under pressure (idiom) /ˈʌndə(r) ˈpreʃə(r)/ being forced to do sth
under scrutiny (idiom) /ˈʌndə(r) ˈskruːtəni/ being watched or examined closely
under the radar (idiom) /ˈʌndə(r) ðə ˈreɪdɑː(r)/ used to say that people are not aware of sth
under the weather (idiom) /ˈʌndə(r) ðə ˈweðə(r)/ slightly ill/sick and not as well as usual
under your belt (idiom) /ˈʌndə(r) jɔː(r) belt/ to have already achieved or obtained sth
update (n) /ˈʌpdeɪt/ the most recent improvements to a computer program that are sent to users of the program
(bring) up to speed (idiom) /ʌp tə spiːd/ having the most recent and accurate information or knowledge
useless (adj) /ˈjuːsləs/ not useful; not doing or achieving what is needed or wanted
virus (n) /ˈvaɪrəs/ instructions that are hidden within a computer program and are designed to cause faults or destroy data

Unit 10

abolish (v) /əˈbɒlɪʃ/ to officially end a law, a system or an institution
adversary (n) /ˈædvəsəri/ a person that sb is opposed to and competing with in an argument or a battle
alternative (n) /ɔːlˈtɜːnətɪv/ a thing that you can choose to do or have out of two or more possibilities
arms (n) /ɑːmz/ weapons, especially as used by the army, navy, etc
ballot paper (n) /ˈbælət peɪpə(r)/ a slip of paper used to register a vote
boil down to (idiom) /bɔɪl daʊn tə/ to have sth as a main or basic part
candidate (n) /ˈkændɪdət/ a person or group that is considered suitable for sth or that is likely to get sth or to be sth
capitalize on (idiom) /ˈkæpɪtəlaɪz/ to gain a further advantage for yourself from a situation
civic engagement (n) /ˈsɪvɪk ɪnˈɡeɪdʒmənt/ individual and collective actions designed to identify and address issues of public concern

class-based (adj) /klɑːs beɪst/ a status hierarchy in which individuals and groups are classified on the basis of economic success and accumulation of wealth

collateral (n) /kəˈlætərəl/ property or sth valuable that you promise to give to sb if you cannot pay back money that you borrow

come under fire (idiom) /kʌm ˈʌndə(r) ˈfaɪə(r)/ to be criticized severely for sth you have done

common good (n) /ˈkɒmən ɡʊd/ the benefit or interests of all

communal (adj) /ˈkɒmjənl/ involving different groups of people in a community

constituency (n) /kənˈstɪtjuənsi/ a district that elects its own representative to parliament

country (n) /ˈkʌntri/ an area of land that has or used to have its own government and laws **(at everyone's) disposal** (idiom) /dɪˈspəʊzl/ sth is available to be used by everyone

distribution (of wealth) (n) /ˌdɪstrɪˈbjuːʃn/ the way that sth is shared or exists over a particular area or among a particular group of people

diversify leadership (v) /daɪˈvɜːsɪfaɪ ˈliːdəʃɪp/ to make leadership become more varied

economical with the truth (idiom) /ˌekəˈnɒmɪkl wɪð ðə truːθ/ euphemism for deceitful, whether by volunteering false information

egalitarian (adj) /iˌɡælɪˈteəriən/ based on, or holding, the belief that everyone is equal and should have the same rights and opportunities

electorate (n) /ɪˈlektərət/ the people in a country or an area who have the right to vote, thought of as a group

enemy (n) /ˈenəmi/ a person who hates sb or who acts or speaks against sb/sth

equal opportunities (n) /ˌiːkwəl ˌɒpəˈtjuːnətiz/ the right to be treated without discrimination, especially on the grounds of one's sex, race, or age

eradicate (v) /iˈrædɪkeɪt/ to destroy or get rid of sth completely, especially sth bad

ethnic diversity (adj) /ˈeθnɪk daɪˈvɜːsəti/ having a wide variety of races in a given situation

extreme (adj) /ɪkˈstriːm/ very great in degree

foe (n) /fəʊ/ an enemy or opponent

freedom (n) /ˈfriːdəm/ the right to do or say what you want without anyone stopping you

freeloaders (n) /ˈfriːləʊdəz/ a person who is always accepting free food, accommodation or help from other people without giving them anything in exchange

general election (n) /dʒenrəl ɪˈlekʃn/ an election in which all the people of a country vote to choose a government

get rid of (phr v) /ɡet rɪd ɒv/ to remove sth that is causing a problem from a place, group, etc.

humanity (n) /hjuːˈmænəti/ people in general

law enforcement (n) /lɔː ɪnˈfɔːsmənt/ the activity of making certain that the laws of an area are obeyed

left-wing politics (n) /left wɪŋ ˈpɒlətɪks/ a political outlook that favours social change

liberty (n) /ˈlɪbəti/ freedom to live as you choose without too many restrictions from government or authority

local election (n) /ˈləʊkəl ɪˈlekʃən/ an election to select members for a local council

mainstream (n) /ˈmeɪnstriːm/ the ideas and opinions that are thought to be normal because they are shared by most people

majority rule (n) /məˈdʒɒrəti ruːl/ a system in which power is held by the group that has the largest number of members

manifesto (n) /ˌmænɪˈfestəʊ/ a written statement in which a group of people, especially a political party, explain their beliefs and say what they will do if they win an election

mankind (n) /mænˈkaɪnd/ all humans, thought about as one large group

minority rights (adj) /maɪˈnɒrəti raɪts/ normal individual rights applied to members of racial, ethnic, class, religious, linguistic or sexual minorities

moderate (adj) /ˈmɒdərət/ having or showing opinions, especially about politics, that are not extreme

(lose) momentum (n) /məˈmentəm/ the ability to keep increasing or developing

nation (n) /ˈneɪʃn/ a country considered as a group of people with the same language, culture and history, who live in a particular area under one government

pledge (n) /pledʒ/ a serious promise

pluck out of the air (idiom) /plʌk aʊt ɒv ðə eə(r)/ to say a name, number, etc. without thinking about it, especially in answer to a question

politically correct (adj) /pəˌlɪtɪkli kəˈrekt/ used to describe language or behaviour that deliberately tries to avoid offending particular groups of people

polling station (n) /ˈpəʊlɪŋ steɪʃn/ a building where people go to vote in an election **(human)**

population (n) /ˌpɒpjuˈleɪʃn/ all the people who live in a particular area, city or country

private (adj) /ˈpraɪvət/ belonging to or for the use of a particular person or group

promise (v) /ˈprɒmɪs/ to tell sb that you will definitely do or not do sth, or that sth will definitely happen

quick off the mark (idiom) /kwɪk ɒf ðə mɑːk/ fast in reacting to a situation

radical (adj) /ˈrædɪkl/ concerning the most basic and important parts of sth

reactionary (n) /riˈækʃənri/ a person who is opposed to political or social change

right-wing politics (n) /raɪt wɪŋ ˈpɒlətɪks/ political outlook that are least in favour of social change

secular (adj) /ˈsekjələ(r)/ not connected with spiritual or religious matters

set the record straight (idiom) /set ðə ˈrekɔːd streɪt/ to give people the correct information about sth in order to make it clear that what they previously believed was in fact wrong

social responsibility (n) /ˈsəʊʃl rɪˌspɒnsəˈbɪləti/ an ethical theory that an entity, be it an organization or individual, has an obligation to act to benefit society at large

spiritual (adj) /ˈspɪrɪtʃuəl/ connected with the human spirit, rather than the body or physical things

swear (v) /sweə(r)/ to use rude or offensive language, usually because you are angry

talk up (idiom) /tɔːk ʌp/ to talk about (sth or someone) to make it seem as good as possible or to draw positive attention to it

toe the line (idiom) /təʊ ðə laɪn/ to say or do what sb in authority tells you to say or do, even if you do not share the same opinions, etc.

turnout (n) /ˈtɜːnaʊt/ the number of people who vote in a particular election

vote (n) /vəʊt/ a formal choice that you make in an election or at a meeting in order to choose sb or decide sth

wear the trousers (idiom) /weə(r) ðə ˈtraʊzəz/ to be the person in a marriage or other relationship who makes most of the decisions

Definitions adapted from *Oxford Advanced Learner's Dictionary* 8th edition